ISRAEL AND SOUTH AFRICA

THE PROGRESSION OF A RELATIONSHIP

RICHARD P. STEVENS

Richard P. Stevens, Professor of Political Science at Lincoln University, Pennsylvania, and former chairman, Department of Political Science, Pius XII University College, Lesotho (Basutoland), is the author of American Zionism and US Foreign Policy: 1942-1947 *(1962;* Lesotho, Botswana and Swaziland, the Former High Commission Territories in South Africa *(1967); the editor of* Zionism and Palestine Before the Mandate: A Phase of Western Imperialism *(1972); and* Weizmann and Smuts: A Study in Zionist-South African Cooperation. *He has also published numerous articles on South Africa in* Africa Report, Journal of Modern African Studies, *and* Africa Today.

ABDELWAHAB M. ELMESSIRI

Abdelwahab M. Elmessiri, Assistant Professor of English and American Literature at Ain Shams University, Cairo, and at present Advisor on Cultural Affairs, Office of the Permanent Observer of the League of Arab States to the U.N., is the author of A Lover from Palestine and Other Poems *(1971); and, in Arabic,* The End of History: An Introduction to the Study of the Structure of Zionist Ideology *(1973);* The Encyclopedia of Zionist Concepts and Terminology: A Critical View *(1975); and* Judaism, Zionism and Israel *(1976). His most recent book in English is* The Land of Promise: A Critique of Political Zionism *(1977).*

ISRAEL AND SOUTH AFRICA

THE PROGRESSION OF A RELATIONSHIP

RICHARD P. STEVENS
and
ABDELWAHAB M. ELMESSIRI

REVISED EDITION
with Foreword by John Henrik Clarke

NORTH AMERICAN
NEW JERSEY

Copyright © Abdelwahab M. Elmessiri 1977 (Revised Edition)
Copyright © Abdelwahab M. Elmessiri 1976 (First Edition)

All Rights Reserved

North American, Inc.
P.O. Box 65
New Brunswick, N.J. 08903

Library of Congress Cataloging in Publication Data

   Stevens, Richard P   1931-
     Israel and South Africa.

     Includes bibliographical references and index.
     1. South Africa—Foreign relations—Israel—
Addresses, essays, lectures. 2. Israel—Foreign
relations—South Africa—Addresses, essays, lectures.
3. Jews in South Africa—History—Addresses, essays,
lectures. I. Elmessiri, Abdelwahab M, 1938- joint
author. II. Title.
DT771.I7S74   1977   327.5694'068   77-10049
ISBN 0-930244-00-1

Cover design by Kamal Boullata

CONTENTS

FOREWORD 7
PREFACE 11
PREFACE TO REVISED EDITION 15

PART I: ESSAYS

    1. CULTURAL ORIGINS AND HISTORICAL PARALLELS

        A. Zionist Apologetics and the White Man's Burden   18
           Abdelwahab M. Elmessiri

        B. Settler Colonialism and *Herrenvolk* Democracy   25
           Samih Farsoun

    2. SOUTH AFRICA, ZIONISM AND ISRAEL

        A. Smuts and Weizmann   34
           Richard P. Stevens

        B. Zionism, South Africa and Apartheid: The Paradoxical Triangle   57
           Richard P. Stevens

        C. Israel and South Africa: A Link Matures   74
           Abdelwahab M. Elmessiri

PART II: READINGS AND DOCUMENTATION

    3. READINGS   84

    4. UNITED NATIONS AND INTERNATIONAL RESPONSE   198

INDEX 227

FOREWORD

In this book, *Israel and South Africa: The Progression of a Relationship,* Professors Richard P. Stevens and Abdelwahab M. Elmessiri open a door and examine one of the most delicate issues of our time. In order to understand this issue and its dimensions beyond the book, there is a need to consider the interplay of forces in South Africa, and in the world at large, that created the state of Israel and the *apartheid*-dominated state of South Africa.

Both Israel and white South Africa are artificial settler states created by the political backwash of Europe. While mentally and culturally they are parts of Europe, they are removed from it geographically. This is the basis of the schizophrenia that prevails in Israel and South Africa. These European settlers are involved in a perpetual contradiction. They are stubbornly trying to establish a nationality in nations that never belonged to them. They are doing this at the expense of the indigenous population in the countries where they have settled. In making an assessment of the relationship of Israel to white South Africa, this dilemma must be taken into consideration.

This dilemma has long historical roots that predate the European settlement of South Africa and parts of Palestine now called Israel. The contents of this book can be understood much better after a review of the antecedents of the present situation.

When the European age of exploration started in the fifteenth century, the Portuguese were searching for a sea route to India by way of the Cape (now Capetown, South Africa).* During one of their early expeditions they attempted to establish a refueling station along the coast of South Africa. This expedition was undertaken upon the advice of Abraham ben Samuel Zacuto, a Jew, who was then the Royal Astronomer for the King of Portugal, Manuel II. Before the edict of expulsion was issued against Spanish Jews in 1492, Abraham ben Samuel Zacuto had been a renowned teacher of astronomy and mathematics at the University of Salamanca in Spain, then the greatest institution of learning in the world.

*The information on the early settlement of the Jews in South Africa was taken from the book: *A History of the Jews in South Africa,* by Louis Herrman, published in Capetown, 1935.

One of the first Jews to land in South Africa was a seaman, Ferado Martins or Fernam Martinz. He was a mariner on Vasco da Gama's ship, *San Gabriel*. He was with the Portuguese fleet that landed at St. Helana Bay in November 1497. Between 1492 and the end of the sixteenth century, nearly a half million Jews left Spain and Portugal. The status of Jews varied from one European country to another. In Holland, Jews participated in the formation of the Dutch East India Company. When the company's undertaking included the occupation of the Cape of Good Hope in 1652, the Amsterdam Jewish community was part of this settlement. Holland had absorbed a large number of Jewish refugees who had spread throughout the provinces. When Jan van Riebeek and his company of servants were preparing to sail for the Cape of Good Hope, the Jews of Holland were petitioning Oliver Cromwell for readmission to England. By the end of the seventeenth century, the Jews of Holland were the principal stockholders in the Dutch East India Company.

Small Jewish settlements at what is now Capetown and other parts of South Africa developed in the seventeenth and eighteenth centuries. On September 17, 1828, the Zulu King Tchaka granted Nathaniel Isaacs the use of a large tract of land for himself and the Jewish people. This was a gesture of friendship from the powerful king who was assassinated by two of his half-brothers before the end of the year 1828.

The discovery of diamonds and gold in South Africa profoundly affected the economic status of the Jews. They had a tradition of dealing in precious minerals. From the 1800s to the present time the Jews of South Africa have been closely related to the marketing of gold and diamonds.

The politics of Zionism in South Africa is mainly a vintage of the twentieth century. This is where Professors Stevens and Elmessiri began their examination of the background of the relationship between Israel and South Africa. This was for many years a quiet relationship with no appreciable international attention. The so-called Six-Day War in 1967 changed this picture and made a larger number of people examine Zionism in general and as a worldwide political force.

In the ten years after the independence explosion starting in 1957 with Ghana, the new state of Israel had more goodwill in Africa than any other white-controlled nation. By November 1973, most of this goodwill had been lost and nations of Africa, like the Ivory Coast, Ethiopia, Zaire, and Liberia (otherwise considered conservative) had broken off diplomatic relations with the state of Israel. There are many factors involved, and the assumption is that Arab influence is the main one. That is not true. The main reason for the break and the change of minds and hearts among African states is Israel's long relationship with the *apartheid* regime of South Africa. There are, of course, many other factors. The Africans seemed to have been slow to learn the fact that the Israelis in Africa were no different from other whites who wanted to control the resources of this vast continent by any means necessary.

When the thirtieth session of the United Nations General Assembly adopted, with a large majority, the resolution equating Zionism with racism, African nations continued to examine their relationship with Israel with a sharper political focus. The relationship of Israel with white-ruled South Africa was the most sensitive area of their examination.

The collaboration between the *apartheid* and Zionist systems is a subject that most "scholars" have been reluctant to examine. The opening of the door also opens other doors, where the rooms, figuratively speaking, are overflowing with political embarrassments.

In the book *Israel and South Africa: The Progression of a Relationship,* the authors deal in depth with many of the neglected dimensions of Israel's relationship with South Africa and the role of the Jews in South Africa, and their non-Jewish allies, such as General Jan Christian Smuts, in the development of Zionism in the twentieth century.

The mentality that went into the making of the South Africa-Israeli alliance was developing in Europe and in the colonial world long before the creation of the state of Israel. The seeds of the future alliance were first planted in late nineteenth-century Europe. The formation of a Jewish state was not seriously considered until the imperialists of Europe found a way to benefit from its creation. Theodor Herzl, the founder of Political Zionism, promised his colonial sponsors that the Jewish state was destined to "form a part of a wall of defense for Europe in Asia, an outpost of civilization against barbarism." In a letter appearing in the *Manchester Guardian,* written in November 1914, Chaim Weizmann, the Zionist leader and first President of Israel, stated:

> We can reasonably say that should Palestine fall within the British sphere of influence, and should Britain encourage Jewish settlement there, as a British dependency, we could have in twenty to thirty years a million Jews out there, perhaps more; they would develop the country, bring back civilization to it and form a very effective guard for the Suez Canal.

Both Theodor Herzl and Chaim Weizmann promised to use the state of Israel to protect European colonial interest in this part of the world. The promise was repeatedly projected until it culminated in the Balfour Declaration in 1917; both Herzl and Weizmann accepted allies wherever they could find them and had no compunctions about linking the Zionist quest for Palestine with British imperial interests. The Balfour Declaration was the reward for this linkage of interest. The Declaration was written, debated, and announced without consulting a single Arab person. In fact the word "Arab" does not appear in any part of the Declaration. This high-minded arrogance was the basis of trouble still to come. In the meantime, Chaim Weizmann searched for additional support and built on the Zionist foundation that had been started by Theodor Herzl. He found a friend and ally in the person of Jan Christian Smuts, South Africa's first celebrated Prime Minister.

While both Herzl and Weizmann preferred Palestine as a homeland for the Jews, they were willing to consider other areas of the world where Jews could live under their own government. At the Sixth Zionist Congress in 1903, Herzl accepted the British proposal for the settlement of Jews in Uganda. He did not give up the claim for Palestine. His goal was to win over world leaders to the general idea of planned Jewish settlement. Though the Ugandan scheme was dropped without fanfare, it was seriously considered. It is noteworthy that the most overt offers of support for the Zionist Commission established to visit East Africa came from South African Zionists.

Such is the background for the book *Israel and South Africa: The Progression of a Relationship.* This book is essential to the understanding of the crisis in South Africa today and the relationship of Israel, another European settler state, to that crisis. Both Israel and South Africa are at the crossroads, on a collision course, in opposition to the full citizenship status of the indigenous people in their respective countries. Geographically, the position of Israel and South Africa epitomizes this point. South Africa is located at the back door of Africa. Israel is the side door of Asia and the front door of Africa. Figuratively speaking, one of the most tragic power struggles in the history of the world is waiting to explode behind one or all of these doors.

JOHN HENRIK CLARKE

PREFACE

With the release of the *Report on the Relations Between Israel and South Africa* in August 1976 by the United Nations Special Committee Against *Apartheid,* world attention was called to a relationship having special importance for the international community as it attempts to cope with the two outstanding problem areas of our day—the Middle East and southern Africa. It is not without significance that both of these problems have their roots in the same historical matrix and that the dynamics of conflict, as well as the linkages of the principal elements daily become more evident. In view of the fact that both problems are bound up with the social fabric of those Western states which have supplied the support, if not the impetus, for South African and Israeli growth, the question of their interrelationship is doubly significant.

The focus of world attention on the Israeli-South African connection has not only embarrassed many Israeli supporters but it has also unleashed a most predictable offensive. Indicative of this trend was the release on September 6, 1976 by the American Jewish Congress of a study naming nineteen Black African states engaged with South Africa in trade relations. The study, prepared by Moshe Decter, was "undertaken to expose the double standard" purportedly applied to Israel by critics of its trade with South Africa. Considerable attention was paid to the economic relationship between Mozambique, Angola, Zambia, Lesotho, Botswana and Swaziland (including the customs union of the latter three) with South Africa as further rationalization of Israeli action. However, as any objective analysis will reveal, the southern African relationship, particularly in its Mozambique dimension, is in itself one of the most glaring instances of the exploitative imperial-colonial legacy. The effort of these states to transform, indeed negate, this relationship is the very essence of the independence period. Of the remaining states, their total trade with South Africa is small. Where it exists, it not only parallels the close ties which previously existed with Israel, buttressed by cooperative "status quo" western powers, but points to vestiges of economic dependence from the colonial era. Three of the states singled out by the AJC for their South African trade—Malawi, Lesotho and Swaziland—are the three states which have not broken their ties with Israel. The transformation of their relationship to the white redoubt of South Africa has in fact been proportionately restrained by the very forces which today hold up African weakness as rationalization of Israeli-South African cooperation.

On the other hand, the relationship between Israel and South Africa is something more than pragmatic. Whatever the degree of shock registered in various circles about the ripening South African-Israeli relationship, that relationship, in its philosophical-historical setting, in its cultural, economic and political expression, is both ordinary and natural, for it flows from the nature of Zionism and its access to the bases of power in the western world. It is this character which puts the Israeli-South African relationship in a different genre from that vestigial relationship of an exploitative African past radiating out from Rhodesia and South Africa. For it is in this white redoubt that one of the richest Jewish communities in the world, a community long committed to political Zionism, has used its abundant energies in pursuit of the Zionist goal. Yet, having derived its sustenance from a social structure whose inequalities were the very condition of white economic growth, *apartheid* is treated from the Jewish organizational point of view as "political." In short, as various Jewish critics in South Africa have pointed out, only those situations or issues are to be characterized from the communal point of view as "immoral" which directly affect the Jewish community or Zionist cause. In terms of Zionist morality, on the other hand, there is an imperative for Christian church leaders, for Black American civil rights groups, for any group which claims to speak in the name of principle, to respond on request to Israeli needs as a condition for Jewish cooperation and support. Needless to say, even for such Black American pro-Israeli supporters as Mr. Bayard Rustin, the relationship has its problems.

Although the racist character of South Africa's *apartheid* policy is today universally acknowledged, it should be remembered that it was only over the strong objections of Britain, France and the United States that *apartheid* was raised at the international level. As a founding member of the League of Nations and the United Nations, the Union of South Africa enjoyed a special place in the Western comity of nations. Thus, despite the fact that South Africa's racial policies were brought to the attention of the United Nations in 1945 by India, the issue was set aside as a matter of domestic jurisdiction and outside the competence of the United Nations. In 1957, however, the General Assembly, considerably more representative of world opinion than in 1945, called upon South Africa to revise its racial policies. In 1961, even the United States and Britain reluctantly concurred that *apartheid*, because of its exceptional character, was a fit topic for United Nations debate. Three years later, in 1964, every member of the United Nations except South Africa and Portugal, saw fit to vote in condemnation of *apartheid*. In 1975, it was a tripartite American-British-French veto which saved South Africa from UN expulsion. Earlier, in October 1973, South Africa's credentials were rejected in the General Assembly.

Preface

Just as expanded United Nations membership and the realities of a changing world economic and political order led to South Africa's isolation, so also over the next decade those very same factors led to a reappraisal of Israel and Zionism on the part of many states, expecially after Israel's expansionism in 1967. Accordingly, by the resolution of November 10, 1975, the United Nations General Assembly determined "that Zionism is a form of racism and racial discrimination." Although denounced by the United States and some of its dwindling number of allies as "obscene," "racist" and "immoral," this United Nations action was a measure of Israel's growing isolation. American and allied prevention of South Africa's ouster the same year from the United Nations further underscored the dependence of both states upon American support.

Although South African and Israeli cooperation has recently become a topic of discussion, the subject, from an academic point of view, can be seen as both too broad and too narrow. Viewed simply as a relationship between two settler colonialist states, the subject is of relevance to liberation movements and holds significance for the militant and the activist, but the full historical and political significance is thereby overlooked. On the other hand, to view the link between the two states as an empirical manifestation of the phenomenon of settler colonialism and Occidental cultural and economic encroachment on the peoples of Asia and Africa, while broadening the scope, relegates the specific link between the two states to a secondary status.

Hoping to reach some kind of reconciliation between these two extremes, we have tried, in this volume, to provide the reader with a broad structural and historical perspective, placing against it a more direct outline of the actual link and the supporting data and documents. The first part includes an essay by Abdelwahab M. Elmessiri on Zionist white supremacist apologetics and their roots in nineteenth century imperialist thought. The piece also refers to the accommodating *apartheid* perception of the Jew as a "white man." Samih Farsoun's essay explores the parallelism between South Africa and Israel and the striking similarity in their political practice (land acquisition, expansionism, immigration laws, etc.). The second section, made up of two essays by Richard P. Stevens, moves from the structural parallelism to the historical links. The first essay, on the relationship between Weizmann and Smuts, explores the political and historical basis and significance of the lifelong friendship between the South African and Zionist leader, and its relevance to the history of South African and Zionist upbuilding. The second essay, a study of Zionism, South Africa and *apartheid,* explores the complex roots of Zionist strength in South Africa, the moral and political implications of Jewish institutional attitudes and the early unfolding of South African-Israeli ties.

The third essay by Elmessiri is a study of the political, economic and military links between South Africa and Israel at the present time.

This last piece is also meant to serve as an introduction to the next two parts of the book, readings and documents. The first section consists primarily of South African Jewish materials relating to the nature of the Jewish community, its economic growth and its contributions to Zionism and Israeli-South African relations. Pieces appear which also question Jewish institutional attitudes toward the *apartheid* issue. Although Israeli-South African ties, up until 1970, are primarily seen only through Jewish organizational reports, after that date they become more common topics of the press. As the relationship between Israel and South Africa has assumed more open form, it has proportionately attracted African and United Nations attention. The relevant documents are presented in the final section.

PREFACE TO THE REVISED EDITION

Since the publication of the first edition of this book, Israel came under attack for its growing collaboration with South Africa. Vague statements and hints were made in Tel Aviv and Zionist circles, assuring the world of Israel's plans to lessen that relationship. Such statements and hints are duly quoted and publicized to cover up the actual intensification of the military, economic, and political collaboration between the two states. The newspaper excerpt [30] in Chapter 3 document the reality and update of this situation, as reported in the American and South African press.

Of far deeper significance is the positive development in the area of Afro-Arab cooperation. The Cairo Summit Meeting, held in March 1977, and similar conferences, are a clear indication of the growing awareness, shared by Africans and Arabs alike, of the common fate and struggles of both peoples. Parts of the declarations of some of these conferences are included in the last chapter.

The revised edition also includes a foreword by Professor John H. Clarke, the American author and historian, and an index.

It is hoped that this new edition will keep the reader apprised of the latest developments and will prove to be an even more valuable reference.

PART I

ESSAYS

1 CULTURAL ORIGINS AND HISTORICAL PARALLELS

A. Zionist Apologetics and the White Man's Burden

ABDELWAHAB M. ELMESSIRI

European settler colonialism was predicated on certain racist assumptions concerning the genetic and cultural superiority of western civilization and the white man. It was these assumptions, in turn, which bestowed legitimacy in the eyes of the colonists on the introduction of an alien western demographic element on the continents of Africa and Asia. In other words, assumption of superiority went hand in hand with colonialism and formed a more or less organic part of it. Lord Balfour, an actor in the South African as well as the Palestinian context, described the process of settler colonialism as being an expression of the "great rights and privileges" of the races of Europe, and he considered the inequality of the races "to be the plain historic truth of the situation."[1]

European settler colonialism, according to Crossman, was launched in terms of the white man's right to bring civilization to the "less civilized 'natives'" of Asia and Africa by physically occupying the two continents even at the cost of "wiping out the aboriginal population," a curious way of civilizing a people by exterminating them.[2] Even before his espousal of Zionism, in keeping with his racist colonialist outlook, Max Nordau suggested the settlement of unemployed European workers, with the European emigrants taking "the place of the 'lower races' who were not surviving in the struggle of evolution."[3]

The Nazi theoretician Rosenberg, to prove his innocence or at least normality during his trial at Nuremberg, advanced a similar argument, underscoring for his judges the organic relationship between racism and colonialism. He pointed out that he had tumbled on the terms "superman" and "super race" in a book on the life of Lord Kitchener, a man who "had conquered the world." He also claimed that he had come across these lines in the writings of the American ethnologist Madison Grant,

*From the author's forthcoming book, *The Land of Promise: A Critique of Political Zionism.*

and those of the French ethnologist Lapouge. He underlined his remark by asserting that this kind of western ethnology was but a "biological discovery which was the conclusion of 400 years of European research."[4]

It seems that with the growing need for markets and territories, and the intensification of Europe's economic and demographic crises, racist theories gained in depth and intensity. The writer of the entry "Race Relations" in the *International Encyclopedia of the Social Sciences* indicates that "the era of race relations can be said to have begun with the overseas expansion of the major European powers from the fifteenth century onward."[5] Gentile Zionism and Christian restorationist views began to flourish at that time. It is no coincidence either that the modern pseudo-messianic movements in Judaism also became more frequent from that time on. The most dangerous of all the false messiahs, Shabettai Zvi, came from a mercantile background and his father worked for a British overseas trading company.

But all of these myths and ideologies were mere adumbrations for the fullfledged global imperialism and racism of the late nineteenth century. The author of the entry on "Race" in *The New Encyclopedia Britannica* finds it "no accident that racism flourished at the second great wave of European colonial expansion and the scramble for Africa." He then adds that the ideology of colonialism and the white man's burden was "often expressed in racist terms."[6]

The fraudulent messiah of the age of imperialism and scramble for Africa was Zionism, and it was in the late nineteenth century imperialist-racist frame of reference that the Zionist theoreticians conceived of their project and implemented it. In order to take advantage of the colonialist formula and to share the privilege and right of shouldering that most onerous burden of civilizing the non-white races and of engaging in the noble *mission civilisatrice* of Europe, one had to be a white man. There was indeed no alternative for the Zionists, they simply had to think in these terms, for they were, after all, the product of their historical background, and one does not expect them to be either angels transcending common historical failures or devils sinking far below them.

In his study *The Jews Today,* Arthur Ruppin sides with a certain von Luschau, one of the many Zionist theoreticians of the "Jewish race," whom he credits with the discovery of the physical resemblance between the Jews and the races of Asia Minor, especially the Armenian. Ruppin prefers to see the Jews as members of "the white race,"[7] and lauds such theoretical efforts that strike a "blow at the Semitic theory." The racial difference between Jews and *Europeans,* according to him, is "not great enough to warrant an unfavorable prognostic as to the fruits of a mixed marriage."[8]

There is a whole strain in Zionist thought which confines the term "Jew" to European Jews, the Ashkenazim. Ruppin talks of how "the Zionist movement has already stirred the Jewish consciousness of many a Western Jew,"[9] with the obvious omission of Sephardic (Oriental) Jews. Accordingly, Zionist settlement efforts aimed till 1948 at recruiting European Jews only, and rarely tried to recruit Oriental Jews, despite the fact that it would have been "a far easier task to settle Oriental Jews (Jews from Yemen, Morocco, Aleppo and the Caucasus) in agricultural colonies." Ruppin even saw them as "already *drifting* toward Palestine" presumably without conscious Zionist efforts. This Oriental drift did not please him, however, because "the spiritual and intellectual status of these Jews is so low that an immigration *en masse* would lower the general cultural standard of the [Ashkenazi] Jews in Palestine and would be bad from several points of view"[10] — words which Abba Eban echoed half a century later in his *Voice of Israel.*

Only pragmatic considerations, however, made a dent in the Zionist white supremacist outlook. Oriental Jews, provided they come "in small numbers, might be extremely useful by virtue of their knowledge of Oriental conditions, their small needs,"[11] but above all their capacity for "competing in wages with the Arab agricultural laborer." The problem with the [white] east European Jew is that he "cannot possibly live on such [low] wages" as those given to Arabs. Moreover, the European Jew, given the fact that he lives "in Palestine only by work which makes demands on his intelligence and reliability," employs Arabs "for purely manual labor."[12] This would have been an acceptable arrangement had it not been imperative from the Zionist standpoint to segregate the "Jewish economic system in order to achieve 'separate development' through the pure Hebrew labor of the Zionist settlers." The hiring of an Arab would represent a "breach" of the Zionist closed system and therefore it had to be "bridged by the Oriental Jew who can do the rough work at the same price as the Arab."[13]

In other words, the Zionist myth of rights, according to Ruppin's view, applies only to the Ashkenazi; as for the Sephardim, they were to be admitted into the enclave out of dire economic necessity and pragmatic consideration.

The language of Ruppin's analysis might sound terribly immoral and racist, and excessively utilitarian, for he speaks of the Sephardic Jews as very useful creatures with very small needs, an *instrumentum vocale,* but such was the language common to Europe at the time. To the extent that Zionism functioned within that framework the universal ethical values of Judaism could not inhibit the accomplishment of its goal.

In point of fact, and in fairness to Ruppin, it should be indicated that he proved far more generous, far more sensitive and concrete, than his abstract theories. When he went to Palestine to supervise Zionist colonial activities there, he developed an awareness of the specificity of the situation far more complex and tragic than his questionable theory of the white Jew's burden.

Theodor Herzl was also part of that colonial culture and he fully realized that his Zionist efforts had to be coordinated with similar projects so that different "white" rights would not come into conflict with each other. Before meeting "Joe" Chamberlain, as Herzl affectionately called the British colonialist, he wrote in his diary that he had to show the Colonial Secretary "a spot in the English possessions where there were no *white people* as yet" before they "could talk about that"[14] Zionist project for settlement.

Throughout all of the discussions involving the Zionist proposals for white penetration into Africa and Asia, it was assumed that the white people of the Occident have these rights and privileges because of their high level of civilization. Herzl, in the manner of nineteenth century imperialist thinkers, spoke of imperialism as a noble activity destined to bring civilization to the benighted members of the other "races."[15] Viewing the Jewish state with these occidental white binoculars, he wrote in 1896 a letter to the Grand Duke of Baden assuring him that when the Jews return to their "historic fatherland," they will do so as "representatives of Western civilization" who will bring "cleanliness, order and the well-established customs of the Occident to this plague-ridden, blighted corner of the Orient."[16] The Zionists, as fervent advocates of European progress, will "build railroads into Asia—the highway of the civilized peoples."[17] Herzl, operating within the myth of the white Jew, asserts that the Jewish state was designed to "form a part of a wall of defense for Europe in Asia, an outpost of civilization against barbarism."[18]

The defense of the Jews as a white, occidental race sounds somewhat ironic, especially after the holocaust, but it was quite natural to the age and almost universal among the Zionists. In a language clearly smacking of the colonial racism of Europe, Jabotinsky, no "great admirer of Oriental culture," described the "Jews as Europeans" who have nothing in common with the Orient where "everything" as he claimed, was "doomed."[19]

The perception of the Jews not merely as a separate racial entity, but as members of the white race and western civilization, underlies many of the statements of the Zionists and their image of themselves.

In *Rebirth and Destiny,* Ben Gurion draws a number of analogies between the Zionists and other colonists which reveal his strong white orientation. In 1917, in an essay entitled "Judea and Galilee," he saw the Zionist settlers in the Land of Israel "as not just working" but rather as "conquering, conquering a land. We were a company of conquistadores." Even though the analogy with a white settler colonialist enterprise is clear, the conquest in this essay is narrowed down to the land, not people.[20]

In another piece entitled "Earning a Homeland," Ben Gurion, extending the conquest to include the people as well, compares the Zionist settlement to the American settlement in the New World, conjuring up the image of the "fierce fights" the American colonists fought against "wild nature and wilder redskins."[21] It is significant, from the standpoint of the present argument, how the Zionist leader identifies the natives of America by color; but more significant was his reduction of the Indians to the level of nature, even lower than it, for they are "wilder."This process of abstracting man, reducing him to mere natural cycles, which is an extension of the Darwinian ethics and outlook, renders extermination quite a palatable act and depopulation of an area an act of survival. The Nazis later on made full use of that logic on a more massive and more systematic and "scientific" scale. They declared it their duty "to depopulate," as part of their mission of preserving the German population. "If nature is cruel,... we too must be cruel."[22]

Although frequently at odds with Ben Gurion on tactics, Weizmann in *Trial and Error* preferred to use the image of the French *colons* in Tunisia[23] and British settlers in Canada and Australia as models, while demonstrating marked sympathy for the settlers in South Africa.[24]

In a note sent by him to President Truman, on November 27, 1947, we note the colonial tendency to draw a sharp line of demarcation between a technologically advanced "European" community and backward natives. Describing the Zionist community in Palestine, Weizmann said that it consisted mainly of "an educated peasantry and a skilled industrial class living on high standards." To this bright image he contrasted the bleak one of "illiterate and impoverished communities bearing no resemblance to the Zionist community."[25] Weizmann of course did not bother to explain to the American president the reason for this state of affairs, and why, after fifty years of British and Zionist colonialism and enlightenment, the light of civilization had not yet dawned.

Given the white racist colonial myth of rights, the Balfour Declaration did not hesitate to refer to the Arab Moslems and Christians of Palestine, who made up over 90 percent of the population, as the "non-Jewish communities." In other words, the indigenous majority was already being ruthlessly relegated to the status of a minority in the name of the superior rights of Europe's forthcoming surplus. Balfour himself once wrote, "in Palestine we do not propose ever to go through the form of consulting the wishes of the present inhabitants of the country, though the American [King-Crane] Commission has been going through the form of asking what they are."[26] As for those public proclamations and liberal safeguard clauses, they were to be dumped: "The Powers have made no declaration of policy which, at least in the letter, they have not always intended to violate."[27] The dominant colonial powers took the decision, and the Zionist settler colonialists took full advantage of the international power structure.

The "civilizing mission enjoyed by Gentiles can [from that point on] be emulated by Jews,"[28] as indicated by an Israeli writer or, to put it more simply, the white Jews should have the rights and privileges of other white settlers in Africa and Asia.

After the establishment of Israel, the same white orientation of the state persisted with the attendant tension between an Ashkenazi myth of rights pitted against the exigencies of multi-racial Jewish immigration and Middle East geo-politics. The tension is quite manifest in Ben Gurion's claim that Israel is only geographically in the Middle East but not of it,[29] and in his declaration that he would like to see more Western Jews settling in the Zionist state to stop Israel from becoming a Levantine state.[30]

Moshe Dayan, Israel's national military hero, chose South Africa to explore his own fears of Oriental Jews. In 1974, at the annual conference of the South African Zionist Federation, he described the fact that "Oriental Jewish immigrants outnumbered immigrants of European origin" as "Israel's biggest problem." He appealed to his audience to help solve Israel's demographic problem by immigrating there.[31]

The classical Israeli expression of this tension is in Abba Eban's *Voice of Israel,* where the author, with his customary eloquence, defined his concept of the ideal relationship that should exist between Israel and her neighbors. "The idea should not be one of integration. Quite the contrary: integration is rather something to be avoided." Turning to the subject of the Oriental Jews, Eban, a South African Ashkenazi Jew himself, speaks of "the great apprehensions which afflict" the Western-born Israelis, stemming from their feeling of "the danger lest the predominance of immigrants of Oriental origin *force* Israel to equalize its cultural level with that of the neighboring world,"[32] i.e. Asia and Africa. He then goes on to say that "far from regarding our immigrants from oriental countries as a bridge toward our integration with the Arabic-speaking world, our objective should be to infuse them with Occidental spirit, rather than to allow them to draw us into an *unnatural orientalism.*"[33]

If Ben Gurion evoked the image of the *conquistadores* and Weizmann that of the *colons,* Eban evokes that of the Yankee in Latin America; Israel, he said, should work toward establishing a relationship akin to that which obtains between the United States and the Latin American continent.[34]

The South African settlers saw themselves in more or less the same terms as members of a superior white civilization, cast themselves in the same missionary role as carriers of that civilization, and, in the name of that cultural and racial superiority, tried to depopulate their promised land from the aborigine to carve out another Western democracy in the middle of the jungle. The white supremacist logic used by *some* Zionist theoreticians, is central to the apologetics of *apartheid,* for both ideologies grew within the same cultural ambience and drew from the same sources and myths. Probably a detailed exploration of the apologetics of *apartheid* might be unnecessary since most people are familiar with the logic of the South African segregationists who, unlike the Zionists, never tried to conceal their logic of conquest and its underlying outlook. What might be of some interest in the present context is the fact that the South African apologists included "the Jews" in the category of a white people. On November 3, 1919, at a reception held in Johannesburg under the auspices of the South African Zionist Federation and the South African Jewish Board of Deputies, Smuts spoke of the Jews as a "little people" having "a civilizing mission" in the world. He cited the language of the Old Testament as the basis of "our white culture" and "your Jewish culture."[35] When Smuts drew the analogy, it was probably greeted with approval, but with the growing isolation of the white minority in South Africa, Zionism thought it fit to minimize the importance of the common cultural, historical origins it shares with *apartheid.* Prime Minister Vorster, however, brushed the whole thing aside, decrying those embarrassed Zionists who want to set up a distinction between Israel's "policy of separate development" on the basis of religion and South Africa's comparable policies on a racial basis.[36]

This viewing of the Jew as a white man is quite manifest in various South African government acts and regulations. When a literacy test to read and write "in the characters of a European language" (designed to exclude Asiatics) was adopted, Yiddish, a language written in (Asiatic) Hebrew characters, was nevertheless accorded official recognition as an acceptable language in the Cape immigration law of 1906 as well as in the basic Immigration Act of 1913.[37]

This labeling of the Jew as "white" accounts for the fact that South African Jewry views itself as an "integral part of the white population," feels that its destiny is "bound up with the rest of the white community,"[38] and "leans as heavily as the rest on the Government which can and is providing order and security."[39]

The idea of the white man's burden, be he a gentile or a Jew, is a theme that both Zionism and the philosophy of *apartheid* have in common. As much as mankind is rigidly divided along racial lines, separate economic development and segregated political structures become only logical and even desirable. It was in the name of this racial separateness, and superiority, that waves of European immigrants, Europe's demographic surplus, flooded South Africa and Palestine, expropriating the natives, then expelling them. In view of these common cultural and historical roots, it is quite natural that the two states, in the face of mounting historical pressures, close their ranks and solidify their relationships.

---

[1] Richard Stevens, "Settler States and Western Response: Israel and South Africa," Abdeen Jabbara and Janice Terry, eds., *The Arab World: From Nationalism to Revolution* (Wilmette, Illinois: The Medina University Press, 1971), pp. 167-168.
[2] Richard Crossman, *A Nation Reborn: The Israel of Weizmann, Bevin and Ben Gurion* (London: Hamish Hamilton, 1960), p. 58.
[3] Desmond Stewart, *Theodor Herzl* (Garden City, New York: Doubleday and Company, 1974), p. 192.
[4] *Trial of the Major War Criminals Before the International Military Tribunal: Nuremberg, 14 November 1945—1 October 1946* (Nuremberg, Germany, 1947), XI, 450.
[5] Edited by David Sills (New York: The Macmillan Company of the Free Press, 1968), XIII.
[6] *Encyclopedia Britannica,* (Chicago: William Benton, 1973), XV.
[7] Ruppin, *The Jews Today,* trans. Margery Bentwitch (London: G. Bell and Sons, 1913), p. 213.
[8] *Ibid.,* p. 227.
[9] *Ibid.,* p. 296.
[10] *Ibid.,* pp. 293-294.
[11] *Ibid.,* p. 294.
[12] *Ibid.*
[13] *Ibid.*
[14] *Complete Diaries of Theodor Herzl,* ed. Raphael Patai, trans. Harry Zohn, 5 volumes (New York: Herzl Press and Thomas Yoseloff, 1960), IV, 1361.
[15] "Race,"*Encyclopedia Britannica,* XII.
[16] *Diaries.* I, 343.
[17] *Ibid.,* I. 338.
[18] Arthur Hertzberg, ed., *The Zionist Idea: A Historical Analysis and Reader* (Westport, Connecticut: Greenwood, 1959), p. 222.
[19] Joseph B. Schechtman, *Fighter and Prophet: The Vladimir Jabotinsky Story, The Last Years* (New York: Thomas Yoseloff, 1961), p. 324.

B. Settler Colonialism and *Herrenvolk* Democracy

SAMIH FARSOUN†

[The text printed below is an abridged part of a paper titled "South Africa and Israel: A Special Relationship" submitted to the Conference on Socio-Economic Trends and Policies in Southern Africa, which, under the aegis of the United Nations African Institute for Economic Development and Planning, Dakar, took place in Dar-es-Salaam between November 29 and December 12, 1975. Some of the details and illustrations, contained in the original, had to be left out.]

The nature of South African settler colonialism historically and contemporaneously has been amply studied from varied perspectives. Less so Rhodesia. And, perhaps because of traditional Western bias, Israel even less. But, since June, 1967, and the emergence of the 'new left' internationally, Israel has been analyzed directly in those terms.[1]

*From *Third World Magazine* (Bonn, Germany). Special issue, "Israel—South Africa: Cooperation of Imperialistic Outposts," 1976.

†Samih Farsoun, Ph. D., is on the staff of the Department of Sociology, The American University, Washington, D.C.

---

[20] David Ben Gurion, *Rebirth and Destiny*, (New York: Philosophical Library, 1954), p. 9.
[21] *Ibid.*, p. 6.
[22] Jacob Bernard Agus, *The Meaning of Jewish History*, 2 volumes (London: Abelard-Schuman, 1963), II, 386.
[23] Chaim Weizmann, *Trial and Error* (New York: Harper and Row, 1949), p. 191.
[24] *Ibid.*, P. 277.
[25] Harry S. Truman, *Memoirs* (Garden City, New York: Doubleday, 1955), II, 159.
[26] Leonard Stein, *The Balfour Declaration*, (London: Vallentine, Mitchell, 1961), p. 649.
[27] *Ibid.*
[28] N.A. Rose, *The Gentile Zionists, A Study in Anglo-Zionist Diplomacy 1929-1939* (London: Frank Cass, 1973), p. 75.
[29] Ben Gurion, *Rebirth and Destiny of Israel*, p. 489.
[30] Philip Sigal, "Reflections on Jewish Nationalism," *Issues*, Fall 1961, p. 21.
[31] *Third World Reports*, Vol. 5, No. 7, September 1974.
[32] Abba Eban, *Voice of Israel* (New York: Horizon Press, 1957), p. 76.
[33] *Ibid.* Emphasis added.
[34] *Ibid.*
[35] "Smuts' Vision for Zion and World Jewry," *Jewish Affairs*, August 1970.
[36] *Contemporary Links Between South Africa and Israel* (Madison Committee on Southern Africa), cited in *127 Questions and Answers on the Arab-Israeli Conflict* (Beirut; Palestine Research Center, 1973), p. 136.
[37] "South Africa," *Encyclopedia Judaica* (Jerusalem: The Macmillan Company, 1972), XV.
[38] *Ibid.*
[39] Neville Rubin, "The Impact of Zionism and Israel on the Political Orientation of South African Jews," in *Settler Regimes in Africa and the Arab World: The Illusion of Endurance* (Wilmette, Illinois: Medina University Press, 1974), p. 171.

The interests of the settler-colonists are in contradiction to both those of the natives and the finance capitalists of the 'mother country'. When an accommodation between the colonial power and the indigenous population begins to emerge (usually leading to political independence of the natives) the colonists are threatened and fight violently.

"This highly retrograde and reactionary element led the struggle (historically) on two fronts—unyielding and wholeheartedly against the natives ... relatively and occasionally, but often very violently against the great capitalists 'back home.' "[2]

Independence of the Colonialists

The colonists attempt to secede from the parent country and set up their own supremacist regime whose hallmark is severe oppression of the natives. Rhodesia is the most recent example of this phenomenon. The violent struggle between the South African settlers and Britain while economic in essence was also related to British policy concerning the natives. When the local whites eventually won independence and control of the state, they imposed one of the most oppressive structures in history, *apartheid*.

"As for Israel, it is all too often forgotten that if this country represents a spearhead of imperialism in the particular present international context of antagonism between the two great blocs, this is only a result of special circumstances. Its true nature is to be a mass of small 'white' settlers spreading out more and more to colonize an under-developed territory. It is this that makes their conflict with the peoples of the region so ruthless, even where the latter live under pro-Western regimes which are themselves the satellites of imperialism. In spite of its ... alliance with American imperialism ... Israel is a secessionist colonial state. Its foundation was the object of a long and bloody struggle with England, who played the role of the imperialist parent country."[3]

Upon secession or independence of the colonists, the pivotal attribute of settler colonial regimes is their relationship to the indigenous population and land. Politically, the European colonists establish what van den Berghe calls a "*Herrenvolk* democracy," a political duality with parliamentary democracy for the settler colonialists and a colonial regime for the natives. This is a "parliamentary regime in which the exercise of power and suffrage is restricted, de facto, and often de jure, to the dominant group."[4] In short, the colonists rule themselves democratically and impose their political, social and economic tyranny over the natives.

Land Acquisition

A colonial settlement needs land. Thus, an immediate antagonism erupts with the indigenous population when colonists take (conquer or even buy) the land. To secure the colony, more immigrants are needed, thus increasing the population and land pressure over the natives. Native resistance ensues. But a dynamic process is set in motion: colonist expansionism, immigration, and expulsion and/or subjugation-segregation of the natives. This process expresses itself in a series of battles and wars culminating in land control, native expulsion and subjugation. At times such conflicts become genocidal. In North America, these wars are known as the Indian Wars, in South Africa the Kaffir Wars and in the Middle East as the Arab-Israeli conflict (this is not to deny that other factors have entered into the picture here).

Expansionism at the Expense of the Natives

The particulars of this dynamic process vary in the different settler-colonial situations, but the essence and end result are the same. In South Africa land acquisition was made by force supported by (and at times ignored by) the imperial power. Indeed, beginning with the 19th century, the conflict between the British imperial interests and the settler Afrikaner community led to further wide-ranging expansionism. This expansionism was, needless to say, at the expense of the natives, first the Bushmen and Hottentots, and later, the Bantu. The Afrikaners pushed the Black South Africans into certain lands which were "reserved" for them. The Natives Land Act of 1913 set aside for the Black natives 7 % of the territory (subsequently increased to 13% in 1936) of South Africa, although the Africans numbered four times as many as the white Afrikaners. This pattern was repeated in Rhodesia except that it was done in a shorter period of time, beginning in 1890 and the population ratio of African to white was nearer 20 to 1.

Land Acquisition through Purchases

In the Arab world, the particulars were slightly different. Although supported by imperial Britain, early Zionist settlement in Palestine was not accomplished by conquest as it would have generated a war with a long-established empire and regional power, the Ottoman Empire. Early land acquisition by Zionists was made through purchases financed by European Zionists and sympathizers. And yet, all such activity amounted to little before the British mandate was imposed on Palestine in the wake of World War 1.

The British Mandate, acting in concert with the Balfour Declaration's intent of establishing a 'national homeland' for the Zionists, facilitated settler land acquisition. This set in motion a pattern of settler immigration and of dispossession of Palestine peasants. This was felt as a threat by the native Arab population who resisted in varied ways, including an all out rebellion against the British and Zionists in 1936-1939. Nonetheless, by 1947, when the British turned the Palestine question to the United Nations, Zionist and Jewish landholding in Palestine did not exceed 7% of the whole territory.[5] And yet, by 1948 settler population in Palestine had come to number close to 700,000, nearly one third the total population of the country. Wholesale Zionist land acquisition in Palestine was not accomplished until after the Palestine war of 1947-48. Here also, land acquisition was accomplished by force. It should be pointed out that the then Western dominated U. N. provided the formal basis for the Zionist settler state, without reference to the natives' wishes, in a partition of Palestine resolution adopted on November 29, 1947. Apart from the Union of South Africa, only one African and one Asian nation voted for the Partition Plan. The resolution passed on the strength of voting European and Western hemisphere countries.

Military Expansionism

The new settler state of Israel expanded its territory in Palestine from the 56% allocated by the U.N. to 77% in 1948. Israeli expansionism continued further in 1967 in the wake of the June war. Territory of the rest of Palestine and of two neighboring states was conquered by Israel. Israel unilaterally annexed Arab Jerusalem and the surrounding area. Over two dozen collective and para-military settlements were established by the Israelis not only in the rest of Palestine (the West Bank) but also in Syrian and Egyptian territory.

Settler State Laws

Once a settler state is erected on native land then the process of land acquisition is promulgated through settler state laws. These are statutes whose consequence is the alienation of native land and the regulation of settler acquisition. They also "legalize" such a pattern. The Absentee Property Law of 1950 in Israel is a case in point. This law and such other statutes as Article 25 of the Emergency Regulations authorizing the military government to expel villagers and close off their areas, contributed to the transfer of Arab property into settler Israeli hands.[6] After the June 1967 war the Israeli government expropriated Arab homes inside the old city of Jerusalem, first in January and then in April 1968. About 5,000 Palestinians lost their land and were subsequently transferred to the East Bank of the Jordan. These "legal" processes of settler acquisition of land were not different in essence or consequence from the statutes and native land acts of South Africa and Rhodesia.

Immigration

Together with land acquisition, settler colonialism is concerned with immigration of new settlers to help secure and strengthen the settler society. This is a thrust which is in direct contradiction to the native population. Thus, the presence of the natives is a problem. As Patrick Keatley says of white Rhodesians: "One cannot help feeling ... that in their heart of hearts, the white Rhodesians bear a wordless wish that the Africans would disappear."

The 'wordless wish' in South Africa takes the form of enforced

Settler Colonialism and *Herrenvolk* Democracy

geographical and social segregation of Blacks. Similarly, the Zionists in their rhetoric and policy exhibit this same 'wordless wish'. An early Zionist philosopher activist, Israel Zangwill, coined the slogan that Palestine is a land without a people to be given to a people without a land (i. e. European Jews). As recently as 1969, Golda Meir, then Prime Minister of Israel, stated in an interview: "It was not as though there was a Palestinian People in Palestine considering itself as a Palestinian People and we came and threw them out and took their country away from them. They did not exist." *(Sunday Times,* London, June 15, 1969).

Zionist settler colonialism, fueled by religio-historical ideology and coupled with the desire to have a modern nation where there are Jews of all classes, was especially concerned with the wish for a native-free, that is Arab-free, country. Erskine Childers has analyzed the history, plans and warfare (military, terroristic, and psychological) which made possible a Palestine, in Ben Gurion's words, "virtually emptied of its former owners."[7] Israel refused to repatriate hundreds of thousands of Palestinian Arab refugees after the 1948 war and again after the 1967 war. After the latter, a token fraction of refugees were permitted back into their homes on the West Bank. It was the unrepatriated refugees whose property was confiscated under the Absentee Property Law.

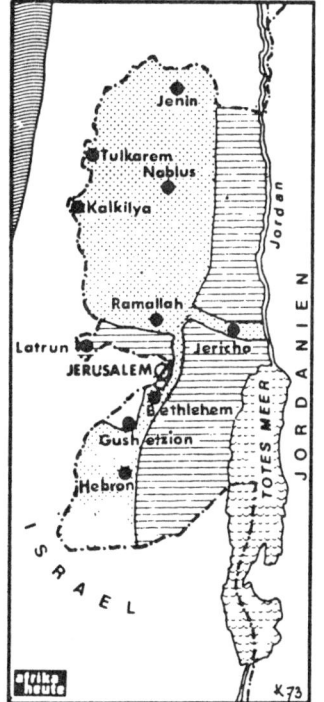

Allon' Westbankplan (1973)
Israeli Palestinustans

Southafrican Bantustans

Biblical Justification

Settler states facilitate immigration of qualified immigrants: White Europeans for South Africa and Jews for Israel. The Israeli Law of Return gives the right to any Jew (legally defined according to religious statutes) to settle in Israel and acquire citizenship. As with South Africa, immigrants are helped socially, economically and in housing. Simultaneously the citizenship laws discriminate against the native. In short, settler colonist movements usurp native land, expel or control the natives and encourage qualified settler immigration. They justify that in terms of an ideology which includes notions that they are civilizing the native, but often such justification is Biblical. South Africa and Israel are especially strong in this.

The Dutch Reformed Church, church of the Afrikaaner settlers, relies on some Old Testament passages. It believes that the inequality of the races is ordained by God. The Blacks, considered by the church as the descendants of Ham, are destined to serve the whites, descendants of Sham. The Boers considered the abolition of slavery as contrary to Biblical precepts.[8] The Afrikaners saw the Blacks as inferior, degraded and uncivilized. The mission of the whites is to civilize them.

The Zionists, too, depend upon Biblical passages to justify their claim to and colonization of Palestine. In addition to their function of bringing civilization to a backward Asiatic region (see T. Herzl), the Zionists saw Palestine as the promised land, given to them by God. The colonization of the country is nothing more than reclaiming what is Biblically theirs and the fulfillment of Biblical prophecy. Statements of the leaders continue to speak of Eretz Israel which includes much of the present territory occupied since the 1967 war.

Colonial Regime for the Natives

As van den Berghe points out, the settler colonists establish a *herrenvolk* democracy in which they impose on the natives—those that remain under their control—a colonial regime characterized by three major attributes:

a) political disfranchisement and control,
b) social segregation, and
c) economic exploitation.

The methods of achieving political control over the natives and bringing about native disfranchisement are both direct and indirect. By virtue of the contradictory claim of parliamentary democracy, the settler regimes resort, most frequently, to indirect and subtle means to curb native political freedoms. In South Africa and Rhodesia where the native Black population is in the majority numerically, the right to vote is denied outright to the natives. In Israel proper where the remaining natives are in the minority (about 12 %) the right to the franchise was not denied although it was highly controlled. Freedom of expression and of association have been severely restricted through the Publications and Entertainment Act of 1963, and the Suppression of Communism Act of 1950 in South Africa. "Communism" is defined as any doctrine "which aims at bringing about any political, industrial, social or economic change within the Union by the promotion of disturbance or disorder, by unlawful acts or omissions or by the threat of such acts or omission."[9] Such a broad definition of the law has meant the suppression of any native activity. In 1963 alone, 7,500 publications were banned. Israeli statutes curbing native freedom of expression are more discreet but just as effective. Independent Palestinian publications in Israel are either not permitted or circumscribed and controlled.[10]

Political Oppression

The freedom of association and political organizations of natives are also curtailed by the colonists. In South Africa the Unlawful Organization Act of 1960 (similar to an identical one in Rhodesia) and the Prohibition of Improper Interference Bill of 1966, not only empowered the authorities to declare the natives' Pan-African Congress and the African National Congress illegal, but also prohibited racial groups from participating in joint political activities. Additionally, the Law and Order Maintenance Act imposes restrictions on the freedom of association. No African can hold, address or chair a gathering except with the permission in writing of the white district commissioner. While these are declared statutes of political control of natives in South Africa, Israel uses informal but recognizable procedures to curtail independent native Palestinian activity. All attempts at establishing independent Arab parties were frustrated by the Israeli Government.[11] Israeli techniques against native activism include arrest and imprisonment of leaders, legal and other types of harrassment of activists, denial of registering of associations, etc.

Social Segregation

Perhaps one of the most effective mechanisms for political and social control of the natives in all settler colonial states including South Africa and Israel is the restriction and regulation of their freedom of movement. Such restriction is justified on a variety of grounds, including security. South African *apartheid,* through several laws, such as the Group Areas Act, the Bantu Urban Areas Consolidated Act, and the Bantu Law Amendment Act of 1964, restricts the natives to certain designated areas. Departure from and entry into African areas of the reservations is strictly controlled. Africans in white areas (over three quarters of the country) travel and reside there only if they can officially show cause. This has to be done through official travel documents.

In Israel, similar restrictions are imposed on the native Palestinian Arabs. Since the creation of the State of Israel in 1948, over 80% of Palestinian Arabs have lived, for at least a time, under military government. The laws which govern these "military zones" are the State of Emergency Laws promulgated by the British Mandate in Palestine in 1945. Additional statutes, the Zones of Security Regulations, were enacted by Israel in 1949. Articles of this law give the military governors near dictatorial rights in restricting not only freedom of movement but all civil liberties. There is no recourse for the native except higher military-administrative authorities. These laws and military government were applied to the areas of greatest native Arab population concentration in Galilee, the Negev and the 'Triangle Area' in the central region of the country. This military rule lasted from 1948 until 1966, when it reverted to police control. During and since the 1967 war, military rule was reimposed in these areas, as well as in the West Bank region. These zones were not only near the Israeli border, but also in areas far from the frontier. Exit out of and entry into these 'closed zones' were by official military passes for the natives.

In 1948 Israel, Arabs who remained in urban areas were forced to move, even abandon their own property, into specified areas designated for them. This forced ghettoization led to de facto segregation of the newly created minority native Arabs. This process along with the military governance system emerged as the basis of social segregation of the native Arabs.[12]

Economic Exploitation

Of course, as in South Africa, there are token natives in certain official and institutional capacities, but these are 'safe' and 'loyal' natives. This pattern of encouraging and supporting conservative and collaborative native leadership is not unlike the pattern of South African support to Black African tribal leaders.

Finally, political and social control of the natives is allied with, and necessary for, economic exploitation of these people. In both South Africa and Israel the natives are concentrated in the lower occupational categories: manual, unskilled and semi-skilled occupations. Such restrictions are either a matter of practice of sometimes provided for by law. Indeed, natives in Israel are paid only a fraction of what the settlers earn for the same job.[13] The usual pattern of last-hired, first-fired is also operative here. Typically, native workers are either denied the right to organize themselves or this right is severely circumscribed. In South Africa, the Industrial Conciliation Act of 1956 defines African workers in such a manner that they are denied union organizing.

In Israel, the powerful settler union organization, the Histadrut, has had a long antagonistic history with native Arab workers. In Mandate days, the Histadrut's slogan was for Jewish work only; after the creation of the Israeli state, the new slogan was to hire 'organized workers'. As Arab workers were not unionized and were not admitted into the Histadrut, this last slogan meant denial of employment of native Arabs. In 1960, Arabs were finally admitted into the Histadrut and yet their earning power is still a fraction of that of equivalent Israeli workers.

Most of Arab labor in Israel is 'itinerant' commuting sometimes long distances for work and returning only periodically to their homes. Since 1967, nearly 70,000 Arabs from the occupied territories also commute daily into Israel for work. These Arab workers have been used as very cheap labor in Israel.[14]

Cultural Discrimination

Similar discrimination in the educational sphere is evident. In South Africa, despite some progress, 60% of the natives of primary school age are out of school while in Israel the rate is about 30%.[15] Native educational institutions and facilities are distinctly inferior and suffer native cultural deprivation. According to Jiryis, native students who studied in primary schools can hardly read and write their native language. Native history is taught in a distorted manner while settler history is gloriously portrayed.[16]

In conclusion, the *herrenvolk* democracy the colonial settlers erected in both South Africa and Israel is quite similar in thrust and in general features, although not in details. The similar social structures, dilemmas in handling the natives, justifications for their settlements and subsequent histories tend to bring about similar ideologies, world views and mutual sympathy.

---

[1] The best example is the book by the French historian and social scientist Maxime Rodinson, *Israel: A Colonial Settler State?*, New York 1973. See also A. El-Kodsy and E. Lobel, *The Arab World and Israel*, New York 1970.
[2] A. Emmanuel, "White Settler-Colonialism and the Myth of Investment Imperialism," in *New Left Review*, No. 73, May-June 1973, p. 39.
[3] A. Emmanuel, *op. cit.*, p. 47.
[4] *Race and Racism*, New York 1967, p. 29; see also L. van den Berghe, *South Africa, A Study in Conflict*. Middletown, Conn. 1965.
[5] See J. Ruedy, *Dynamics of Land Alienation*, in. I. Abu-Lughod (ed.) *The Transformation of Palestine*, Evanstown 1971.
[6] See the account of this process in S. Jiryis (a 'native' lawyer), *The Arabs in Israel*, Beyrout 1969.
[7] Israel *Yearbook*, 1952, p.38.
[8] See G. Jabbour, *Settler-Colonialism in Southern Africa and the Middle East*, Kartoum/Beyrout 1970, p. 58.
[9] *Ibid.*, p. 67.
[10] The best illustration of this pattern is the case of Al-Ard publication. See J. Landau, *The Arabs in Israel*, London 1968, p. 96; and S. Jiryis, op. cit.
[11] See J. Landau, *op. cit.*, p. 54 ff.
[12] Evidence to illustrate this is collected by the Israeli League for Human Rights. See Israel Shahak (ed.) *The Non-Jew in the Jewish State*, Jerusalem 1975. Shahak is the Chairman of the League.
[13] Cited in S. Jiryis, from parliamentary debates; see also Y. Ben-Porath, *The Arab Labor Force in Israel*, Jerusalem 1966; and A. Cohen, *Israel and the Arab World*, Paris 1964.
[14] S. Ryan, "Israeli Economic Policy in the Occupied Areas: Foundations of a New Imperialism." *Merip Reports* No. 24, Washington/Boston, January 1974.
[15] See G. Jabbour, *op. cit.*, p. 83; S. Jiryis pp. 146 ff.
[16] S. Jiryis, pp. 146-155.

2 SOUTH AFRICA, ZIONISM AND ISRAEL

A. Smuts and Weizmann*

RICHARD P. STEVENS

Introduction

Perhaps few personal friendships have so influenced the course of political events during the twentieth century as the relationship between General Jan Christian Smuts, South Africa's celebrated prime minister, and Chaim Weizmann, the charismatic Zionist leader and Israel's first president. But the importance and significance of this little publicized relationship far transcends the personal elements involved or its contribution to Zionist success; rather, it helps to throw into perspective both the contradictions of western liberalism and the psychological climate which rationalized the dominant position of a white minority in South Africa on the one hand and of a new European settlement in Palestine on the other.

Both Weizmann and Smuts stood in much the same way towards their respective "constituencies" and both represented in their "constituencies" the imperial factor in its economic, political and strategic dimensions. Without Weizmann there would have been no Balfour Declaration and without Smuts the Union brought forth in 1910 in South Africa might well have foundered. On the personal level it must be noted that during the entire thirty-three years of this relationship, extending from 1917 to Smuts' death in 1950, both men took for granted the moral legitimacy of each other's respective position. Thus, not a word is to be found in Weizmann's correspondence or writing questioning the racial basis of the South African state on which Zionism was so dependent or Smuts' own role in upholding its racist system. Similarly, Smuts assumed without question "the right" of Jewish settlers to occupy Palestine without regard to the rights of the indigenous Palestinian Arabs. In both cases, Smuts and Weizmann projected at the highest level the capacity of western civilization to rationalize domination and exploitation, conquest and control as Christian civilizing mission or ethnocentric Judeo-Christian fulfillment.

*Journal of Palestine Studies, Vol III, No. 1, Autumn 1973.

Smuts and Zionism

Smuts and Weizmann were introduced to each other for the first time in London in June 1917.[1] At that time Smuts was the "Special Delegate from South Africa" to the British Government and War Cabinet and was the only representative of the British dominions to play a full role in the wartime policies adopted by Great Britain.[2] Weizmann, who had obtained recognition from the British Cabinet for his success in producing acetone to aid the British war effort,[3] was President of the English Zionist Federation and actively attempting to convince the British Cabinet of the soundness of the Zionist programme and its usefulness to British policy aims. Weizmann records that he was received by Smuts:

> in the friendliest fashion, and given a most sympathetic hearing. A sort of warmth of understanding radiated from him, and he assured me heartily that something would be done in connection with Palestine and the Jewish people. He put many searching questions to me, and tried to find out how sincerely I believed in the actual possibilities. He treated the problem with eager interest, one might say with affection.[4]

There were several elements in Weizmann's character and approach which appealed naturally to the sensibilities of the South African leader, and on at least three major grounds, Smuts could share a kindred feeling with the Russian Jewish exile. Not least of these was Weizmann's candid avowal that Zionism was naturally and organically linked to British imperial interests. This was the crucial test for Smuts, who saw in the British Empire the buttress of world order and civilized development. Smuts himself was identified with the vision of an Anglo-Boer union within the framework of the British Empire; Weizmann's own plans for a Zionist entity within this framework meant that he, like Smuts, was spared any problem of conflicting national and imperial loyalties. As Leonard Stein, the historian of the Balfour Declaration, observed:

> From the outset it was clear to him [Weizmann] that British sponsorship of Zionist aspirations in Palestine was not only more likely to be obtainable but was beyond all comparison more to be desired than that of any other Power. In presenting their case to the British, the Zionists would not be approaching them merely as suppliants, still less as suppliants for something not manifestly in line with British interests. As he wrote to Israel Zangwill on October 10, 1914, he thought it self-evident that England needed Palestine for the safeguarding of the approaches to Egypt, and that if Palestine were thrown open for settlement by the Jews, then "England would have an effective barrier, and we would have a country." This was while Turkey was still neutral. With her entry into the war on the side of the Central Powers, the future of her Asiatic Empire, and, as part of it, the future of Palestine, became an open question. This was an invitation, of which Weizmann took full advantage, to insist on the community of interest between Great Britain and the Zionists. The common interest was something in which he genuinely believed. For him the Zionist cause came first, but in doing his best to promote it he was not speaking merely from an advocate's brief when he dwelt upon what Great Britain

stood to gain by a pro-Zionist policy. "Dr. Weizmann," says Webster, "could not have attained the position which he held in official circles had not all those with whom he came into contact believed absolutely in his probity and sincerity and learned to work with him as a partner in a great enterprise which would be of advantage to Britain as well as to his own people."[5]

A second reason for the appeal of Zionism to Smuts was that, in Weizmann's mind, the Zionist cause was justified in the same way as European civilization had rationalized its expansion over the Americas, Asia and Africa. It was, explained Weizmann, a simple question of the "desert versus civilization."[6] Disclaiming any "arrogance" in his analysis, Weizmann explained:

> Yet even today we hear people saying: "Well, yes, perhaps what you have done is all very good, but the Arabs in Palestine were used to a quiet life. They rode on camels; they were picturesque; they fitted into the landscape. Why not preserve it as a Museum, as a National Park? You came in from the West with your knowledge and your Jewish insistence. You are not picturesque. You do not fit into the landscape. You drain the marshes. You destroy malaria. And you do it in such a way that the mosquitoes fly on to the Arab villages. You still speak Hebrew with a bad accent, and you have not yet learned how to handle the plough properly. Instead of a camel you use a motor car." It reminds one of the eternal fight of stagnation against progress, efficiency, health, and education. The desert against civilization.[7]

At the same time, there was Weizmann's simple conviction of the righteousness of the Zionist cause—a conviction so fundamental that, like the claim of the Europeans to South Africa, it seemed self-evident. "The basis of our whole existence," said Weizmann, "is our right to build up our National Home in Eretz Israel. This is a right which has belonged to us for thousands of years ... which originated in the promise of God to Abraham, and which we have carried with us through the whole world, throughout a career of many vicissitudes."[8]

In his attitude towards Jewry itself in South Africa, Smuts had already shown favorable leanings. He believed that the defence of South African civilization (which he equated with "white civilization") required white unity. No sooner had Smuts and his colleague General Botha set about forming their *Het Volk* party after the Boer War, than they declared that it was "open to all white men whether Boer, Jew or Briton."[9] Since it was only through white unity that "civilization" could be preserved, anti-Semitism was rejected.

In a more personal vein, it has been suggested that Smuts' affinity for Jews reflected his sense of a similar background between them and the Boers. In the words of H.C. Armstrong, the Jews

> ... had the same background as his [Smuts] own people: the Dutch of the veld and the Jews of the desert. They had the same characteristics. Both were sour, bitter people; strictly religious with their lives based on religion learned from

the same Book—from the Old Testament.[10]

But to champion the Zionist cause—"to see the Jews great again"[11] of necessity meant oppostion to the Arab renaissance. "Justice apart, he [Smuts] had natural sympathy with neither French nor Arabs."[12] In short, Smuts' attitude towards the Arabs was essentially racist. Whereas some Europeans might tolerate a romantic attitude towards the Arab, Smuts, like most South Africans, could not be so inclined. As his biographer noted:

> As to Arabs, a Bedouin Arab quite naturally cannot seem so romantically strange to a South African as to a European, for the South African very well knows dark skinned peoples; peoples resembing, indeed, the Arabs—and with reason since Arab blood is in them. All his life the South African has been surrounded by millions of these dark peoples who, like the Bedouins, live in huts or wander over the land; are more courtly, courageous and poetic than he will admit; and (unless civilization compels them) like the Bedouins again, do, make, grow, want and own nothing.
> Smuts thinks as a European rather than as a South African—yet dark skinned people cannot seem exotic to him.[13]

Although Smuts' cultural and racial bias undoubtedly worked in Jewish favor, the fact remained that there were also sound domestic reasons for supporting Zionism. From its inception, the party of Botha and Smuts— the South African Party, and the United Party, its successor—was the party "that represented mine owners, industrialists and bankers"[14] and in at least two of these categories Jews were well represented. While not the dominant economic force in South Africa, Jews clearly controlled certain industries such as clothing manufacture and later the cinema. Although few Jews were farmers, those who turned to agriculture were heavy investors in machinery, and both the "potato king" and the "maize king" were Jews.[15] The vast majority of the group, some 80 per cent, traced their origins to Lithuania, thus making for an unusual degree of homogeneity.[16] Despite their original poverty, Jewish immigrants, like all white immigrants to South Africa, quickly discovered that the racial inequalities of the country allowed for upward group mobility; the working class element soon became a small minority. According to many observers, the South African Jewish community had become, by the end of the First World War, the wealthiest Jewish community in the world on a per capita basis.[17] Nor was the size of the Jewish community, as Rabbi Dr. Andre Ungar observed, a true reflection of the position of the Jews in South African life:

> ...it would be a grievous mistake to underestimate the significance of the Jewish minority. Even purely numerically speaking, under the absurd rules of South African ethnic arithmetic, the size of the Jewish population constitutes a factor necessary to reckon with ... in the two main cities, Johannesburg and Cape Town, the Jews constitute one-tenth of the citizens "that count": the Whites...[18]

Jewish institutions reflected the Zionist priorities and interests of the community. Fully 99 per cent of South African Jews were Zionist-affiliated.[19] With the small but influential South African Jewish community committed to Zionist philosophy, Smuts readily saw the political wisdom of embracing the Zionist vision. Since Zionism would obviously fit in with the imperial scheme of things, there was all the more reason to accept it wholeheartedly.

Smuts and Weizmann From World War I to World War II: Aspects of their Relationship

While the names of Lloyd George and Lord Balfour and Lord Milner have long been identified with the Balfour Declaration, the role of General Smuts has not received the same attention, despite the fact that by the General's own account he figured prominently in that decision.

Smuts' intriguing role in the Balfour Declaration has occupied the historian of that document, Leonard Stein. Now the first meeting with Weizmann, as mentioned above, took place in June 1917, in which month one of Weizmann's associates had advised that since Smuts was joining the War Cabinet rather than accepting an offer to command British forces in Palestine, "we must try to win him for our cause."[20] While Weizmann described the friendly reception accorded him by Smuts he gave no details of the conversation. On September 25, Weizmann's correspondent, Sacher, expressed satisfaction that Weizmann had "found Smuts so very understanding."[21] Concluding that "the part actually played by Smuts in helping to secure the approval of the Declaration is, however, difficult to assess," Stein nevertheless admitted that "he must rank among the architects of the Declaration" even though his contribution "was not of the same order as that of Balfour, Milner, or Lloyd George."[22]

Yet the whole story is not told, as Stein admits, because Smuts, as was his custom, "exerted his influence in the background."[23] It is this "influence in the background," so amply demonstrated on Zionism's behalf over the next three decades, that concerns us.

Over the three decades following the Balfour Declaration General Smuts and Chaim Weizmann would in large part respectively dominate or influence the course of events affecting South Africa and the Zionist movement. Smuts, in or out of office, never abandoned his support of the Zionist cause nor ceased to use his considerable influence in London on its behalf. Weizmann, ousted from the presidency of the Zionist Organization and Jewish Agency in July 1931, and without official position until 1935, continued to cultivate his friendship with General Smuts. Thus, as Britain found it increasingly difficult to honor the Balfour Declaration without jeopardy to other imperial interests, Smuts responded to Weizmann's appeals for assistance. Whether it was the White Paper of 1922, the Passfield White Paper of 1930, the Royal Commission Report of

1937 or the White Paper of 1939, Smuts was heard championing the Zionist cause and demanding the fulfilment of the Balfour promise.

While attending the Imperial Conference in late 1923 Smuts stayed in close contact with Weizmann and the Zionist Organization Central Office and was brought up to date on difficulties encountered by the Zionists in Palestine.[25]

On October 21, 1930 the MacDonald government published the Passfield White Paper (later withdrawn), a document which stated that in view of disorders which had taken place in Palestine, Jewish immigration and land purchases should stop. This threatened to repudiate the Balfour Declaration and threw the Zionist Organization into turmoil. At Weizmann's request Smuts cabled the Prime Minister "as one of those who is responsible for the Balfour Declaration" against what he considered "a retreat from that Declaration":

> As one of those who is responsible for the Balfour Declaration, I feel deeply disturbed because of the present political situation in Palestine which is a retreat from that Declaration. The Declaration was a definitive promise to the Jewish world, that the politics of a national home would be actively pursued and its intention was to win powerful Jewish influence for the cause of the allies in the lowest hours of the war. As such it was approved by the United States and the other allies and supported in good faith by the Jews. It cannot be altered unilaterally by the British. It now represents a pledge which must be honoured. The accompanying ceremonies of that declaration were so celebrated that there can be no backing off. I wish to insist that the government issue a declaration that it will carry out to the fullest the provisions of the Balfour Declaration in good faith, and that the Palestine politics of the government will be altered accordingly.[26]

MacDonald's immediate and lengthy telegraphic reply allayed Smuts' fears. In response, Smuts declared:

> I welcome especially your assurance that the recent declaration does not crystallize the policy of the government as regards the national home, as my impression remains, that as regards the purchase of land as well as immigration, the governments declaration does not deny the active duty to establish a Jewish national home as called for in the Balfour Declaration.[27]

Smuts also prepared the way for Weizmann to see Lloyd George on October 23.[28]

In spite of British modifications of the 1930 White Paper, the Seventeenth Zionist Congress, which met in 1931, was in no mood to tolerate Weizmann's sympathetic attitude to Great Britain. Having failed to win majority support, he left the Congress in anger and spent the next four years out of office. In late 1931 he decided to go off "on a money-raising expedition to South Africa."[29] This trip, described in Weizmann's autobiography, *Trial and Error,* and also in his wife's memoirs, *The Impossible Takes Longer,* was significant in that it brought forth no critical comment from Weizmann on the race problem of South Africa. This was despite the fact that during their extensive visit through all parts of the Union, the Weizmanns were brought face to face with African wretchedness. As his wife observed:

> The condition of the African population appalled us. The train stopped at every station and always naked children came round, their tummies distended from hunger, their little legs crooked from rickets. The Africans did not know how to cultivate their land properly. Their farms did not grow in size with the increase in the size of their families. The young generation had to go to the big towns to make a living. Emigration into the larger cities such as Capetown, Durban and Johannesburg became a problem. Africans were not allowed to come into shops: except by the back door![30]

In the face of this misery Mrs. Weizmann consoled herself with the thought that "there has always been a bond of sympathy between the Jewish people ... and other people seeking to emerge into nationhood" and that "many members of the Jewish population in South Africa have played a notable part in trying to alleviate and improve the lot of those in that country less fortunate than themselves."[31] She gave no indication that the problems of African servitude and white domination by Boer, Jew and Briton merited further analysis. Weizmann's own memoirs make no mention of Africans whatsoever, except for the fact that at 4 a.m. one morning "excited Kaffir boys"—the derogatory term used by white South Africans in speaking of Africans—awoke them in the Kruger game park with word that lions were in the vicinity. Even more paradoxical was Weizmann's reflection on the beauties of the park and the happy lives of the animals:

> Here they were, I thought, in their home, which in area is only slightly smaller than Palestine; they are protected, nature offers them generously of her gifts, and they have no Arab problem ... It must be a wonderful thing to be an animal on the South African game reserve: much better than being a Jew in Warsaw—or even in London.[32]

Weizmann failed to ask what it would be like to be an African in South Africa. Perhaps a key to Weizmann's obvious aloofness from the issue of racial injustice in South Africa while insisting upon "justice for the Jewish race" is provided by his English admirer, Richard Crossman, at an earlier period:

> It has been suggested that Weizmann's refusal to theorise was something he had learnt from Britain. There is as little evidence for this view as there is for the suggestion that he learnt anything from the British democracy. When I was reading in the Rehovoth Archives, I asked to be shown any references in Weizmann's lectures either to British politics or to social conditions in Lancashire, where he lived for so many years. One single letter was found for me, in which he mentions to his wife the terribly sad look of the workers as they go

into a factory. But that is all. When I learnt this, I couldn't help contrasting Weizmann's concentration on the plight of his own Jewish people with the attitude of another foreigner who lived for many years in Manchester, Friedrich Engels. Engels came to Lancashire as a cotton manufacturer, but as the collaborator of Karl Marx he concerned himself passionately with the condition of the workers and, as we all know, the Marx-Engels analysis of class war was worked out in terms of Lancashire. Weizmann had just as acute a mind and, when he was dealing with his own people, was just as interested in social conditions and social policies. But, unlike Marx and Engels, he did not feel moved by the condition of the workers and the problem was not his problem. Marx and Engels were self-conscious internationalists who believed in the unity of the working class. He was a self-conscious Jewish nationalist who believed that the Jewish worker of the Diaspora was separated by his Jewishness from the workers around him. That is why he conducted himself throughout his sojourn in Britain as a stranger and always refused to interfere or even to interest himself in British domestic politics, except insofar as they affected the Palestine question. The only obligation he felt was to persuade British politicians of all parties to espouse the Jewish cause.[33]

Similarly, the only obligation Weizmann felt vis-a-vis South Africa was to maintain Jewish support of the Zionist cause and to secure the political support of its famed world statesman, General Smuts.

In the latter part of the decade, between 1937 and 1939, the Smuts-Weizmann correspondence largely reflects Weizmann's concern with the partition proposal put forward by the Peel commission and Smuts' efforts to prevent its adoption.

When the Woodhead Report, which was intended to draw up plans for the implementation of the Peel commission proposals, was prepared, Smuts stated that London had already provided him with an advance copy of the still secret document (no small tribute to his influence in Whitehall). He commented:

There remains the larger question of the Palestinian settlement. I have had for more than a week an advance copy of the Woodhead Report of which I have made a fairly careful study. By the time you receive this letter, you will be in full possession of the facts and therefore I break no secrecy by at once giving you my impression of the Report.

I thought the original [Peel] Royal Commission Report unacceptable for a number of reasons, and can understand that you could only have been driven to entertain its consideration under severe compulsion of circumstances. The Woodhead Report however makes acceptance of partition by the Jews even more difficult. From the purely British point of view it is undoubtedly an improvement on the Royal Commission Report. It gives the mandatory authority greater elbow room for strategic purposes, and it avoids some of the pitfalls from a military and an air point of view which I saw at once in the original Report. From the Jewish point of view, however, the area for the Jewish National State is now so very contracted and exiguous that one doubts whether it is worthwhile accepting a little mouse that the mountains in labour have produced.[34]

Despite its unacceptable tenor, Smuts seemed confident that the report would not be implemented:

> My impression on the whole is that the Woodhead Commission is against partition, and does not really intend its recommendations to be carried out. Under the circumstances, I look with some curiosity to the statement of policy to be made by the British Government as I am now doubtful whether they will go on with partition, but I say this without any authority except my personal impressions of the Report. The question therefore remains what future policy is going to be laid down.[35]

In conclusion, Smuts expressed his pleasure in seeing "that American Jewry had taken a very firm line over the question, and it may be that with their strong support, you may carry the day";[36] an awareness, perhaps, that the real center of power behind the Zionist enterprise would soon shift from London to New York.

With Britain's entry into World War II on September 3, 1939, the situation with regard to Palestine took on new dimensions. Although Weizmann had earlier cabled to Smuts his concern that Britain might repudiate the National Home concept by adopting a rigorous immigration policy, he also indicated a new theme—repudiation of solemn undertakings to Jews "would constitute the gravest moral blow to this country (i.e., Britain) in the United States."[37]

Throughout the remainder of the war years, the immigration restrictions imposed by the White Paper of 1939, the question of a Jewish army, Jewish gun running, and the outbreak of Jewish terrorism against the British administration and armed forces in Palestine were chief topics of conversation between Weizmann and Smuts.[38]

Zionist determination to resist partition,[39] a proposal formally put to Weizmann on November 4, 1944,[40] was reflected for some time in Weizmann's correspondence. In September, Weizmann cabled his concern about rumors of decisions pending likely to affect the situation and urged Smuts to repond to a June 14 memorandum of his rejecting partition.[41] Smuts' response to this cable and a memorandum of October 6, 1944 was conveyed on November 14, 1944. By this time, however, Smuts had undoubtedly been informed of Churchill's proposal of partition and regarded it as inevitable:

> In spite of your cogent argument for a whole and undivided Palestine, I am afraid there will and must be partition. Too many chances were missed since 1919 in the carrying out of the spirit and intention of the Balfour Declaration. Probably the chief failure was the limitation on immigration in the early years when a strong immigration policy was possible. If by now the Jewish population of Palestine were in the majority a far-reaching solution would be possible. Now, with a majority of Arabs, and the Arab world in uproar, and British policy afraid to antagonize Arabs and Muslims, the best one could accept is a partition which will do substantial justice to the Jews and create a viable

Jewish State. The atmosphere has been worsened by the insane assassination of poor Moyne, and a malign fate has done the Jewish cause great harm at a critical moment—one of the worst strokes of luck you have had to endure. I am not all *au fait* with the present British proposals and speak only of the knowledge I have of the situation as it was six months ago.[42]

Smuts enclosed a copy of a statement made at the request of a local Jewish paper on the approach of Weizmann's 70th birthday.

In early 1945 Smuts received a confidential aide-memoire from Weizmann occasioned by the latter's visit to Palestine the previous November. In this remarkable document, entitled "Changes of Outlook in Palestinian Jewry since 1939, and the Causes," Weizmann passed on to Smuts a number of thoughts undoubtedly intended to reach British and American ears. With regard to the Yishuv (Jewish population of Palestine), Weizmann affirmed that during his five and half years' absence, there had been a deterioration in Jewish-British relations. "But I soon discovered," said Weizmann, "that this, as yet, had not gone deep, at any rate on the Jewish side. In the eyes of the Yishuv I stand for the link with Britain, and never have I had such a reception ... " After this reaffirmation of his leadership position and British connection, Weizmann went on to condemn what had been conceded or promised to the Arabs in Syria, Lebanon and Libya "without any stipulations regarding us." In short, in Zionist eyes no concessions should be made to "extreme" Arab nationalism without Arab agreement to an unpartitioned Jewish state in the whole of Palestine. "If the British Empire and the USA lay down their policy with regard to a Jewish State as an undiscussable decision," disclosed Weizmann, then "I believe that Ibn Saud and the others will acquiesce."

Aside from his advice regarding coercion of the Arabs, Weizmann went further and intimated another element in the Zionist approach seldom articulated, namely, that Jews could never be assimilated even in liberal western countries. Was it a warning to the West or a prediction of disaster for the Zionist cause should it occur? Whatever the case, Weizmann stated that Jewish emigration was a necessity. If they were not allowed to go to Palestine argued Weizmann, they "may be forced in a different direction." Moreover, argued Weizmann, "unless the gates of Palestine are opened the pressure will be directed towards the USA and the British Empire, where almost every European Jew has relatives or friends." In the long run, concluded Weizmann,

> ...the Jewish problem is the problem for these two great Commonwealths, which after the war will include considerably more than half of world Jewry. Unless through a Jewish State in Palestine they introduce an element which has been absent for 2,000 years, they are in danger of being poisoned by the Jewish question as others have been before them.[43]

In this context an earlier remark by Weizmann that anything and everything must be done to save the Jewish population of Europe and at any cost *except at the cost of Zionism itself* becomes more intelligible. It was precisely the Zionist determination not to press for massive Jewish immigration into the United States and Britain which gave Weizmann additional bargaining power with the "western democracies." Now Weizmann would raise a virtual spectre, if necessary, to secure the Palestinian area, of a flood of Jews pounding at their doors.

After the end of the war, the issues of the fate of Jewish refugees and the future of Palestine came up for consideration once more. In 1946 Smuts responded to a request by Weizmann concerning the newly created Anglo-American Inquiry Committee which Weizmann expected would recommend the abolition of the Jewish Agency and the establishment of a Palestine government (i.e., Arab majority) which would then control Jewish immigration. Under these circumstances Weizmann requested that Smuts once more involve his "powerful aid in the interests of Zionism and Palestine."[44] Specifically, Smuts' assistance was needed in securing immediately from the British government 100,000 certificates for Jewish immigration. Should these certificates be granted, said Weizmann:

> The Jewish position in Europe will be to some extent relieved, and it will then be possible to consider the wider issues of the Palestine problem as a whole, with which I believe to be linked up the future of the Middle East and Great Britain's position and interests there. It is not for me to speak of the last-mentioned problem but I believe you have always shared our view that a Jewish Palestine is the surest of all available bulwarks for British power in the Middle East.[45]

Once immigration on a large scale had been resumed then it was expected, declared Weizmann, that the pheonomenon of terrorism would disappear "and the cooperation with Britain, which has always been the firm basis of our policy, will be reestablished."[46] In conclusion, Weizmann appealed to Smuts' own sense of Afrikaner loyalty as well as Jewish-British mutual interest:

> I am appealing to you as one of our oldest friends—one of the few still left to us of the group of great statesmen to whom we owe the National Home policy. You know what is at stake in the coming critical weeks. May I invoke your powerful aid for another people in dire need—small, like your own, and like your own, old and proud? Now is the time when our friends can help us if they will. What we can do for ourselves, we have done; our fate now rests with England and America.[47]

Although Smuts did not reply to this letter for some weeks he almost immediately submitted a lengthy statement to the Anglo-American Committee of Inquiry, "as the one surviving member of the War Cabinet of the last war and one who in 1917 took an active part in the planning of the

Balfour Declaration."[48] Throughout his statement Smuts argued that the Declaration was not meant as "a mere temporary expedient out of a present difficulty" but as "a declaration of long range policy for the future." Thus, said Smuts:

> The White Paper of 1939, which purports to limit the immigration policy under the Mandate, by a term of years and a limit of numbers, was merely the unilateral act of the British Government and—it seems to me—in conflict with the real character of the Mandate. I do not think that it can be used as an argument in the interpretation either of the Declaration or the Mandate. All I wish to emphasize in this statement is that the Balfour Declaration made by the British Government, assented to by the American and French Governments, and subsequently solemnly confirmed in the Mandate by the nations of the League—is a solemn and sacrosanct document, embodying a long range policy of Jewish immigration into Palestine, that it should be treated with respect as such, and that the fundamental rights thereby assured to the Jewish people should not be abridged or tampered with more than is absolutely necessary under all the circumstances of the case.[49]

On June 9, Smuts was able to respond personally to Weizmann's letter of April 14. His delay in replying was simply attributed to the fact that "nothing has happened that is not known to you." "And until the two governments have finished the discussions now going on between them," said Smuts, "there [was] really nothing to report."[50] Smuts was convinced, however, that Britain would do nothing without American backing, and that the near future would show "whether and how far America is prepared to go." He accurately predicted that "the American indications [were] on the whole favourable" for the Zionist cause and promised to be in touch with Weizmann upon his return to London.[51] After the South African Prime Minister's departure from London Weizmann confessed to Smuts: "I can scarcely tell you how much I miss your guidance and advice in these terribly difficult times."[52]

The Creation of Israel

Following the British decision to submit the Palestine question to the United Nations, the United Nations Special Committee on Palestine (UNSCOP), drawn from eleven states held to be "neutral" on the Palestine issue—Australia, Canada, Czechoslovakia, Guatemala, India, Iran, Netherlands, Peru, Sweden, Uruguay and Yugoslavia—could not but bring encouragement to the Zionists. These "neutrals" included such staunch Zionist champions as Jorge Garcia Granados of Guatemala and Enrique Rodriguez Fabregat of Uruguay, and it was before this committee that Weizmann testified in Jerusalem during its sitting from June 16 to July 24. As part of his testimony he quoted a portion of a letter by Smuts as a commentary upon Jewish sufferings by "one of the last surviving statesmen who formulated the Balfour Declaration."[53] On September 1, UNSCOP proposed partition and recommended Jewish statehood to the

General Assembly.

After arriving in New York in October Weizmann advised Smuts that the situation seemed favorable:

> The main point is the positive attitude both of America and of Russia and it is almost tantamount to a miracle that these two countries should have agreed on our problem.
>
> It looks as if the UNSCOP majority report is meeting with a great deal of favour. There may be some slight modification here and there but on a whole, it seems to be an excellent basis for discussion.[54]

With the United Nations now the focus of activity Smuts was able to assist Weizmann in still other ways through the South African delegation. Weizmann expressed his gratitude to Smuts for putting him

> in touch with your delegation here whom I have seen twice and with whom we have discussed all the various details. Mr. Lawrence and his colleagues are thoughtful and sympathetic men and they listened very attentively to what I had to say.[55]

Smuts indicated to Weizmann that he had spoken in favor of the partition of Palestine before the South African parliament in May. Even before that statement the Prime Minister spoke of South Africa's support for the convening of a special session of the United Nations to consider the Palestine question. In reply to a question in mid-April Smuts declared,

> I myself have been very doubtful about that 1939 White Paper. I have been very doubtful about it. I think the British Government is doubtful about it. I believe in fact it has been practically withdrawn, that it is largely in abeyance ... The Jewish people have been driven to desperation. I look upon these criminals among them as real desperadoes, driven mad by the suffering of their race and constant frustration. I hope the Jewish people will get that solution from UNO.[56]

In this same question period, however, Smuts, the steadfast friend of Zionism, revealed how consistent support of Zionism was with professedly discriminatory immigration policies against Jews. Turning to a plea made in the House of Assembly that displaced persons from Europe, including Jews, should be admitted to prevent invasion from India, China and Japan, General Smuts said that

> Referring to the above suggestion by Mr. Kentridge, General Smuts said that that would not be a solution to the Jewish problem. To overload the country with Jews would merely create anti-Semitism. He always held that view. South Africa would do her share by helping to find a solution which in his view was the establishing of a Jewish National Home in Palestine.[59]

The Jewish deputy who followed, Dr. Friedman of Smuts' own party, did not challenge the Prime Minister's logic. Instead he expressed appreciation for what Smuts had said on Palestine. The brief debate succinctly summarized the fact that Zionism and anti-Semitism, in South Africa as in the rest of the "liberal" West, were mutually interdependent. That South Africa, whose support for Zionism was exceeded by no other country on a per capita basis, could yet accommodate anti-Semitic policies thereby becomes more intelligible. Thus, while General Smuts argued against any general policy of Jewish immigration he could also congratulate Jewish citizens for playing "a foremost part from the very beginning in the building up of the greatest centre of European population in the Union."[58]

The close financial relationship between South African Jewry and the Zionist enterprise in Palestine throughout the years served to underline the very special role of South African capital in the Jewish colonization scheme. In recognizing this relationship and encouraging its continuation Smuts was able to cement his own political fortunes with the Jewish community in a manner fully consistent with his traditional support of the country's strongest capitalistic interests.

Jewish capital funded the South African Palestine Enterprise (Binyan) Corporation, which was presented as not merely a means of South African support for Zionist efforts, but as a sound business proposition as well.[59] According to the South African Zionist leader, Mr. Bernard Alexander, "Zionism in action expressed in terms of practical assistance, had been its [the Jewish community's] most distinguishing characteristic," although "the not unprosperous material situation of South African Jewry enabled it to indulge this propensity."[60]

Recently, said Alexander, the "practical work" of South African Zionists had entered a new and vitally important field. Within the previous 15 or 20 years, he explained, something like a South African "aliyah" had set in. He reported that while in 1947 the number of ex-South Africans in Palestine was small, it was perceptible, and, in spite of all difficulties of entry, was steadily on the increase. In kibbutzim in all parts of Palestine, South African *chalutzim* were to be found; ex-soldiers in the extreme north, Shomer Hatzair youngsters in the Sharon and the Negev, former youth leaders in the Huleh and the Emek Zebulun, young Mizrachi in the Hebron hills. Ex-South Africans were to be found here and there running private farms. In the towns, business and professional men and women were to be found aplenty, and all were doing a pioneer job, and at the same time strengthening the nexus between South Africa and "Eretz Israel." At the same time, he declared, the numerous and active South African companies were engaged in a very real "practical Zionism"—being instruments for the creation and maintenance of productive undertakings, calculated to foster Palestine's economic development, and to widen the field of settlement and absorption. As to individuals in South

Africa who made investments in Palestine, their number, said Alexander, was legion. The significant part which South African Zionists, individually and collectively, played in the upbuilding of Palestine was evidenced, he said, by the large number of "institutions" which perpetuated South African names or were known to owe their existence, wholly or in part, to South African benefactions. The list was long and impressive. Still, when all was said and recognized, said Alexander, it remained true that, in a community of over 100,000 souls, living thousands of miles from "Eretz Israel," the main work for Palestine would continue to take the form of financial contributions to the "constructive tasks" of the Jewish National Home. And indeed the growth of more personal and direct ties with Palestine had gone hand in hand with an ever increasing support of all such undertakings. During the war and post-war years, in particular, he affirmed, the results had been most impressive, both in magnitude and in range, embracing not only the main fields of Jewish construction, but also cultural, rescue and philanthropic objects of a varied nature. But the Zionists of South Africa had long since come to the conclusion, said Alexander, that the "normal" methods were hopelessly inadequate: that to secure the land, and secure it in time, the Jewish people must have much larger liquid resources; and that as far as South African Jewry was concerned, this meant special campaigns over and above the ordinary collection means. Indeed it was the devotion of South African Jewry to Zionism, as demonstrated by ever increasing financial commitments, which undoubtedly assured the permanency of the Smuts-Weizmann friendship and which served both so conveniently.

Weizmann, meanwhile, was anxious lest British resentment over recent developments in Palestine turn into outright opposition to a Jewish state. While recognizing that Britain was no longer a key factor influencing the Palestine issue, on November 15, as a General Assembly vote neared on the UNSCOP report, Weizmann asked Smuts, then in London,

...most respectfully, whether you could, with your great influence, at the last moment, try and bring about a change in the attitude of the Foreign Office ...[61]

Again, a few days later, Smuts received another urgent appeal:

Attitude British delegation here disturbing and may endanger success all our efforts which otherwise reasonably certain stop. Could you use your great influence to induce a more friendly relationship at last crucial hour? Many thanks.[62]

On November 29, 1947, after an unparalleled example of "behind the scenes" negotiations and outright political intimidation, the partitioning of Palestine into Jewish and Arab states became the declared policy of the United Nations. The day before the Zionist victory was carried, Smuts had confirmed to a Jewish Agency official in London that:

> I have instructed my UNO Delegation to be helpful in your support and to keep in close touch with Dr. Weizmann. I have also discussed on the highest level the matters we touched upon a few days ago, and am hopeful of good results.[64]

With victory in hand, Smuts was one of the first to be thanked by Weizmann for his unfailing support. Having arrived back in Pretoria the Prime Minister penned a personal reply:

> My dear Weizmann,
>
> I was deeply moved by your kind wire from New York on the passing of the Partition motion. I received the wire at Rome on my way back to South Africa and have had no earlier opportunity to thank you, for a wire I deeply appreciate. My service in the cause has been small, but it has been wholehearted all the way and in all weathers...
>
> With the leading people in the British Cabinet I have discussed the necessity of a fair ending which will not leave Palestine in a mess. It must be an orderly and proper ending of a great chapter of history. I hope this appeal will have a good response. Great Britain has been the friend although sometimes a difficult friend... It must retain Jewish friendship in the difficult chapter ahead. It is to be hoped that nothing will jeopardise that friendship...[65]

With violence mounting in Palestine in the aftermath of partition, the United States backed off from enforcing partition. Instead, the United States seemed to suggest on February 24, 1948 that the Security Council could not enforce partition and urged a trusteeship arrangement. As Zionists responded to what was considered a threat to partition, every device, including the formation of the "Emergency Conference to Save the United Nations by Supporting the Palestine Resolution" was adopted.[66] Weizmann was summoned back from Palestine to New York in mid-February to assist "in the gathering crisis."[67]

On March 24 Weizmann dispatched an urgent cable to Smuts:

> Anxious draw your attention Evatts statement concerning partition would be most grateful if you could support partition at this critical moment particularly in view of American change in policy. Thankfully and affectionately yours.[68]

Smuts, however, was convinced that the United States did not intend to block partition but merely wished to prevent a vacuum of public authority after the British withdrawal set for May 15.[69]

On April 21, Smuts was asked in a cable for South African assistance.

> We are reaching decisive point in deliberations stop. Attitude of New Zealand

and Australia demanding fidelity to Assembly resolution and resistance to aggression has raised morale and hopes of all here stop. Similar attitude by South African delegation in conformity long tradition would be most helpful.[70]

To this request Smuts cabled a reply through the South African UN delegation:

> My delegation has instructions to continue our support partition and press for special truce Jerusalem if general truce fails.[71]

On May 15, 1948 Britain withdrew as promised from Palestine and the state of Israel was officially declared. Recognition followed from various countries but Great Britain remained silent. According to Weizmann, it was thought that Mr. Bevin was bringing pressure to bear on the British Dominions and Western Europe to withhold recognition.[72] He therefore addressed a cablegram to General Smuts urging immediate recognition:

> Now that Balfour Declaration has been consummated by establishment state of Israel I take opportunity of expressing to you as one of architects of Declaration and most constant supporter of Jewish cause my deepest appreciation and gratitude for manifold kindnesses which you have shown to Zionist movement and to me personally during intervening years stop. I understand that new state has approached you for recognition and I venture express hope it will be possible for you to crown your lifelong encouragement of our national aspirations by giving speedy recognition stop...[73]

Replying through the South African Legation in Washington Smuts welcomed Weizmann's message and expressed his hope for Israel's success. But official action of recognition, he said, was "held up by considerations [of] new situation and necessary consultation."[74] Weizmann returned to press the issue a few days later. His cable, quoted in full below, gave specific reasons for the urgency of South African recognition:

> Personal and confidential
>
> Deeply appreciate your encouraging message stop. Consider prompt recognition would not only crown long-standing support your country yourself for revival Jewish nationhood but would also have important effect present situation firstly by giving lead other dominions secondly by strengthening efforts prevent further bloodshed through Security Council thirdly by helping promote better relations with Britain stop. As life-long protagonist British-Jewish friendship am deeply distressed present British role allowing invasion by Arab Legion including destructive assault on Jerusalem with British commanders weapons finance also continuing arms supplies to other Arab armies operating Palestine also leading opposition in Security Council to American cease-fire initiative stop. Your unofficial influence to mitigate unfriendly British policy and promote satisfactory relations between new state and Commonwealth would be signal contribution stop. As ever my heartfelt good wishes
>
> Chaim Weizmann

(Major Comay suggests that this cable be teletyped to our Washington office, who will hand it to the South African Minister in Washington requesting him in the name of Dr. Weizmann to convey the message to General Smuts.)[75]

On May 24, in a cable to Moshe Shertok, Foreign Minister of Israel, the Union government accorded *de facto* recognition.[76] Two days later, on May 26, the Smuts government fell. Immediately after the narrow Nationalist victory the Malan government extended *de jure* recognition to Israel. Weizmann's May 26 cable of thanks came to Smuts on his last day as prime minister.

As the 1948 general election approached there had been growing signs indicating a switch in traditionally anti-Semitic South African Nationalist thought towards South African Jewry. Not only did the Afrikaans press support Zionist opposition to British policies in Palestine, which since 1939 had moved away from endorsing Jewish statehood against the wishes of the Arab majority, but it compared the determination of the Afrikaners to break the Union's British ties with the Zionist undertaking. In various localities Nationalist politicians began to seek openly the favor of influential Jews and a dialogue was opened in Cape Town between several prominent Jews and leading Nationalists. Although in October 1947, Malan repeated his party's opposition to additional Jewish immigration, he argued that opposition was not because of anti-Jewish feeling but "because we want to prevent these feelings."[77] But it was the creation of the state of Israel on May 14, 1948, only a few days before the May 26 election, which especially influenced Nationalist attitudes. According to Dr. Leslie Rubin, a South African exile and co-founder of the Liberal Party,

> ... A strange mixture of motives made it easy for Malan (and Strijdom has faithfully followed his lead since) and the Nationalists to offer enthusiastic support to the new state. There was a sense of affinity with the Israelis in having thrown off the British yoke. A psychologist might have called it admiration for the achievement by another of what was for them still a suppressed desire.[78]

Under Nationalist Party leadership relations with Israel were carried to their logical conclusion of cooperation. Various South African Jews, including Abba Eban, Mr. Arthur Lourie and Major Michael Comay, and many others, would now join the top ranks of Israel's decision makers.[79]

The Final Years

In the aftermath of defeat, Smuts' contribution to Zionist victory would not be forgotten. His role over thirty-one years was recognized by the South African Jewish press, the South African Jewish Board of Deputies and by the Zionist Federation. Weizmann, soon to be elected Israel's first president, cabled his affectionate regards.[80] During the final two and a half years of his life Smuts' ties with Weizmann and the Balfour Declaration would be celebrated as one of the greatest contributions to the success of the Jewish state.

The first anniversary of the proclamation of Israel's independence was celebrated in South Africa with a banquet in the Johannesburg City Hall tendered by the Executive of the South African Zionist Federation with General Smuts as guest of honor. Surrounded by all the important personalities of the Zionist movement, Smuts was greeted with tremendous enthusiasm and tributes were paid to him for his devoted labors to the Zionist cause. In his response, Smuts observed that it was in fact most astonishing that the birth of Israel had occurred in their lifetime. And South Africa, he said, had played a fine part in this achievement. "There was no country in proportion to its population which had done more, materially, for the National Home than South Africa according to its means." He took special pleasure, he said, in thinking that his last act as Prime Minister of the Union was the recognition of the state of Israel. "It put Israel 'on the map,' but it also put South Africa 'on the map'."[81]

In August of 1949 Weizmann sounded out Smuts on the possibility of attending a great dinner celebration in London planned for his own 75th birthday. Smuts was asked to attend and to be the chief speaker. Smuts quickly replied that despite a "very tight political time-table," he was "anxious to join in any move to do honour to you. Our long association in the great cause is of course an added reason for my accepting the invitation, if made."[82]

As promised, Smuts flew to London to join in honoring Weizmann, one he called "a great friend, a great man, with whom I have had the privilege to be associated for much of a lifetime." Recalling Weizmann's rise from a Russian ghetto, his scientific studies and his arrival in England, Smuts said that Weizmann was more than a scientist; his imagination and heart had been fired with the vision brought by Herzl and "he remained faithful when many, even Herzl himself, began to quail before the enormous difficulties." The case itself, said Smuts,

> and Weizmann's way of presenting it, together with his personal prestige as a scientist and war worker, carried the day with some members of the then War Cabinet. Mr. Balfour was persuaded, and became a convinced supporter. Likewise Mr. Lloyd George, who had not only been educated on the Book, but was particularly sensitive as a member of a small people to Weizmann's arguments....
>
> We were persuaded, but remember it was Weizmann who persuaded us. But for Dr. Weizmann there would have been no Balfour Declaration.[83]

While saddened by Jewish terrorism in Palestine, Smuts nevertheless attempted to put it in an acceptable historical context—an approach rendered somewhat more paradoxical considering subsequent condemnation of "exasperation" from Africans in his own country and displaced Palestinians:

> There was a growing exasperation among the Jewish remnants, into whose soul the iron of suffering had entered, and who could bear no more. No wonder extremist elements got out of hand and forced the pace towards solutions such as no Commission or endless palavers could have brought about. We know that sad story. One need not approve the violent policies of Irgun Zvai Leumi, nor need one abate one's abhorrence of the criminal proceedings of the Stern Gang. But history does not always proceed along the way of law and order. Where reason fails force takes charge, and speeds up conditions. Long delays and continual frustrations do sometimes create an abnormal state of mind, and Jewry as a whole should not be held responsible for such aberrations.[84]

As for Israel's relations with her neighbors, Smuts hoped for an accommodation and acceptance. Still, in Smuts own inimitable style, even conflict and violence could be elevated to a "sport" by those carrying the message of civilization:

> Life would become too drab and too much living human interest would be taken out of it. Sport, fun, a certain amount of tension and excitement, and even unruliness have their function in human society. Life is interest, and that interest takes many strange forms. Some sparring among the Semitic elements in Palestine may therefore not be an unmitigated evil.[85]

And finally before concluding his praise of Weizmann and the Jewish state, Smuts showed his loyalty to the British tradition. In the final analysis, he declared, it was the identification of the National Home with Britain which had brought success:

> Nor should we tonight forget the great Commonwealth which stood by the National Home from the Balfour Declaration to the achievement of national sovereignty. It has been a hard way, sometimes marred by misunderstanding due to the conflicting duties laid on Britain under the Mandate. But let Israel never forget that it was Britain that first took Weizmann by the hand, and that grip should never be relaxed. Forget the smaller differences which have developed on the way. The historic comradeship should continue unbroken for the fruitful service of mankind.[86]

Smuts' last two years could hardly add to the record of his service to the Zionist cause. But with the end drawing near Smuts put a visible capstone upon his lifetime service by presenting on December 4, 1949 a bust of himself by the South African Jewish sculptor, Moses Kottler, to the Hebrew University in Jerusalem. Handing the bust over to Justice L. Greenberg, President of the South African Friends of the Hebrew University, Smuts again affirmed his belief in the historical role of the Jewish people:

> I do not think that at any other stage in history has there been an event of such far-reaching importance as the return of the Jewish people to their ancient homeland, he said.[87]

General Smuts then proceeded to discuss the effect of the establishment of Israel on the Middle East. He thought that the fact of the Jewish state would alter the entire situation in that area. "The Middle East has been asleep for centuries, and I want to see Israel emerge as the vital force, leading its neighbouring countries along the paths of progress. It is this I want to see, and not strife and warfare. It is my wish that we will soon witness the dawn of a new era in the Middle East, with Israel exerting a tremendous influence for good." The Hebrew University, said General Smuts, could become the spearhead of this cultural advance, and it was to be hoped that it would realize the hopes and aspirations of its many friends and fulfil its noble mission:

> I am happy to be here tonight, and to have been associated with at least one thing in my life which has been successful, and I am glad that South Africa has played a part in the realization of the return to the Jewish homeland. This great achievement has been brought about by an act of historic justice and it was good to realise that there were forces for good at work in the world.[88]

In thanking General Smuts, Justice Greenberg declared that "It would remind Jews of future generations of this great man who had busied himself with the aspirations of the Jewish people and who was big enough to allow his interests to stretch from his birthplace in the Western Province to the Middle East."[89] Indeed, it was to Smuts' transformation from a Boer soldier of the "Western Province" of South Africa into the foremost champion of the British imperial "mission," a mission which so happily embraced the Zionist cause, that Israel's birth in part was due.

On September 11, 1950 General Smuts passed away on his farm at Irene. Among the many tributes in his honor none were more fervent or heartfelt than those from South African Jewry, Zionist and Israeli leaders. Throughout South Africa Smuts would be eulogized in Jewish synagogues as a "life-long Zionist," a "framer of the Balfour Declaration" as well as "the architect of South African Union." As for Israel itself, said the then Acting Prime Minister, Joseph Sprinzak, "General Smuts is written on the map of Israel and in the heart of our nation."[90] Two years later on March 18, 1952 Israel would dedicate its "living memorial" to General Smuts. That day on the southern slopes of the Judean Hills the Smuts Forest, overlooking the Weizmann Forest, was formally dedicated. With the South African flag flying alongside the Israeli banner and representatives of the Israeli Government, the Jewish Agency, the Keren Keyemeth and the South African Jewish community in attendance, a message of tribute from Winston Churchill, the sole survivor of the Imperial statesmen associated with the Zionist programme, was read to the assembled gathering. With the passing of General Smuts a chapter in the South African-Zionist-Israeli relationship was brought to a close, but the foundations had been securely laid. The importance of South Africa for the Jewish state was incontestable; a new and more intriguing relationship lay ahead.

[1] Leonard Stein, *The Balfour Declaration* (London, 1961), p. 480. This dating contradicts that of Weizmann in *Trial and Error*, p. 159.
[2] A.P. Thornton, *The Imperial Idea and Its Enemies* (New York, 1968), p. 214.
[3] Samuel Shikor, *Hollow Glory* (New York, 1960), pp. 23-26.
[4] Chaim Weizmann, *Trial and Error* (New York, 1966), p. 159.
[5] Stein, pp. 14-15.
[6] Chaim Weizmann, "The Position in Palestine," *Palestine Papers*, No. 2 (Jewish Agency for Palestine, London, 1929-30), p. 24.
[7] *Ibid*, pp. 24-25.
[8] *Ibid.*, p. 24.
[9] Sarah Gertrude Millin, *General Smuts*, Vol. II (London, 1936), p. 109.
[10] H.C. Armstrong, *Grey Steel: J.C. Smuts, A Study in Arrogance* (London, 1937), pp. 300-301.
[11] Millin, p. 110.
[12] *Ibid.*, p. 111.
[13] *Ibid.*, pp. 112-113.
[14] J.H. and R.E. Simons, *Class and Colour in South Africa, 1850-1950* (Baltimore, 1969), p. 288.
[15] Bernard Sacks, "South Africa: Life on a Volcano, The Jewish Community in A Caste Society," *Commentary*, IX (June, 1950), p. 530.
[16] Dan Jacobson, "The Jews of South Africa: Portrait of a Flourishing Community," *Commentary*, XXIII (January, 1957), p. 39.
[17] *Ibid.*
[18] Andre Ungar, "The Abdication of a Community," *Africa South*, III (January-March 1959), pp. 29-30.
[19] Sarah G. Millin, *The People of South Africa* (New York, 1954), p. 236.
[20] Stein, p. 480. Smuts had already promised a local Zionist to "help 'Zionism'" while in South Africa in 1916, according to the *South African Zionist Record*, September 22, 1950.
[21] *Ibid.*
[22] *Ibid.*, p. 482.
[23] *Ibid.*
[24] Weizmann to Smuts, November 6, 1923.
[25] Cable, Johannesburg, South African Zionist Conference to Zionist Organization Central Office, March 5, 1924.
[26] Smuts to MacDonald, October 22, 1930.
[27] Smuts to MacDonald, October 24, 1930.
[28] Vera Weizmann (David Tutaev writer), *The Impossible Takes Longer* (New York, 1967), p. 113.
[29] Vera Weizmann, p. 122.
[30] *Ibid.*, p. 123.
[31] *Ibid.*, p. 124.
[32] Weizmann, *Trial and Error*, p. 347.
[33] Richard Crossman, *A Nation Reborn* (New York, 1960), pp. 30-31.
[34] Smuts to Weizmann, November 4, 1938.
[35] *Ibid.*

[36] *Ibid.*
[37] Weizmann to Smuts, March 8, 1939.
[38] See, e.g., Weizmann to Smuts, February 17, 1940; August 15, 1941; November 10 and 23, 1943; June 12, 1944.
[39] On June 12, 1944, Weizmann had noted that while he had been willing to compromise and accept a partition proposal in 1937, the idea was now untenable.
[40] Meyer Weisgal and Joel Carmichael, *Chaim Weizmann* (New York, 1963), p. 275.
[41] Weizmann to Smuts, September 12, 1944.
[42] Smuts to Weizmann, November 14, 1944.
[43] Memorandum on the Position in the Yishuv to Field Marshal J.C. Smuts, March 20, 1945.
[44] Weizmann to Smuts, April 14, 1946.
[45] *Ibid.*
[46] *Ibid.*
[47] *Ibid.*
[48] *South African Jewish Chronicle (SAJC),* April 19, 1946.
[49] *Ibid.*
[50] Smuts to Weizmann, June 9, 1946.
[51] *Ibid.*
[52] Weizmann to Smuts, July 12, 1946.
[53] Shikor, p. 48.
[54] Weizmann to Smuts, October 28, 1947.
[55] *Ibid.*
[56] *South African Zionist Record,* April 18, 1947.
[57] *Ibid.*
[58] *SAJC,* July 4, 1947.
[59] *SAJC,* July 18, 1947.
[60] *Ibid.*
[61] Weizmann to Smuts, November 15, 1947.
[62] Weizmann to Smuts, November 22, 1947.
[63] See Richard P. Stevens, *American Zionism and US Foreign Policy, 1942-1947* (New York, 1962), pp. 175-85.
[64] Smuts to Linton, November 28, 1947.
[65] Smuts to Weizmann, December 5, 1947.
[66] Stevens, pp. 186-210.
[67] Weizmann, *Trial and Error,* p. 471.
[68] Weizmann to Smuts, March 24, 1948.
[69] Smuts to Weizmann, March 29, 1948.
[70] Weizmann to Smuts, April 21, 1948.
[71] Permanent Delegation of Union of South Africa to Weizmann, April 26, 1948.
[72] Weizmann, *ibid.,* p. 479.
[73] Weizmann to Smuts, May 16, 1948.
[74] Legation of Union of South Africa to Weizmann, May 17, 1948.
[75] Weizmann to Smuts, May 21, 1948.
[76] *SAJC,* May 28, 1948.
[77] *Die Transvaler,* October 30, 1947 as quoted in translation in Alexander Hepple, *Verwoerd* (Baltimore, 1967), p. 226.
[78] Leslie Rubin, "Afrikaner Nationalism and the Jews," *Africa South* (April-June, 1957), p. 29.
[79] See *SAJC,* June 11, 1948 for detailed background on Lourie and Comay.
[80] Weizmann to Smuts, June 13, 1948.
[81] *SAJC,* September 15, 1950.
[82] Smuts to Weizmann, September 1, 1949.
[83] *South African Zionist Record,* November 25, 1949.
[84] *Ibid.*
[85] *Ibid.*
[86] *Ibid.*
[87] *SAJC,* September 15, 1950.
[88] *Ibid.*
[89] *Ibid.*
[90] *SAJC,* September 22, 1950.

B. Zionism, South Africa and Apartheid: The Paradoxical Triangle*

RICHARD P. STEVENS

The Nationalist Party and Anti-Semitism, 1930-1947
Professor Keppel-Jones' prediction of an officially sanctioned pogrom for 1956[1] appeared fully consistent with the anti-Semitic record of the Nationalist Party in South Africa in the years preceding its electoral victory of 1948. It was, after all, as recently as 1930 that Dr. Daniel F. Malan introduced his immigration quota bill restricting immigration from Eastern Europe. This bill, fathered by the man who led the Nationalist Party to victory in 1948, was adopted as the Quota Act of 1930 and effectively reduced Jewish immigration from Eastern Europe to a trickle. When Hitler's attacks upon German Jewry led to the immigration of several thousand German Jews, Nazi-inspired elements within the Nationalist Party openly advocated the adoption of similar methods in South Africa. Dr. Hendrik F. Verwoerd, Malan's close associate and eventual successor as Prime Minister, also launched his political career at the same period of anti-Semitic outpourings. One of Verwoerd's first political actions was to lead a deputation to Prime Minister Hertzog asking that he refuse admission to Jewish refugees.[2] In 1936 an Aliens Act instituted a new system of controlling immigration which meant in effect that until the end of the war no more than fifty Jews a year entered the country.

The blatant anti-Semitic policy of the Nationalist Party continued until 1945. Through its attacks on "Jewish democracy" and "Jewish capitalism," the Party clearly indicated that Jews were not far behind "kafirs" in terms of its defined prejudices. During this period some Afrikaners favored the disfranchisement of all "un-assimilable" groups in which Jews were specifically included. Rarely was a person of Jewish background admitted to the Nationalist Party and through its recognized organ, *Die Transvaler,* edited by Dr. Verwoerd, the "Jewish imperialistic war machine" and Jewish immigration were attacked. The anti-Jewish policies of the Nationalist Party were officially proclaimed in their elec-

---
**Phylon,* The Atlanta University Review of Race and Culture; Vol. 32 (No. 2, 1971).

tion manifesto of 1938 and reaffirmed three years later. Not even the defeat of Nazi Germany in April, 1945, brought an immediate end to Nationalist support of Nazi principles.[3]

The South African Jewish Community and Zionism

By 1945 the South African Jewish community was estimated at something over 105,000 and grew to 120,000 five years later.[4] While not the dominant economic force in the country, Jews clearly controlled certain industries such as clothing manufacture and the cinema. Although few Jews were farmers, those who turned to agriculture were heavy investors in machinery and both the "potato king" and the "maize king" were Jews.[5] The vast majority of the group, some 80 per cent, traced their origins to Lithuania thus exhibiting an unusual degree of homogeneity.[6] By 1948, however, approximately 46 per cent were South African born. Despite their original poverty, Jewish immigrants, like all white immigrants to South Africa, quickly discovered that the racial inequalities of the country permitted upward group mobility; the working class element soon became a small minority. According to many observers, the South African Jewish community had, by the end of the war, become the wealthiest Jewish community in the world on a per capita basis.[7] Nor was the size of the Jewish community, as Rabbi Dr. Andre Ungar observed, a true reflection of the position of the Jews in South African life:

> [I]t would be a grievous mistake to under-estimate the significance of the Jewish minority. Even purely numerically speaking, under the absurd rules of South African ethnic arithmetic, the size of the Jewish population constitutes a factor necessary to reckon with.... South Africa is the land *par excellence* where minorities can have a say—and a vast majority be deprived of it—quite without regard to what, in a democracy, their numbers would warrant. And in the two main cities, Johannesburg and Cape Town, the Jews constitue one-tenth of the citizens "that count": the Whites.... [8]

Despite the economic gains of the Jewish community there was no commensurate cultural flowering or peculiarly South African focus of development. According to Bernard Sachs, a well-known Jewish literary and political writer in South Africa, the weakness of cultural development had as its corollary an expression of Jewish interests and activities "almost entirely through the channels of Zionism and philanthropy."[9] Rabbi Ungar also saw the effects of Jewish separateness both from the Afrikaner and British groupings as taking the form of "two main quasi-religious preoccupations ... a numinous awe surrounding the separate sports club, and an enshrinement of Zionism in its most uncritically chauvinistic form."[10] Like other Jewish communities which left Czarist Russia after the pogroms of the late 19th and early 20th centuries, South African Jews were especially attracted to the idea of political Zionism with its promise of a Jewish state. Statehood seemed the logical alternative to an existence where assimilation had either been prevented by government edict or fostered by Orthodox belief in the security offered Judaism by ghetto separation. Rejected on the social plane by both major white groups in South Africa, Jews found little stimulation to develop a South African Jewish culture.

Jewish institutions, which correspondingly reflected the Zionist priorities and interests of the community, were represented foremost by the South African Zionist Federation, founded in 1895 and the South African Jewish Board of Deputies (1912). These bodies were not mutually exclusive, however, and even before 1948 Zionists not only "formed the majority of the Board of Deputies but also occupied the leading posts in the Jewish community."[11] By 1948 fully 99 per cent of South African Jews were Zionist affiliated.[12] In short, Zionism was without question the primary cultural expression and group concern of South African Jewry. Sachs estimated that the right-wing or revisionist form of Zionism accounted for only 15 per cent of the total Jewish strength while the moderate United Zionist Party attracted the bulk of Jewish membership. By 1944 considerable numbers of all factions were expressing strong contempt for British opposition to extreme Zionist demands regarding Palestine.[13] Thus, while Jews traditionally favored British attachments as a bulwark of democracy against the philosophy of the Nationalist Party, confrontation between Jewish terrorist groups and British soldiers in Palestine brought a substantial decline in British orientation at the precise moment when the Nationalist Party was preparing its assault on continued South African attachments to the British Crown. Ironically, however, South African Jewish concern for Palestine was not merely the outgrowth of ordinary Zionist interests which, during the aftermath of Hitlerism, had won over American and British Jewry to Zionist political goals. It also reflected community concern that the increasing strength of the Nationalist Party might in fact necessitate a Jewish exodus.

The Nationalist Party Adopts A New Jewish Policy

Notwithstanding its legacy of virulent anti-Semitism, by 1948 the Nationalist Party dramatically modified its attitude towards the Jewish community. Not only was it a case of perceiving the necessity of white solidarity if a minority racial regime were to be maintained, but rather the nature of the Jewish community itself and events involving Britain in Palestine made a new policy both attractive and expedient. According to Dr. Edwin S. Munger, a long-time observer of the South African scene, the post-war Jewish-Afrikaner *rapprochement* was also due to the opinion among highly influential Afrikaners that "the elimination of Jews from South Africa would shake the country to its foundations"[14] since any implementation of discrimination would lead to the withdrawal by wealthy Jews of sufficient capital to precipitate an economic slump.

As the 1948 general election approached, signs indicated a switch in Nationalist thought. Not only did the Afrikaans press support Zionist opposition to British policies in Palestine, which since 1939 had moved away from endorsing Jewish statehood against the wishes of the Arab majority, but it compared the Afrikaners' determination to break the Union's British ties with the Zionist undertaking. In various localities Nationalist politicians openly sought the favor of influential Jews and a dialogue was opened in Cape Town between several prominent Jews and leading Nationalists. Although Dr. Malan repeated his Party's opposition to additional Jewish immigration in October 1947, he argued that opposition was not because of anti-Jewish feeling but "because we want to prevent these feelings."[15] But it was the creation of the State of Israel on May 14, 1948, only a few days before the May 26 election, which strongly influenced Nationalist attitudes. According to Dr. Leslie Rubin, a South African exile and a co-founder of the Liberal Party (also Jewish and former senator representing non-Whites):

> A strange mixture of motives made it easy for Malan (and Strijdom has faithfully followed his lead since) and the Nationalists to offer enthusiastic support to the new state. There was a sense of affinity with the Israelis in having thrown off the British yoke. A psychologist might have called it admiration for the achievement by another of what was for them still a suppressed desire. Then—this is the view which was put to me by a leading Afrikaner intellectual with genuine feeling—many Nationalists saw the success of the Jews against the Arabs as a victory of White over non-White. Malan himself, growing old, displayed and voiced with much fervor a highly emotional people-of-the-book enthusiasm for the restoration of the Jews to their ancient homeland in accordance with Biblical prophecy.[16]

Richard Weisbord has also observed that it was "not coincidental that the turning away of the Nationalist Party from overt anti-Semitism occurred at the same time as the goal of the political Zionist movement, the creation of the State of Israel, was realized."[17]

Israel's declaration of independence raised the question of diplomatic recognition and brought immediate repercussions on South African politics. Despite the fact that Prime Minister Smuts was a life-long supporter of Zionism and a close, personal friend of Chaim Weizmann, the Zionist leader,[18] Smuts extended only *de facto* recognition to the new state. Although reticence in this matter might be attributed to Smuts' own regard for British sensibilities as to Anglo-South African sentiment, he also feared the Nationalist Party would make political capital of an action so clearly welcome in the Jewish community.[19] However, the Prime Minister's action not only had the effect of alienating some English-speaking voters ("who had no love for Jews of any kind and a bitter hatred of the gunmen of Palestine who were murdering British soldiers...")[20] but it enabled Dr. Malan to use Smuts' action to proclaim by way of contrast his own "true friendship" for the Jewish people, a people whose race-consciousness would enable them to "more easily understand and respect the same feeling in the case of every other section of the community."[21] Immediately after the narrow Nationalist victory of May 26, the Malan Government extended *de jure* recognition to Israel.

Diplomatic recognition of Israel was succeeded by other actions calculated to win Jewish support. Six weeks after taking office Dr. Malan declared that both he and his Government stood for a policy of non-discrimination against any section of the White population and looked forward to the day when there would no longer be any talk of the Jewish question in the country.[22] Malan exceeded the position of most other countries favorable to Israel: he not only permitted Jewish reserve officers to serve in Israel, a procedure officially contrary to law,[23] but was the first Prime Minister in the British Commonwealth to pay a courtesy visit to the new state. When, despite serious financial problems, the Government permitted the export of needed commodities and currency to Israel, Malan's victory with the Jewish community was virtually complete. Thereafter the Jewish South African community sent more money per capita to Israel "than any Jewish group in the world—far exceeding the Americans—and a higher percentage of settlers ... [emigrated] to Israel from South Africa than ... from other countries where Jews are relatively prosperous."[24]

The Consequences Of Rapprochement

Nationalist support of Israel and its official abrogation of anti-Semitism engendered acceptance of Nationalist Party policies at all levels of formal Jewish expression. In 1951 the Chairman of the Jewish Board of Deputies extended sincere thanks to the Government for its pro-Israeli sentiment and for appreciating the feelings of the Jewish community towards Israel.[25] At the same time, however, he expressed disappointment that Jews were still barred in most regions from Nationalist Party membership. Within a few months the Transvaal Congress of the Party lifted its ban on Jewish membership with the Orange Free State and Natal Congresses following suit. Subsequent elections in South Africa witnessed a growing number of Jews backing the Nationalist Party.[26] When Dr. Malan retired from official life in 1954, succeeded by Prime Minister Strijdom, South African Jewry paid him its highest honor by inscribing his name in its Golden Book as recognition of his "contribution to better racial understanding in South Africa...."[27] Mr. Strijdom's Government continued to display a cordial attitude towards Israel and "as if to seal this strange interracial harmony, the Minister of Justice appointed Mr. Simon Kuper, the president of the South African Zionist Federation, to the Transvaal bench."[28]

Upon the election of Dr. Verwoerd as Prime Minister in 1958 a deputation from the Jewish Board of Deputies extended formal congratulations. His Government's appointment of Dr. Percy Yutar as Deputy Attorney-General of the Transvaal in 1960 put to rest any possible lingering doubts concerning the ability of Jews to attain high governmental positions.

Yutar, as president of the Johannesburg United Hebrew Congregation and president of the South African Board of Education Fund, distinguished himself as prosecutor in the infamous Rivonia trial of the African National Congress leader, Nelson Mandela and his associates, several of whom were Jewish; in 1968 he was elevated to Attorney-General of the Orange Free State.

Verwoerd's policy permitted South African Zionists to continue sending some $700,000 annually to Israel.[29] Dr. M. Nurok, a visiting member of the Israeli parliament, formally expressed Israeli gratitude in April, 1959:

> We are very grateful to the South African Government for the part it has played in helping Israel to attain its present status. South African Jews who have settled in Israel are staunch patriots of the Union.[30]

Before leaving South Africa Dr. Nurok invited the Prime Minister to visit Israel.

This cordial state of relations between the Nationalist Government and the Jewish community raised the moral question of Jewish complicity in *apartheid,* a complicity beyond that which might be attributed to other religious groups in South Africa. As Henry Katzew, assistant editor of the Johannesburg *Zionist Record* acknowledged, the Jewish community after 1948, was in a unique situation "in which the government was sympathetic to the Jewish community and harsh and discriminating against other elements in the population, in this case, Africans, Coloreds and Indians."[31]

The change in Nationalist Party attitudes and concomitant response on the part of organized Jewry has been fully documented. Under the Smuts Government, the Jewish Board of Deputies' monthly journal *Jewish Affairs* (established in 1946), freely expressed itself on issues of color and discrimination. Editions featured articles reminding readers that "Judaism enjoins upon its preachers the fearless demand for social justice."[32] On the eve of the 1948 election, *Jewish Affairs* commented editorially on *apartheid:*

> [It is] a policy which the social and industrial realities of the day reduce to hopeless contradiction.... It is doubtful whether there can be a specific Jewish viewpoint, but something, nevertheless, can be expected of the Jew. On racial issues he should take as liberal a view as possible. He should be profoundly sensitive to injustice arising from discrimination based on race or caste. He can and must be progressive.[33]

Immediately following the Nationalist Party victory the editor of *Jewish Affairs* again pointed out that "the only safeguard for peace lies in just treatment and the progressive promotion of the well-being and development of these underprivileged groups."[34] But as Katzew admitted, "[T]his was the last time *Jewish Affairs* was to speak in such emphatic terms."[35] The columns of *Jewish Affairs* quickly mirrored the impact of Dr. Malan's June 1948 meeting with leading members of the Board. The next editorial simply expressed hope that an unhappy chapter in the attitude of the Nationalist Party toward the Jewish community had been closed; no reference was made to continuing discrimination against non-white groups. Thus, within a matter of weeks, the Board of Deputies buried its expressed doctrine that Jewish security was best assured by support of all liberal causes in favor of the doctrine that "the Board of Deputies is a non-political body which refrains from taking any position on party political issues and does not express views on the various race policies being advocated...."[36]

According to Katzew, the Jews were simply responding as a people, not paragons, and thus "did not balk at a reconciliation which relieved them, but not the Africans, Indians and Colored." In the Afrikaners, said Katzew, the Jews were now able to see "a brave people and we could not but note in them certain tenacities and identities of purpose similar to our own. We also deeply valued their attitude to Israel."[37] The Board of Deputies was thus of its own volition a casualty of *apartheid.*

The silence which descended upon the Jewish Board of Deputies and *Jewish Affairs* enfolded the rest of the Jewish press. Synagogues fell silent as well except for occasional challenges to *apartheid* delivered by Chief Rabbi L. I. Rabinowitz, who soon found reason to emigrate to Israel. Speaking to the Eighth International Conference of the World Union for Progressive Judaism in London in July, 1953, Rabbi Dr. J. C. Weiler candidly explained that:

> The Jews as a community had decided to take no stand on the native question, because they were involved with the problem of assisting Jewry in other lands. South African Jewry was doing more to help Israel than any other group. The community could not ask for the government's permission to export funds and goods and at the same time, object to the government.[38]

Even the Sharpeville massacre of March 1960—which brought condemnation of South Africa from most governments (including the United States) and virtually all religious bodies—did not break the silence of the South African Jewish press or the Board of Deputies. Instead, as Mr. Charles Hoppenstein, a member of the Board for thirty years affirmed in London a few months later, "A majority of us are supporting the Union Government's policy in connection with *apartheid."* Hoppenstein appreciated the fact that South Africa had opened its doors to more than 1,500 Jewish refugees from the Congo.[39]

The first comprehensive history of the South African Jewish community, edited by Gustav Saron and Louis Hotz and entitled *The Jews in South Africa,*[40] was published in 1955. It was written to demonstrate that the Jewish community had made a substantial contribution to the development of South Africa. While much attention was paid to Zionism, significantly Judaism or any religious developments were ignored. The Zionist movement, according to the authors, received greater financial (and political) support on a per capita basis from the South African Jewish community than from any other in the world.[41] The anti-Semitic period of Nationalist Party history was passed over in a few pages and general political and social matters were ignored except when "issues directly affecting Jews as a group came into the political arena."[42]

A review of *The Jews of South Africa* by Dan Jacobson, a prominent South African Jewish writer, in the January, 1957, issue of *Commentary* precipitated an interesting exchange with Ronald M. Segal, also a Jew, and editor of *Africa South,* which was published in Cape Town until Segal's exile. The Jacobson-Segal exchange most forcefully revealed the issues at stake.

Jacobson held that "no government could have been more scrupulously correct in its attitude [than Dr. Malan's] towards the Jewish community and its successor under Strijdom [has] continued the tradition of friendship toward the State of Israel initiated by General Smuts."[43] Jacobson argued that Jews in South Africa were no more immune to race prejudice than other groups and that to identify Jewish 'radicals' with the community at large was a mistake. Although non-South African nationals might feel that Jews have a duty to oppose racialism *because* they are Jews, this point of view did not apply in South Africa where:

> [R]acialism ... is not a government, not a movement, not a political party, but the very basis of society: South Africa has never been anything but racialist, and yet so far it is a country in which Jews have managed to fare rather well. Many South African Jews see no *necessity* that South African color-consciousness must give rise to anti-Semitism: if there is, it is a necessity that after three hundred years in which to mature has not yet issued into action.[44]

Although a few leaders—whose concern for conditions in the country arose from their interpretation of Jewish ethic and experience—would speak out, they were not inclined "to speak wildly with the natives...." Finally, contended Jacobson, the only group in South Africa which persistently called upon the Jews to so associate themselves with Blacks were the Communists, "who like Communists everywhere else in the world, make appeals that are permitted by contempt for the fate of particular people in particular situations...."[45]

In reply to Jacobson's assessment of the realities of South African life, Segal charged that South African Jewry's concern for "justice" had been confined to narrow Jewish interests. He recalled:

> How many South African Jews of status in the community have I not heard condoning and even casually commending the worst horrors of "apartheid" and, almost within the same breath, pleading for the world to acknowledge at

last the cruelties of the Nasser regime? The South African Jewish community was outraged by the seizure of Jewish property and the internment of Jewish civilians in Egypt. It protested publicly and vigorously against the injustice. Yet, when the Africans of Sophiatown were dispossessed of their homes and their right to own land and property in Johannesburg, when they were driven from their houses in the early morning between lines of armed police, how many leaders of Jewish communal organizations protested? There was not one public statement, not one deputation; no deputations to the government were made. No wonder then that the late Field Marshal Smuts is a folk hero of the South African Jewish community.[46]

The excuse that Jews could not protest officially against particular legislation was not only "ludicrous" but in the context of the Jewish community's general pattern of behavior, "hypocritical" since they "persistently deliver themselves of communal opinions on the conduct of affairs in the Middle East, and that is surely much less their concern than a law herding into ghettos the various races of South Africa...." Failure to speak out on these issues, said Segal, then raised the fatal question:

If the Jews are not a race like the Indians, nor a religious community like the Anglicans, what precisely are they, in their own eyes? If they are only just South Africans and nothing else, then the Jewish Board of Deputies has no business to exist, and the Zionist Federation works for Israel under totally false pretenses.[47]

In defense of the South African Jewish community, Jacobson concluded that "[no] community will ever sacrifice itself for the sake of another."[48] Other religions condemn *apartheid* because there are black Anglicans, black Methodists, black Catholics, but there are no black Jews. The Jewish community "raises its voice when it feels its own immediate interests are threatened (whether by Soviet-Egyptian policy in the Middle East, or local immigration laws) and for the rest it keeps mum."[49]

A Temporary Reversal: Israeli Condemnation of Apartheid, 1961

From 1948 until mid-1961, Nationalist Party spokesmen, the Government and the Afrikaans press praised Israel unstintingly. This harmonious atmosphere was shattered by Israel's decision to expand her diplomatic offensive in Black Africa which had been under way since 1956.[50] When the President of Upper Volta visited Israel in July, 1961, the Israeli Government issued a statement describing *apartheid* "as disadvantageous to the interests of the non-white majority of the land." In October, 1961, Israel voted in the United Nations' Political Committee to censure a speech by the South African delegate, Mr. Eric Louw, Minister of Foreign Affairs. Finally, in November Israel supported a General Assembly resolution which deprecated South Africa's policy of *apartheid* "as being reprehensible and repugnant to the dignity and rights of peoples and individuals."[51]

The response from the South African Government and the Afrikaans press to Israel's "about-face" was predictably bitter. *Die Transvaler* asked what the government of Israel would think if, uninvited, South Africa concerned itself with Arab refugees who, for thirteen years, "lived on Israel's borders in the most wretched conditions because they are not allowed to return to their original homes." *Die Transvaler* asked:

> And is there any real differences between the way that the people of Israel are trying to maintain themselves amid non-Jewish peoples and the way the Afrikaner is trying to remain what he is? The people of Israel base themselves upon the Old Testament to explain why they do not wish to mix with other people: the Afrikaner does this too....[52]

Mr. Louw accused Israel of "hostility and ingratitude ... in view of the fact that the South African government and individual members of the Cabinet have in the past gone out of their way to foster good relations with Israel."[53] Dr. Verwoerd observed that the Jews "took Israel from the Arabs after the Arabs had lived there for a thousand years. In that I agree with them, Israel, like South Africa, is an *apartheid* state."[54] And in a private letter which was "leaked" to the *Sunday Press,* Dr. Verwoerd said Israel's actions were a tragedy for the Jews in South Africa, but he noted that the pro-South African reaction of the Jewish press had somewhat relieved the situation. He went on to say:

> People are beginning to ask why, if Israel and its Rabbis feel impelled to attack the policy of separate development here, the policy of separate development in Israel is not wrong in their eyes as well ... it may be said that they wish to differentiate in separate states because of religious and not racial differences, because if differentiation is wrong on one score it is also wrong on another ... we believed in the separate state of Israel, but now begin to wonder whether that support should be withdrawn if, according to their own convictions, the ideal of separate development is fundamentally wrong. You see, therefore, that the action of Israel has set in train a new line of thought.[55]

The Government rescinded the special concessions in foreign currency regulations which allowed Jewish organizations to transfer money and goods to Israel; thereafter applications for the transfer of funds were considered on their merits.

South African Jews were also horrified by Israel's actions and severely discomfited by the Prime Minister's remarks. The *Zionist Record,* official organ of the South African Zionist Federation, voiced regret that "Israel's delegation found it fitting to vote with the 67 rather than abstain with the Western group of nations."[56]

The South African Jewish Board of Deputies passed a resolution stating that "Israel should have joined the other western nations in abstaining from voting against South Africa."[57] The Board called upon Mr. Arthur Suzman, a prominent lawyer and chairman of the Board's Public Relations Committee, to explain its action. While the Board of Deputies had no *locus standi* for expressing views on Israel's foreign policy, many Jews could not help but ask, said Mr. Katzew, whether there were "any circumstances at present imaginable in which the Jew of Israel would consent to share power with an Arab majority" any more than Afrikaners would with Africans.[58]

The matter was brought to a close when the Board of Deputies expressed its satisfaction with Dr. Verwoerd's explanation that his criticism of Israel had nothing to do with the Government's attitude towards Jewish citizens. Following the Prime Minister's assassination in September, 1966, the *South African Jewish Times* commented:

> It was one of the marks of [Verwoerd's] statesmanship that he curbed past currents which sometimes washed against the Jewish community, set himself up against any form of discrimination against Jews and appealed for the complete eradication of anti-Semitism from South African life.[59]

At a Cape Town memorial service Chief Rabbi Professor Abrahams said that Dr. Verwoerd was "a man of sincerity and of deep integrity ... a moral conscience underlay his policies: he was the first man to give *apartheid* a moral ground."[60] The Senior Rabbi of the Progressive Jewish Congregation, Rabbi Arthur Super, eulogized Dr. Verwoerd as "one of the greatest, if not the greatest prime minister South Africa has ever produced."

Here was a man, who, like Moses of old, had led his people through the promised land after sixty years of wandering. He had the courage and the strength to establish the Republic of South Africa and so dissolve in one act the old heritage of hatred, communal jealousies, blurred loyalties, old grudges and past grievances which were preventing South Africa from becoming one nation.[61]

Reconciliation: Organized Jewry Defends South Africa Abroad

Whatever the apprehension Dr. Verwoerd's remarks had occasioned, the Jewish community did not rupture friendly relations with the Government. Rather, either through fear of a revival of anti-Semitism, belief in the South African system, or determination to carry on unimpeded with assistance to Israel, the Board of Deputies and Zionist organizations worked to deflect criticism of South Africa abroad by other Jewish bodies. The Board of Deputies resolved that "the Jewish community should take steps to explain South Africa's position to Jews overseas and at home."[62]

Even before Israel's anti-South African stance of 1961, the South African Jewish Board of Deputies had counseled Jewish organizations abroad to refrain from commenting on South African problems. Jewish non-governmental organizations having consultative status with the United Nations—including the World Aguda, the World Union for Progressive Judaism, the World Jewish Congress, the Co-ordinating Board of Jewish Organizations (comprising the British and South African Jewish Boards of Deputies and the B'nai B'rith) and the Consultative Council of Jewish Organizations (American Jewish Committee, the Alliance of France and the Anglo-Jewish Association) —declined to discuss the *apartheid* question at the United Nations.

This sort of non-involvement has been the main concern of Mr. Fritz Flesch of Detroit, a Jewish victim of Nazism at Dachau between 1938 and 1939. His investigations, covering more than a decade of activity, have not only documented the position of the South African Jewish community but, in Rabbi Ungar's words, have revealed the general "pattern of evasion" displayed by world Jewish leadership in response to South African initiatives.[63] When Flesch asked the World Jewish Congress about abstention from the *apartheid* question, Rabbi Maurice Perlzweig told him:

> The Jewish non-governmental organizations have refrained from commenting on South African problems because they do not desire to worsen the already difficult situation in which the Jewish community finds itself. And they know that this restraint, whatever the arguments against it may be, is regarded as important by that community.
>
> Moreover, the World Jewish Congress is precluded by its Constitution from undertaking any activity in relation to any country which has a Jewish community that can speak for itself, unless that community either requests or permits it....
>
> I take the liberty of suggesting that you might usefully turn your abundant energies to the problems of racialism at home in the knowledge that any improvement in this area will be an effective contribution to the fight elsewhere.[64]

The situation in South Africa hardly warrants fear of "worsening the already difficult situation." On the contrary, as Mr. Aaron Mendelow, an executive member of the Board of Deputies stated, "South African Jews have for better or for worse, cast in their lot with other South Africans, and we are proud of the fact that we have always acted as an integral part of the South African community."[65] That the World Jewish Congress should resist any attack on the position of the Jewish community in South Africa is readily understandable in light of an earlier statement by Dr. Israel Goldstein, chairman of the Western Hemisphere Executive of the Congress. After a visit to South Africa late in 1959, Dr. Goldstein reported the Jewish community there was "the most Jewish-spirited community outside of Israel ... and deserves its reputation ... as measured by the criteria of synagogue affiliation, Jewish education and Zionist devotion, including not only their response to fund-raising appeals for Israel but immigration, pioneering and investments in Israel."[66] Dr. Goldstein's remarks were reported in all the various official publications of the South African Information Office.

Efforts to dissuade American Jewish organizations from condemning *apartheid* have had limited success. The American Jewish Congress, for example, has affirmed on various occasions its opposition to South Africa's racial policies. Some outstanding examples of Jewish Americans—such as Mr. Peter Weiss, Board Chairman of the American Committee on Africa, who over the years has devoted considerable time and energy combating *apartheid*—run counter to the efforts of South African Jewish and Zionist organizations.

On the other hand some, like Samuel H. Wang, put the well being of the South African Jewish community first and value its support for Israel more than they devalue racism in South Africa. A man of considerable wealth, Mr. Wang regularly sponsors advertisements in the *New York Times* in support of Israel and against "Arab barbarism." Wang attacked the American Jewish Congress for endorsing an advertisement sponsored by the American Committee on Africa which protested the granting of landing rights to the South African Airways.[67] Wang charged that the Congress, in virtue of its stand against *apartheid,* was "acting contrary to Jewish interests."

> Your effort against the South African airlines is a pertinent example justifying this charge.
>
> Your anti-South African campaign, speaking in the name of American Jewry, is putting the distinguished South African Jewish Community in a serious predicament.
>
> No doubt, it will raise anti-Jewish feeling among the majority of South African citizens who uphold and support their Government. The South African Jews who are noted for their devotion to the cause of Jewry and who are in the forefront with their contribution to Jewish world needs, surely deserve more concern from responsible Jewish organizations.[68]

Zionist efforts were early complemented by South African fear of Communism. Concern over possible Soviet penetration into Africa and fear of Communist subversion of the country's political-social system elicited a favorable response to Middle East defense arrangements advanced by the Western bloc. As Dr. Malan informed the House of Assembly in April 1952, South Africa stood ready to cooperate with the North Atlantic Treaty Organization and the Commonwealth to create a Middle East Command "to stop the enemy from coming through the Middle East and from invading Africa through Egypt in the event of war... what happens higher up in Africa must necessarily affect us."[69] In keeping with this concern, if not reciprocating it, Israel's Foreign Minister, Moshe Sharett, visited South Africa shortly after independence and an Israeli destroyer paid a courtesy call.

The military overthrow of the Egyptian monarchy in July, 1952, and subsequent Pan-African initiatives by the Nasser government occasioned growing South African alarm and concern for North African and Middle East affairs. At the time of the Suez crisis of 1956, the Union conspicuously refrained from condemning the Anglo-French-Israeli invasion of Egypt. "Some among the Afrikaner Nationalists," as Jitendra Mohan has observed, "found in the Suez crisis an opportunity for renewing their faith in the Union's race policies. This was done in the context of the general support enjoyed by Nasser's Egypt among the non-whites of Africa as the standard bearer of their emancipation from the Europeans."[70] Throughout all stages of the Suez crisis the South African press maintained a posture sympathetic to Israel.

In spite of Israel's black-African diplomatic offensive in the post-1961 period, certain economic figures reveal that Israeli-South African relations were not as poor as diplomatic recriminations would have one believe. Between 1961 and 1967 Israeli exports to South Africa increased from $1.4 million to $4 million while imports in 1967 reached $3.3 million.[71] Although Israel's trade with South Africa represented only a fraction of its total, by 1961 South Africa had become Israel's chief partner in Africa.

There seemed to be other efforts to conciliate South African sensibilities. For example, a prominent French Zionist writer, Paul Giniewski, published *The Two Faces of Apartheid* in 1965 in which he advanced a new theory in support of *apartheid*. *Apartheid*, with its Bantustan concept, argued Giniewski, was nothing more than "bantu Zionism" which alone could preserve African interests. Drawing numerous parallels with Zionist efforts in Palestine, Giniewski asserted that "from the Bantu people themselves must come the visionaries who will dream the Bantustans of tomorrow, who will take the people toward the resurrected country, as Herzl dreamed and realized the Jewish state.[72] This counsel to a majority of South Africa's people to acquiesce in accepting abouth 16% of the country's more barren land on a subservient political basis was endorsed in the book's preface by Clarence Randall, president of U.S. Inland Steel, and a prominent American apologist for South Africa.

Whatever official South African resentment remained against Israel by 1967 was mitigated by the June war. In an outpouring of pro-Israeli sentiment, Dr. Vorster's government not only permitted South African volunteers to work in civilian and para-military capacities in Israel, but more than $28 million by Zionist groups was released to Israel.[73] Soon after Israel's new Trade Commissioner to South Africa announced the expansion of existing programs and the South Africa Foundation, the country's most sophisticated propaganda institution, undertook to subsidize the founding of an Israeli-South African Committee which brought the editor of an influential daily to South Africa.[74] Closer political and economic ties between Israel and South Africa were recommended.[75] Furthermore,

Israel strengthened her developmental programs in Lesotho, Botswana, Swaziland and Malawi, states in which South African influence was all but dominant. It was hoped that these states would play a "moderating" role between South Africa and its black neighbors to the north in addition to supporting Israeli policies in United Nation's debates. In short, South Africa found reason to ignore certain Israeli policies and Israel found reason to cultivate South African friendship in practical if unspectacular ways.

Conclusion

The dilemma or quandary of the South African Jewish community has been discussed by various writers as a struggle between conscience and political realism. Professor Edward Feit has observed that it is easy for others to urge upon the Jewish community heroic gestures from many thousands of miles; but it is that community which might feel overt governmental hostility.[76] The moral aspects notwithstanding, it remains that one cannot debate the issue as though an alternate policy might be adopted. If ever there was a meaningful struggle between conscience and "political realism," resistance was extremely short-lived. As Rabbi Miller, an American Reform rabbi, who served in Durban for sixteen years, succinctly observed, any rabbi who supported or engaged in overt civil rights activity would lose his pulpit overnight. "I went to South Africa," said Rabbi Miller, "to serve the Jewish community, not to become a martyr. The laws of the United States and the interpretations by the Supreme Court are in favor of integration, so that people in the civil rights movement are not only following their conscience and their interpretation of Judaism, but at the same time are good citizens. That situation does not exist in South Africa because its laws are for separate development." Rabbi Miller also noted that he intended to live in South Africa for three more years and then move to Israel.[77]

But whether in the minds of the black majority of South Africa the self-interest of any white community, especially as directed abroad and flowing from exploitation of the country's black labor, can override the existential moral imperatives of South African life is highly dubious. That South African Jews might legitimately turn away from the blatant racial injustice of the Republic, and then, if occasion should require, emigrate to Israel, seems even less acceptable. South Africa's Jewish community, in the eyes of South African blacks, shares the same burden as the rest of that country's dominant groups and would consequently share its fate. Given the position expressed by Rabbi Levi A. Olan, president of the Central Conference of American Rabbis, that Christian churches had failed in their moral duty "to support Israel in its struggle to survive,"[78] it would not be unreasonable to believe that the Africans of South Africa will reject a moral framework for the Jewish community which operates without reference to their own determination to survive and claim that which is their own. And in the broader sense, the interrelationship of Zionism, *apartheid* and Israel poses problems of fundamental morality which will be of greater concern to the black American community not only as it ponders its relationship to the moral and political aspects of Israeli-Palestinian Arab relations, but as it asserts its concern for the disenfranchised black majority of South Africa.

[1] A. Keppel-Jones, *When Smuts Goes* (Pietermaritzberg: Shuter & Shooter, 1950), 31f.
[2] Leonard M. Thompson, *Politics in the Republic of South Africa* (Boston and Toronto: Little, Brown and Company, 1966), 157.
[3] R. G. Weisbord, "Dilemma of South African Jewry," *Journal of Modern Studies*, Vol. V (September 1697), 234-35.
[4] Bernard Sachs, "South Africa: Life on a Volcano, the Jewish Community in a Caste Society," *Commentary*, Vol. IX (June, 1950), 530.
[5] *Ibid*, 532.
[6] Dan Jacobson, "The Jews of South Africa: Portrait of a Flourishing Community," *Commentary*, Vol. XXIII (January, 1957), 39.
[7] *Ibid*.
[8] Andre Ungar, "The Abdication of a Community," *Africa South*, Vol. 3 (January-March 1959), 29-30.
[9] Sachs, 533.
[10] Ungar, 31, 32.
[11] Sachs, 533.
[12] Sarah G. Millin, *The People of South Africa* (New York: Alfred Knopf, 1954), 236.
[13] Although the British Government had promised unlimited Jewish immigration into Palestine in the Balfour Declaration of 1917, by the late 1930's the contradiction of this promise (i.e. "it being clearly understood that nothing shall be done which may prejudice the civil and religious rights of existing non-Jewish communities...") as well as the demands of British Middle East strategy led to a reversal of policy. The MacDonald White Paper of 1939 promised to limit Jewish immigration thus guaranteeing an Arab majority. cf. Richard P. Stevens, *American Zionism and United States Foreign Policy, 1942-1947* (New York: Pageant Press, 1962), 78.
[14] Edwin S. Munger, "Jews and the National Party" (New York: American Universities Field Services, 1956), 2.
[15] *Die Transvaler*, October 30, 1947, as quoted and translated in Alexander Hepple, *Verwoerd* (Baltimore: Penguin Books, 1967), 226.
[16] Leslie Rubin, "Afrikaner Nationalism and the Jews," *Africa South*, Vol. 1, no. 3 (April-June 1957), 29.
[17] Weisbord, 235.
[18] General Smuts, who represented the Union at the Imperial War Council, was a supporter of Zionism from 1919. His relations with Weizmann and Zionism in South Africa are described in Gustav Saren and Louis Hotz, *The Jews in South Africa* (Cape Town, London, New York: Oxford University Press, 1955), 281ff. Almost on the eve of the general election he dashed off to London to attend the seventy-fifth birthday celebration of his old friend, Dr. Chaim Weizmann. cf. Walker, 788.
[19] Rubin, 31.
[20] Eric A. Walker, *A History of Southern Africa* (London: Longmans, Green and Co., 1965), 772.
[21] Cited in Weisbord, 236.
[22] Henry Katzew, "Jews in the Land of Apartheid," *Midstream*, Vol. 8 (December, 1962), 68.
[23] E. Feit, "Community in a Quandary: the South African Jewish Community and Apartheid," *Race*, Vol. 8 (April, 1967), 406.
[24] Edwin S. Munger, *Afrikaner and African Nationalism: South African Parallels and Parameters* (London: Oxford University Press, 1967), 20.
[25] *Cape Times*, June 1, 1951.
[26] Hepple, 227.
[27] Walker, 922.
[28] Julius Lewin, "Appeasement in South Africa," *Nation*, Vol. 182 (April 14, 1956), 294.
[29] Hepple, 227.

[30] *South African Scope,* Vol. 2, no. 6 (June, 1959).
[31] Katzew, 68.
[32] *Ibid,* 69.
[33] *Ibid.*
[34] *Ibid,* 70.
[35] *Ibid.*
[36] *Ibid,* 68.
[37] *Ibid,* 72.
[38] Rabbi M. C. Weiler, Speech to Eighth International Conference of the World Union of Progressive Judaism, London, 1953, cited in F. Flesch documentation, 189.
[39] *Jewish Chronicle* (London), September 2, 1960.
[40] Saron and Hotz, *Ibid.*
[41] *Ibid,* 283 ff.
[42] *Ibid,* Preface.
[43] Jacobson, 43.
[44] *Ibid.*
[45] *Ibid,* 45.
[46] Dan Jacobson and Ronald Segal, "Apartheid and South African Jewry: An Exchange," *Commentary,* Vol 24 (November, 1957), 425.
[47] *Ibidem.*
[48] *Ibid,* 430.
[49] *Ibid,* 429.
[50] cf. Samuel Decalo, "Israeli Foreign Policy and the Third World," *Orbis,* Vol. 11 (Fall 1967), 724-745.
[51] Cited in Henry Katzew, "South Africa: A Country Without Friends," *Midstream* (Spring 1962), 73. According to Mr. Harold Soref, a delegate to the Council of the Anglo-Jewish Association in November 1962 (London): "It was ... a complete misunderstanding to look on Israeli action as a moral stand. Israeli diplomats had visited the emergent African States and they sought support from these States against the Arabs at the U.N. They were perfectly entitled to do this, but to regard their action as being based on moral grounds was euphemism." *Jewish Chronicle* (London), November 30, 1962.
[52] Cited in *Ibid,* 73.
[53] Cited in *Ibid,* 74.
[54] *Rand Daily Mail,* November 23, 1961.
[55] Cited in Katzew, *Ibid,* 76.
[56] Cited in *Ibid,* 74.
[57] Cited in *Ibid,* 74-75.
[58] *Ibidem.*
[59] *South African Jewish Times,* September 9, 1966.
[60] *Rand Daily Mail,* September 12, 1966.
[61] *Ibidem.*
[62] *Jewish Chronicle* (London), December, 1962.
[63] Andre Ungar, "Profile of a Stubborn Man" (unpublished manuscript in Fritz Flesch collection).
[64] Maurice L. Perlzweig to Fritz Flesch, April 5, 1963.
[65] *Rand Daily Mail,* July 2, 1964.
[66] *South African Scope,* Vol. 2, no. 8 (September, 1959).
[67] *New York Times,* May 28, 1969.
[68] *New York Times,* June 6, 1969.
[69] *Ibid,* cf. Jitendra Mohan, "South Africa and the Suez Crisis," *International Journal* (Autumn 1961), Vol. 16, 333.
[70] Mohan, 333.
[71] Israel, Central Bureau of Statistics, *Statistical Abstract of Israel,* 1968, no. 19, 212.
[72] Paul Giniewski, *The Two Faces of Apartheid* (Chicago: Henry Regnery Co., 1965), 349.
[73] AMAX, *Summary of Press Coverage, South Africa* (August 15, 1968), 3.
[74] *Newscheck,* March 22, 1968.
[75] *Ibid.*
[76] E. Feit, "Community in a Quandary: the South African Jewish Community and Apartheid," *Race,* Vol. VIII, no 4 (April 1967), 399.
[77] *National Jewish Fact and Opinion,* July 15, 1966.
[78] *New York Times,* June 17, 1969.

C. Israel and South Africa: A Link Matures

ABDELWAHAB M. ELMESSIRI

To view Israel in an exclusively Arab context would be to overlook the wider impact that the creation of the Zionist state has had on the Afro-Asian scene. Ben Gurion, a leading Zionist and Israel's first Prime Minister, firmly believed that Israel's loyalties from the standpoint of its survival and security required it to place its "friendship with European countries" far above the mere "sentiments that prevail among the Asian people."[1]

The same realistic recognition of this identity of interests underlies the statement of Ishar Harari, member of the Knesset and of Israel's delegation to the UN General Assembly in 1955. Outlining graphically, in the *Jerusalem Post* of January 21, 1956, Israel's achievement at the UN, Harari asserted that "the most significant development" in Israel's favor "was the 1955 defeat of the Bandung Conference countries on practically every issue brought before the General Assembly."[2]

In keeping with its realistic view of its primary loyalties vis-a-vis its Afro-Asian neighbors, Israel has vigorously pursued the colonialist policies originally envisaged for it.

However, the objectives of Zionist settler colonialism and its primary concerns can be fully discerned from a close scrutiny of its strong ties with South Africa which date back to the very beginnings of both colonialist ventures. The same political figures who "fathered" the Balfour Declaration were instrumental in issuing the Act of the Union of South Africa. Zionist historians and writers have unfailingly noted the link between the two concepts. The author of the entry on "South Africa" in the *Encyclopedia Judaica* notes, for instance, that "from its earliest days, the Zionist idea elicited goodwill and understanding from non-Jews in South Africa, especially from the Afrikaans-speaking segment of the population."[3] The "efforts of the Jews to return to the Promised Land" have always struck a responsive chord among the deeply religious Afrikaners. According to Yitzhak Unna, Israel's Ambassador to South Africa, the Afrikaners, being a devout Calvinist people immersed in the Old Testament and sharing a common Biblical heritage with the Zionists, are prone to draw an analogy between their own experience of immigration and settlement on African soil and the Jewish exodus from Egypt and eventual establishment of a Zionist state in Palestine.[4]

Such a theo-historical outlook has political implications manifest in the fact that the Afrikaners, from the earliest days of settlement up to the present time, see their own political and cultural aims as quite similar to "the Jewish struggle for survival."[5] Recently Prime Minister Vorster underscored this point clearly when he declared that both South Africa and Israel have "to deal with terrorists across the border" and "to fight against enemies bent on their destruction."[6]

Spokesmen in both states constantly harp on the theme of "survival" and emphasize the need to take "defense" measures, while at the same time ignoring the circumstances that gave rise to the conflict which they see as a threat to their existence. Both settler states believe that their survival is contingent on their ability to deal quick retaliatory blows by sea, air or land and to take "preemptive" measures as they see fit. When Prime Minister Vorster threatened to deal "retaliatory" preemptive strikes against Zambia and Tanzania, "he cited Israel as a model for the tactics that South Africa may adopt against her neighbors."[7]

According to Israeli General Mattityahu Peled, the perception of similarity between the two states apparently so preoccupies the Israeli mind that many Israelis tend to exaggerate it. Significantly, this parallelism in the two situations that could be exaggerated or underestimated, was more or less "officially" recognized during Mr. Vorster's visit to Israel. The South African Prime Minister pointed with pride to the fact that the *apartheid* and Zionist states enjoyed "similarities in many, many instances, from climatic conditions upwards." The Zionist Prime Minister emphasized this point "in a toast to Mr. Vorster." He further expressed Israel's sympathy for South Africa's "historic efforts to achieve detente" in South Africa "without outside interference and threat."[8] What the two prime ministers did not choose to dwell on is the remarkable parallelism in issues relating to their religio-racial outlooks or to the definition of identity, the dispossession of the native inhabitants, the usurpation of the land and various other practices that settler colonialist enclaves have in common.

Recognition of the parallelism in their origin and circumstances has motivated Israel and South Africa to develop various means of cooperation between them on the political, economic and military levels. The ties of cooperation on the first level are probably the oldest, though not necessarily the strongest of the three.

In an article in *Jewish Affairs,* a leading South African Zionist, N. Kirschner, cites such South African national heroes as General Louis Botha, General Smuts and J.B. Hertzog as among the fervent supporters and defenders of the Zionist cause. Titled "Zionism and the Union of South Africa," Kirschner's article further points out that Tielman Roos, Hertzog's lieutenant, actively lobbied for the South African pro-Zionist Declaration which was issued in 1926.[9] According to the writer, General Jan Christian Smuts, the South African military leader and statesman, was a prominent gentile Zionist and a lifelong friend of Weizmann's. Smuts' enthusiasm for the Zionist project and his efforts on its behalf were to be duly remembered by Weizmann at a crucial moment in the history of Zionism. In 1948, the Zionist leader sought the support of General Smuts. As expected, *de facto* recognition of the Zionist state was granted.[10] This was understandable since South Africa had actively supported the idea of a partitioned Palestine. Even though Smuts resigned and his party was eventually replaced by the pro-Nazi Nationalist Party, which at one point banned Jews from membership,[11] South Africa continued to support Israel. Furthermore, Israel was granted preferential treatment under the country's foreign exchange control regulations, [12] and South Africa also extended *de jure* recognition. When Israel applied for membership in the UN, South Africa voted its approval, backing Israel "on a number of subsequent issues in that forum."[13]

In 1950, two years after the creation of the Zionist state, the then Prime Minister, Moshe Sharett, visited South Africa. Three years later South African Prime Minister Daniel F. Malan, the *first* head of government to pay a visit to Israel, returned to his country carrying with him the message that Israel could be a source of inspiration to the *apartheid* state.[14]

A relatively strained atmosphere marred relations between South Africa and Israel during the period of courtship between the latter and a number of African countries. During that phase, Israel cast several votes against South Africa at the UN. This interregnum came to an end under the pressure of reality, and consequently the last ten years witnessed a gradual improvement in the relations culminating in the elevation of diplomatic ties between the two states to full "ambassadorial status."[15] It would not be an overstatement to argue that the tie between South Africa and Israel has become more or less organic. A committee of "Cabinet ministers representing both countries" has been established. It will meet annually "to discuss investment, increased trade, scientific and industrial cooperation, and joint projects to exploit Israeli manpower and South African raw material."[16] The *Jerusalem Post* has noted that Israel "is the first country with which South Africa has set up a joint ministerial committee to promote economic cooperation."[17]

Political cooperation has been translated into more direct forms, both economic and military. The large Jewish population of South Africa, described by an Israeli newspaper as "one of the most vibrant Zionist-minded and supportive in the world,"[18] has made various significant contributions to Zionist settler colonialism. Financial support from the South African Jewish community has been of great value to Israel. "From 1926 South Africa occupied the second place in the world (after the US) in fund raising...its per capita contribution...was by far the largest."[19] During his visit to South Africa in the 30's, Weizmann was extremely satisfied with the results of his visit which were, in his words, "financially quite considerable."[20]

The flow of Zionist funds slackened in 1962. The South African Government, in retaliation for Israel's UN votes against *apartheid*, cancelled the special concessions for the flow of funds to Israel which it had previously granted. But after 1967, the ban was lifted and special regulations were reinstated, allowing the Zionist Federation in Pretoria to transfer some of the funds it raises. The practice is still in effect, and it is believed that during the 1973 war as much as 30 million dollars were transferred to Israel.[21] The Israeli Ambassador to South Africa has stated in this connection that South African Jewry thereby enjoys a special "privilege," since currency regulations forbid such transfer of funds to prevent flight of capital.[22]

South African Zionist funds penetrate to all levels of Israeli society, for they pour into as unrelated and unexpected places as the parasitology laboratory at the Hebrew University and "the first dormitory for women students there."[23]

Important as they are, the direct financial contributions are not comparable in importance to the investments of South African Jews in Israel. In 1922, South African Zionists established the Binyan Mortgage Company which sought to provide the Zionist settlers from South Africa with housing and which contributed to the development of Haifa after 1948. The firm then merged with Migdal Insurance and together they formed the largest insurance company in Israel. South African Zionist funds helped as well in the development of the port of Ashkelon, which was then handed over to the Israeli Government. A furniture company, an Israeli shipping company and El Al, the Israeli national airline, have grown out of South African projects or were funded by South African Zionists.[24]

Apart from the aid provided by the Zionist Jewish community in South Africa, there is the direct economic relationship between Zionism and *apartheid* on the governmental level. The need to strengthen their relations led in April 1968 to the establishment of "an Israeli-South Africa Trade Association ... to promote trade between the two countries," and in June of the same year,[25] an Israeli trade commissioner to South Africa was appointed.

With the bolstering of trade ties, Israel's exports to South Africa began to expand, totalling more than 28.7 million dollars in 1974. During the same year South Africa sold Israel goods worth 43.1 million dollars (an astronomical increase over the 1965 figures: 2.7 million dollars for export and 4.3 million dollars for import). The diamond cutting industry, which represents about 34 percent of Israel's total exports, imports its raw material from South Africa which makes the *apartheid* state "Israel's primary trading partner."[26] The figures for the import and export of diamonds are not included in the statistics for trade between the two countries since sales are carried out through a London agency.

Like all other aspects of cooperation between the two countries, economic cooperation increased after the Vorster visit to Israel. It is believed that the two countries will jointly build "a railroad, a steel-rolling mill and a hydro-electric plant that will use Mediterranean water diverted into the Dead Sea."[27] Israel in turn has placed an order for large quantities of coal from South Africa.

Of special importance are the semi-finished products which Israel "imports" from South Africa. These are prepared in Israel for re-export to African countries which have a trade embargo on South Africa.[28] Benyamin Wainstein, the leader of the South African delegation to the Millionaires' Conference, indicated that South African companies use Israel "as a very useful base" for avoiding sanctions imposed by African states. Disclosing a plan for founding a textile factory in Israel, he added that the said project "was only one of six or seven moves in the pipeline." It was probably for that reason that he expected South African businessmen to invest in Israel "right up to the ceiling imposed by their government."[29] The *Rand Daily Mail* of April 14, 1976 further confirms the story about plans for finishing industries in Israel, adding, in turn, that it is not simply a means of avoiding the African embargo, but also a way of taking "advantage of Israel's free-trade agreements with the [European Economic] Community and the United States."[30]

The military relationship between the two states, another rapidly growing area of cooperation, dates back to 1948 when South African Zionist volunteers fought on the side of the Zionist settlers in Palestine. To quote Zionist/Israeli sources, the small Jewish community in South Africa "contributed more to the Israeli war effort, in terms of skilled volunteers, than any other country in the world."[31] It is significant in this regard that the first pilot to fall in battle in the Israeli Air Force was a South African volunteer.[32] The same holds true for the 1956 and 1967 wars during which many South African Zionists volunteered and a number of them actually did fight with the Israeli forces.

The *New York Times*' C.L. Sulzberger was unofficially told, as reported in the April 28, 1971 issue, that a South African mission had flown to Israel during the 1967 war "to study tactics and use of weapons." The war was subsequently given major attention in South Africa's military literature. Many Israeli generals and top defense officials, such as General Mordechai Hod, Commander of the Israeli Air Force, and Defense Minister Shimon Peres visited Pretoria. General Hod, according to one source, addressed a selected group of officers at the Air Force College, and Shimon Peres who was then the Secretary of the ruling Israeli Labor Party and member of the key Foreign Affairs and Security Committee met with the South African Minister of Defense.[33]

The 1973 war witnessed even wider cooperation—1500 Jews of South African descent took part in actual combat, and about 800 were among the units that crossed the Suez Canal.[34] At least one jet fighter of South African origin was shot over the Suez Canal.

Cooperation in the vital area of arms manufacture is fairly strong. It appears that the two states, heavily dependent on Western aid and technology, are trying to coordinate their efforts to achieve independence in the area of military hardware production.[35] South Africa, for instance, "manufactures the Israeli-invented Uzi submachine gun under a license granted through Belgium." Unconfirmed reports indicate that "after the Israelis secured plans of the French Mirage fighter engine, blueprints of their improved version were made available to South Africa."[36] Israeli businessmen and aviation experts touring South Africa in December 1967 visited the Atlas Aircraft industries near Johannesburg and expressed their hope to bring an "Israeli manufactered short-take-off-and-landing aircraft to South Africa for a series of demonstrations." The South Africans, in turn, decided according to the *Jewish Telegraphic Agency Bulletin* of January 26, 1970, "to organize the export of [Chieftain type] tanks to Israel."[37]

Exchanges related to military aid, know-how and weapons were largely kept secret. Prime Minister Vorster, during his visit to Israel in April 1976, described as "utter nonsense" any talk about an "impending arms deal," and the Israeli Ambassador to Pretoria pointed out that "Israel's and South Africa's defense needs were quite different." However, no matter how hard Israel tries to conceal the link, the facts uniformly filter through. Eventually they find their way into the press and at times they are even admitted.

Vorster's emphatic denials notwithstanding, it was not long before news about the arms deal had become known. Reports concerning it were broadcast by the Israeli radio. During his visit to Israel, Prime Minister Vorster inspected Israeli aircraft factories, naval facilities and an air force base—a tour which the Israeli Ambassador to South Africa tried to pass off as mere sight-seeing. The Israeli Army, Navy or Air Force, according to the Israeli envoy, were viewed by Vorster as more or less tourist attractions, "like the Western Wall and Mount Zion."[38]

But further details of Israeli-South African military collaboration were contained in a report broadcast on Kol Israel. On August 9, 1976, the Israeli radio disclosed that Israel is building long-range gunboats for South Africa. The vessels are to be armed with sea-to-sea missiles (some reports put the number at two, others put it at six). It might be of some interest to point out that these boats are of the same class as the Israeli boats that participated in New York's "Operation Sail" on July 4. The crew that is to man the boats is now being trained in Haifa, and it was expected that the first boat would be ready in January 1977. Kol Israel also reported that "an Israeli designed coastal patrol boat will be built under license in South Africa."[39] It would appear that all these items are part of a larger "arms deal" which is to include "up to two dozen Israeli-built Kfir Jet planes." The South African order is further reported to include advanced military electronic equipment.[40]

As noted earlier, South African volunteers fought on the Israeli side in Israel's numerous wars. As the Black national liberation movement gains strength in Africa, the situation may arise where Israel will find itself forced to repay the favor by sending Israeli "volunteers" to fight alongside South African troops. It may also find itself obliged to put its know-how and expertise at the disposal of its South African benefactors.

Collaboration along these lines may have started already in anticipation of more disturbances in South Africa. According to the *Wall Street Journal*, there have been unconfirmed reports that Israel was preparing to train South Africans in security techniques, in order to prepare them for the potentially explosive situation in South Africa. Signs of trouble were already in evidence a few weeks after Vorster's return from Israel.[41] Although it remains an understandably sensitive issue for both sides, more information concerning cooperation in this area between the two settler regimes is beginning to surface. Some facts can easily be gleaned from remarks and statements by Israelis in high places. General Meir Amit, President of Koor Industries, former chief of the Israeli secret service, declared during his July visit to South Africa last year that Israeli officers "regularly lecture before an audience of South African officers about modern warfare and anti-guerrilla tactics."[42] This report was corroborated in a statement by Marcia Freedman, member of the Israeli Parliament. According to the Israeli legislator, "hundreds of Israeli soldiers were attached to the South African Army units as instructors and participated in training manoeuvres." This report, like many others, was vigorously denied by the Israeli Defense Ministry.[43]

Israeli denials notwithstanding, it is safe to state further that collaboration between the two garrison states goes beyond instruction and training. In its coverage of the Angolan uprising, the British press carried a report indicating that "Israeli officers had been closely involved with South African Army planning in the Angolan campaign." In the same report which appeared over the byline of the Johannesburg correspondent of the *British Telegraph,* on April 3, 1976, a South African general attributed the lightness of the casualties sustained by the South African soldiers in the fighting in Angola to the fact that "Israeli techniques for evacuation and treatment of front line casualties had been closely followed."[44]

Additionally, unconfirmed reports from Africa indicate that there may even be direct collaboration between Israel and South African soldiers in actual combat situations. According to representatives of the South-west Africa People's Organization (SWAPO) who were on a mission to Angola, Israeli soldiers are now actively involved in the fight against their forces. A British press report, quoting the Angolan freedom-fighters, said that "a number of SWAPO wounded... were casualties of clashes with Israelis. The latter are said to be using helicopter-borne commando groups to swoop down on SWAPO fighters, especially in the frontier areas between Namibia and Angola." The Israelis are particularly noted for their skill in the use of helicopters for lightning attacks.[45]

More ominous is the rumor that South Africa is preparing to "supply Israel with uranium."[46] If confirmed, the threat presented by this dangerous development is incalculable given the desperate situation of these two states, and in view of the fact that neither is signatory to the nuclear non-proliferation treaty. A nuclear deterrent might appear to both as the only alternative to their complete dependence on the West. With such a state of military self-sufficiency, they can pursue their policies unhampered by world public opinion, or any pressures from their Western supporters.

This close, and sometimes open, collaboration is consistent and logical when viewed in the context of Israel's position and orientation. That it has taken so long for Israel to be identified publicly as a close ally of South Africa is a testimony to the remarkable effectiveness of Israel's public relations specialists and its image builders. Now that the facade so skillfully erected has crumbled, the need for subterfuge has disappeared. It is now possible for an Israeli journalist, Joseph Lapide, to speak his mind in an article published in *Maariv* before the 1973 war. The writer admits that he had previously been inhibited from telling his Israeli readers his honest opinion about the majority of Black African states. Now, he went on to say, he need not pretend any more. In his article he describes these states as "one nauseating mess." Using a typically Western colonialist idiom, Lapide points out that "the most oppressed Negro in South Africa has more to eat than millions of Africans in 'liberated' countries." This is also true of the Arabs in Israel—they too are well-fed and clothed, yet like most colonized people, they are ungrateful and tend to vent their anger in riots. Revealing his narrow Zionist and colonialist mentality, Lapide asserts that he prefers friendship with a white state that is "orderly and successful and contains a blossoming Jewish community" to friendship with Black Africa.[47]

Perhaps one single act, more than any other, finally served to lift the mask which had long obscured the true nature of Israel's cooperation with South Africa. During his visit to Israel, Vorster, a former "general" in the pro-Nazi South African nationalist movement which opposed the Allied war effort against Nazi Germany, a man who was interned for twenty months for his opposition and who has never repudiated his pro-Nazi stand,[48] laid a wreath at the Yad Vashem Memorial in Jerusalem for the victims of the Nazi holocaust. Even the pro-government *Jerusalem Post* felt compelled to protest, though in muted tones, that it was not "for the Jews to become associated with a former Nazi sympathizer."[49] It is ironic that this self-evident proposition should have had to be reiterated in the Jewish state.

---

[1] Cited in J. Artusky, "The Tragedy of Israeli Chauvinism," *Zionism, Israel and the Arabs* (Berkeley, California: Independent Socialist Clippingbooks, 1967), p. 191.
[2] Cited by Ibrahim Al-Abid, *127 Questions and Answers on the Arab Israeli Conflict* (Beirut: Palestine Research Center, 1973), p. 130.

[3] "South Africa," *Encyclopedia Judaica*, ed. Cecil Roth (Jerusalem: Keter House, 1972), XV.
[4] *Jewish Press*, June 18, 1976.
[5] "South Africa," *Encyclopedia Judaica*, XV.
[6] *New York Times*, April 30, 1971.
[7] *Israel and Southern Africa: A Comparison of the Roles of South Africa and Israel in the Third World* (Madison Area Committee on Southern Africa, n.d.), p. 12.
[8] *Wall Street Journal*, April 23, 1976.
[9] N. Kirschner, "Zionism and the Union of South Africa," *Jewish Affairs*, May 1960, p. 42.
[10] Chaim Weizmann, *Trial and Error* (New York: Harper and Row, 1949), p. 47.
[11] "South Africa," *Encyclopedia Judaica*, XV.
[12] *Ibid.*
[13] *Ibid.*
[14] Kirschner, "Zionism and the Union of South Africa," p. 42.
[15] *Washington Post*, April 8, 1976.
[16] *Christian Science Monitor*, April 14, 1976.
[17] *New Times*, May 14, 1976.
[18] Cited in *Washington Post*, April 8, 1976.
[19] "Zionism," *Encyclopedia Judaica*, XVI.
[20] Weizmann, *Trial and Error*, p. 347.
[21] "UN Report (A/AC.115/CRP.25) on the Relations Between Israel and South Africa," p. 13.
[22] *Jewish Press*, June 18, 1976.
[23] "South Africa," *Encyclopedia Judaica*, XV.
[24] "South African Jews in Israel," *Encyclopedia of Zionism and Israel*, II.
[25] "UN Report on the Relations Between Israel and South Africa," p. 18.
[26] *Israel and Southern Africa*, p. 13.
[27] *Newsweek*, August 23, 1976.
[28] *The Wall Street Journal*, April 23, 1976.
[29] Peter Hellyer, "Israel and South Africa: Development of Relations, 1967-1974." A paper submitted in October 1974 to the United Nations Special Committee on Apartheid and inscribed as an official document of the 1974 UN General Assembly. p. 23.
[30] "UN Report on the Relations Between Israel and South Africa," p. 20.
[31] *Zionist Record*, May 22, 1959.
[32] "UN Report on the Relations Between Israel and South Africa," p. 12.
[33] *Contemporary Links Between South Africa and Israel* (Madison Committee on Southern Africa), cited by Al-Abid, *127 Questions...*, p. 134.
[34] Peter Hellyer, "Israel and South Africa," p. 26.
[35] *Contemporary Links*, cited in *127 Questions...*, p. 135.
[36] Sulzberger, *New York Times*, April 30, 1971.
[37] *Contemporary Links* cited in *127 Questions...*, p. 134.
[38] *Jewish Press*, June 18, 1976.
[39] Jewish Telegraphic Agency *Daily News Bulletin*, August 10, 1076.
[40] *New York Times*, August 18, 1976.
[41] April 23, 1976.
[42] "Military Collaboration and Cooperation in Defense Production," *Third World Magazine* (Bonn, Germany). Special issue "Israel-South Africa: Cooperation of Imperialistic Outposts," 1976, pp. 64, 66.
[43] "UN Report on the Relations Between Israel and South Africa," p. 15.
[44] *Ibid.*
[45] *The Guardian*, July 7, 1976.
[46] *Wall Street Journal*, April 23, 1976.
[47] Les de Villiers, *South Africa: A Skunk Among Nations* (London: Universe Tandem, 1975) pp. 38-39.
[48] "Vorster: Man on a Wagon Train," *Time*, June 28, 1976.
[49] *New Times*, May 14, 1976.

PART II

READINGS AND DOCUMENTATION

3 READINGS

[1] Jews in South African Trade and Commerce*
Eric Rosenthal

The Strength of Zionism in South Africa is directly related to the economic strength of the Jewish Community. The first two readings [1 and 2] outline the course of this development.

From the early days of European colonization in South Africa, Jews have been prominent in those bodies upon which the efficiency of trade, finance and industry so largely depend. Beginning with the Dutch East India Company, under whose auspices Jan van Riebeeck brought his famous expedition in 1652 to set up the first trading post on the shores of Table Bay, we already find them represented. ...

Jewish Commercial Pioneers

In South Africa itself the Jewish role only began at a later date, since the early settlers were restricted to persons of the Christian faith. Indeed, it was not until the beginning of the nineteenth century that Jews began to figure to any extent in the commercial life of the Colony. ...

Of the five Jewish families represented among the 1820 Settlers, nearly all ultimately made a contribution to the development of commerce and industry, though, like most colonists under that experiment, they began as farmers. Thus Maurice Sloman, after disastrous experiences through raids by the Xosas on the Frontier (they incidentally killed his little boy Mark), finally became a merchant in Cape Town and a member of the Commercial Exchange. Similarly Benjamin Norden finished up as a successful Cape Town merchant, while John Norton settled at Grahamstown in a similar capacity.

The Kilians in their turn were responsible for the immigration of sundry other commercial magnates of the future, including Nathan Birkenruth, Abraham Horn and, above all, Joseph Mosenthal, all originally clerks in their counting-house. No less important was the advent in 1834 of Gabriel Kilian's cousin, Jonas Bergtheil, one of the leading figures in the early colonization of Natal and the father of the country's cotton industry.

*South African Jewry 1969 (ed. Leon Feldberg, Johannesburg, 1965) pp.141-153.

The House of De Pass
Pre-eminent in the Cape Commercial Exchange in the middle of the last century was the house of De Pass, who, amongst other things, led the way in the important guano industry. In 1859 they provided the first patent slip in South Africa for the repair of ships at Simonstown, for which they were rewarded with a special vote of congratulation and thanks by the Exchange Committee. ...

Chambers of Commerce
Even more important, in 1860, was the decision to convert the Commercial Exchange into the Cape Town Chamber of Commerce, the historic meeting at which the matter was discussed being presided over by a Jew, Charles Manuel. It is also worth recording that at the final meeting of the old Exchange the chair was taken by Saul Solomon.

In the later part of the 19th century, a converted Jew was pre-eminent in the affairs of the Cape Town Chamber—Ludwig Wiener, who, as a Member of Parliament and head of the firm of Van der Byl & Co., was the then recognized spokesman of the South African business world. Incidentally he was invited, as the official representative of the Cape Town Chamber of Commerce, to attend the opening of the railway line to Bloemfontein on January 17, 1891. Wiener was also the trusted adviser of the Government on such matters as railway rates, and in 1892 was sent to Chicago as the Commissioner of Cape Colony at the World's Fair.

The first Jewish President of the Cape Town Chamber was Meyer Cassel in 1853. ...

When in 1856 the Natal Chamber of Commerce came into existence, there were several Jewish merchants in the country. Jonas Bergtheil and Adolph Coqui, the latter a Belgian Jew, closely associated with the Voortrekkers, played a leading part in the affairs of such enterprises as the Natal Bank and the Natal Insurance Company, as well as the original Natal Railway Company, which in 1860 completed the first line in South Africa, from Durban to the Point. ...

On The Rand
For a considerable period in the early days, Johannesburg had both a Chamber of Commerce and a Mercantile Association. In 1893 David Holt, having seceded from the former, became vice-chairman of the latter; while on the Mercantile Association Committee were also J. D. Elias, L. Hart, J. Jacobson, J. H. Israel and A. H. Jacobs (who, in 1896, was the purchaser of the very first motor car ever imported into South Africa!).

In 1896 the Mercantile Association Committee included Mones Davis and G. Koenigsberg, while the secretary, L. Eisenberg, was a well-known German Jew.

After the Anglo-Boer War the Mercantile Association became the Johannesburg Chamber of Trade, which lasted till 1910, when the obvious unwisdom of two separate bodies led to a merger. Already by 1902 some of the Mercantile members had returned, including J. Jacobson and David Holt, while another well-known old-timer on the Chamber's committee was Alfred Rogaly, elected vice-president in 1911.

For many years one of the mainstays of the Johannesburg Chamber was Alfred Rosenthal (no relative of the present writer), who was on the executive, while J. Raphaely, B. Gundelfinger, J. Heilbronn, S. M. Ismay, Claude H. Leon were other well-known figures on that body. In 1922 Selig Hillman was elected vice-president.

Ever since the foundation of the Association of Chambers of Commerce of South Africa there have been Jewish presidents, starting with Ludwig Wiener, who held office from 1894 to 1899. In 1909 and 1910 there was Wolf Ehrlich, of Bloemfontein, and in 1928 and 1929 Karl Gundelfinger, of Durban. More recently there were Harry Goldberg, of Johannesburg, in 1953-4, and in 1962-3, E. P. Bradlow, also of Johannesburg.

Jewish participation in the mining industry goes back to 1854, when, in consequence of the first great copper boom in Namaqualand, a number of flotations took place at the Cape. Among the directors of the South African Mining Company was Saul Solomon, while among those of the Cape of Good Hope Mining Company was Ernst Landsberg. M. Preuss was chairman of the Western Province Mining Company and Aaron de Pass a director of the Walwich Bay Mining Company, H. Solomon of the Cape Colonial Mining Company and Julius Mosenthal, along with E. G. Landsberg of the Spektakel Mining Company.

Not until the diamond fields of Griqualand West were discovered did circumstances make necessary some form of organization. Out of the primitive "Diggers' Committee," set up along the Vaal, which included men like T. B. Kisch, there grew the Kimberley Mining Board, with F. de Pass, R. Hinrichsen and other Jewish members.

The Chamber of Mines

When, soon after the discovery of gold, the "Witwatersrand Chamber of Mines" came into existence, its first annual report, issued in 1888, showed a substantial participation of Jewish members. Not only was the vice-president and chairman of the Council the redoubtable magnate, Carl Hanau, but the committee included Edward Lippert and Lionel Phillips. Among the members, representatives were Gustav Imroth, on behalf of the Flora Gold Mine, Simon Sacke (Geldenhuis Main Reef), Alfons Lilienfeld (Langlaagte Block B), Richard Lilienfeld (Langlaagte Estates), Sydney Morris (Langlaagte Western), L. Lowenthal (National Gold Mine), Gustav Sonn (Transvaal Coal Trust) and others. In 1891 Lionel (later Sir Lionel) Phillips became the first Jewish President of the Chamber, an honour repeatedly bestowed upon him, and new members of the executive included Wolf Joel, George (later Sir George) Albu,

Adolf Barkhan, J. N. de Jongh, Adolph Epler and C. S. Goldman. Presidents included Louis Reyersback in 1907 and Max Elkan in 1912.

Long before South Africa had an organized Stock Exchange, in the 1850's, individual Jewish brokers operated, like M. L. Bensusan, of Cape Town, but the real flowering came after the founding of Kimberley. Among the famous early figures were N. Abrahams, H. J. Cohen, Gallewski & Hart, P. Herman, H. E. Jacobs, Bernard Klisser, Sydney Mendelssohn, B. Oppenheimer, Philip & Dettelbach, N. Raphael, Alfred Rogaly, Runchman & Hart, A. Saalfeld, B. Solomon, E. Solomon, Sonning & Pollock, C. Stranski, J. Swaebe, Tallerman & Ansell, J. Weinberg and A. Yockmonitz. Many of these moved to Barberton and then to Johannesburg. There we find, in the very early days, A. Benjamin, Cohen & Graumann (Sir Harry Graumann later became Mayor of Johannesburg), E. H. A. Cohen and Lewis & Marks.

The Stock Exchange

Some idea of the prominence of the Jewish element on the Johannesburg Stock Exchange in the early days may be gained from the fact that in 1889 well over 100 Jewish firms were in existence, representing an actual individual membership of probably twice that figure! The earliest committees included among their members Gustav Imroth, H. Solomon, F. Mosenthal, Carl Hanau, J. Friedlander, H. W. Adler, while the secretary was R. Moss. Later committee members were Julius Friedlander and S. B. Joel. In 1894 the Johannesburg Stock Exchange had its first Jewish chairman in Harry Solomon, while another familiar name on the committee was that of Otto Beit (later Sir Otto). Solly Joel became chairman in 1896, with Fritz Mosenthal as his deputy, the committee also including George Albu, E. E. Berlandina, A. Friedlander, L. Joel and Bernard Oppenheimer. The following year Harry Solomon was again chairman and the committee had acquired as members Alfred Benjamin, Hertzberg and Alfons Sprinz. Perhaps it is not suprising to find that the Johannesburg Stock Exchange has always been closed on Jewish holidays!

Similarly there has always been a substantial Jewish participation in the bodies controlling South African industry, starting with the old Cape Manufacturers' Association, forerunner of the present-day Chamber of Industry. Dating back to the beginning of the present century, this had among its founders M. Rothkugel, the furniture maker, Senator Franz Ginsberg of Kingwilliamstown, and Maurice Eilenberg, who started South Africa's garment manufacturing industry with the production of waterproofs at Cape Town, likewise Simon Roytowsky (Roy), who about 1910 put up the first modern clothing factory; Hermann & Canard, who turned out cigarettes by hand in the 1880's; Louis Nathan, cigarette pioneer of Port Elizabeth; and P. Barnett & Co. of that city who were making saddlery in the 1890's. Louis Policansky, of Cape Town, rolled cigarettes by hand before the Anglo-Boer War. David, Albert and Hillier

Holt opened the first cigarette factory in the Transvaal in 1895, parent of the United Tobacco Company of which David in 1905 became the first chairman. Up-country, the Hillman brothers, storekeepers at Norval's Pont during the Anglo-Boer War, rose to dominate the timber and sawmilling business, while Dr. Jaques Schlesinger was vice-president of the Transvaal Chamber of Industries in 1910.

Some Leading Personalties

Coming to our own times, the Jewish contribution is even larger. Taking "ASSOCOM" (the Associated Chambers of Commerce), we find E. P. Bradlow, one of the leaders of the country's furniture trade, as President, while another particularly notable personality is Miss G. Horwitz, who, apart from being prominent in the administration, was the chairman of ASSOCOM's Committee on Consumer Credit. Then there are L. M. Sher, vice-president for the Transvaal, and I. Goldsmith, vice-president for the Orange Free State, K. Karr, chairman of the Parliamentary Liaison Committee, J. H. Levien, chairman of the Tax Committee, and C. B. Kaplan, chairman of the Board of Trade and Export Committees, and A. Bernitz, chairman of the Import Control Committee. We find R. Goldman as the President of the Durban Chamber; L. Salber, of the Cape Town Chamber; and G. Barris, of the Port Elizabeth Chamber. At Bethal, Transvaal, the post is held by E. Feldman, at Randfontein by J. Chait, at Vereeniging by Max Shapiro, at Messina by G. Klaff, at Lichtenburg by A. Melman, at Somerset West by A. Friedman, at Kimberley by G. B. Haberfeld, at Queenstown by B. Levin, at Vredenburg by S. J. Levin, at Leslie by L. Taitz, at Randburg by M. Sklaar, at Roodepoort by I. Simon, at Windhoek by Barney Gamsu, at Boksburg by H. Resnick, at Bellville by C. I. Jawitz, at Goodwood by W. Freedberg. Taken from several hundred Chambers, this list is by no means exhaustive. Similarly, in the Federated South African Chambers of Industries, former Presidents include Morris Kramer of Kingwilliamstown, pioneer of the tanning industry, who served from 1924-1925, and again from 1929-1930. Present office-bearers include S. Goodman, President of the Transvaal Chamber of Industries; S. R. Back, of the Cape Chamber of Industries, well-known shirt manufacturer; L. Dubb, of footwear fame, and on the National Clothing Federation, H. Abramowitz. Philip Frame and Dr. J. Harte head the National Textile Manufacturers' Association. J. Bloom is a leader of the South African Oil Expressers and the Soap Manufacturers' Association. J. Greenstein is director of the Transvaal Clothing Manufacturers' Association and W. Goldberg vice-president of the Cape Chamber of Industry.

Apart from its chairman, J. H. Hyman, the Johannesburg Stock Exchange Committee of 1963-1964 included A. Mennell, R. Lurie and E. Heilbromer.

All these personalities have played their part in taking organized South African commerce and industry to the levels they hold today.

[2] Jewish Contributions to South Africa's Economic Development*

Louis Hotz

South Africa is only six years short of a century since its first "take off" into the stratosphere of a modern industrial economy—to borrow a Space Age phrase coined by the American economist, W. W. Rostow, to describe, more cumbrously, "the surge of industrialization focused in a relatively few sectors." This exactly denotes what happened to South Africa in the early 1870's, for there was indeed an intense concentration on a few sectors of tremendous importance at that stage. In the intervening years after the "take off," South Africa had experienced many setbacks and failures; but there has been a succession of "boosters" that have kept the country steadily orbiting on the path of economic development to undreamt-of heights.

During that period, under the impact of the mineral discoveries—diamonds in 1870, gold rather more than a decade later—South Africa has been transformed from an essentially agricultural and pastoral society, politically torn asunder, into an advanced industrial and constitutionally united State. On those foundations the whole of present-day South Africa, a virile and self-confident community, has been erected.

True, new factors have emerged out of the dynamism of the original "take off," and they have gone to broaden and strengthen the superstructure. In the first half of the century that followed the first mineral discoveries, the mining industry—and this means primarily the gold industry—was by far the most important single contributor to the burgeoning South African economy. In the second half, with the First World War more or less as the dividing line, that was no longer entirely the case.

Gold The Mainspring

South Africa's national income has grown until, today, it has approached the R7,000-million mark. To that impressive figure (more than double what it was only ten years ago) the gold mines contribute directly rather more than one-tenth, compared with about one-fifth at the time of the First World War. This is greater than the contribution of any other individual industry, but it is now a long way behind that derived from the secondary industries as a whole. Here we have a measure of South Africa's second great industrial revolution, which is gaining momentum with every passing year. Yet, as we look at the phenomenal growth of our factory production, we are constantly struck by the fact that the mines continue to be the mainspring of modern South Africa's economy and the impetus at the back of every subsequent development.

*South African Jewry 1965, pp. 51-59

Besides being an immediate source of material wealth and a growth point for a host of other industries, the mines performed another historic function. Directly and indirectly, they were the magnet that attracted from many parts of the world large numbers of newcomers who brought with them new skills, new energies, a fresh spirit of enterprise, new wants and new ways of life.

As Professor D. Hobart Houghton has aptly remarked, when outlining the rise of the mining industry: "Attention has often been drawn to the power of gold to attract foreign capital, but there is another aspect which has become no less significant. This is the way in which gold mining has attracted men from abroad with drive, energy, vision and the courage to take chances; and on the Witwatersrand they found scope for their talents. Some may have been mere adventurers, but others were not; and as a group they brought new vitality, enterprise and progressive notions; and these qualities have been perpetuated in the modern generation of South African industrial leadership. Whether this enterprise would have arisen without this injection from abroad is doubtful."

In a nutshell, this sums up what South Africa owes to the generation of "new South Africans" who appeared on the scene in the latter part of the past century and to their descendants and successors in the present generation.

The Jewish Role

Among those who have thus helped to enrich South Africa's human resources and to develop its natural assets, not the least valuable element has been South African Jewry.

In point of numbers the Jewish community has never exceeded much more than 4 per cent of our total White population; but its contribution to South Africa's economic and cultural progress has been out of all proportion to its numerical size. What the Jews have meant to South Africa could hardly be better or more simply summarized than in a few sentences written by a non-Jewish historian, Leo Marquard, some years ago.

In his book, *The Peoples and Policies of South Africa,* Mr. Marquard said: "From the early days of settlement, when Jewish pedlars wandered about the country with pack-horse or donkey cart, Jewish traders have been foremost in commerce. When diamonds and gold were discovered, individual Jews helped to develop these industries, and subsequently to start secondary industries and to expand trade and commerce. But the contribution of Jews to South African life is not confined to economics. In the encouragement of the arts, in helping to establish universities, and in the spread of enlightenment, Jews have always been prominent. While clinging tenaciously to their religion and in this respect isolating themselves from the rest of the community, they have nevertheless thoroughly identified themselves with South African life."

From this pen-picture of Jewish identification with South Africa's national upbuilding some salient facts emerge. It recalls the role of the humble Jewish pedlar and trader who, in his unobtrusive way, was to occupy an indispensable place in the South African community before the advent of modern transportation and machine-age industry in this country. It records South Africa's indebtedness to the Jews who were among the planners and builders of its ever-expanding economic vistas and achievements; and it recognizes the share which Jews have had in the shaping of the industry which, more than any other, has come to symbolize South Africa in the world economy.

Gold mining today, with a current annual production of not far short of R700-million, is a supremely efficient and streamlined industrial complex. It is the collective creation of many minds and hands; but it still demands, and has room at the top for, the qualities of personal initiative and leadership. Throughout the chequered history of this industry and its formidable record of achievement, Jewish names can be found among those who have provided those qualities and among its formative and executive brains.

Mining Pioneers

Only a few of a long roll of able and frequently picturesque personalities can receive special mention here. Looking down the year we find in the front rank the historic names of B. J. ("Barney") Barnato, Hermann Eckstein, Alfred and Otto Beit, Lionel Phillips, the Joel brothers (Woolf, Solly and Jack), George Albu, Samuel Marks and his partner Isaac Lewis, and Ernest Oppenheimer. Most of these men were contemporaries and associates in the infant days of diamonds and gold in South Africa.

In human interest, no less than for its influence on the development of the mining industry, to this day pride of place belongs to the dazzling and, in its final phases, tragic career of Barney Barnato. Shrewd and nimble-witted, a product of Cockney London, with a flair for daring speculation and risk-taking, Barnato was cut out for the rough-and-tumble of the mining camp. It was not long before he came to the top as the most challenging competitor of that other colossus of Kimberley, Cecil John Rhodes. The struggle for the economic future of the diamond fields ended with Rhodes and Barnato joining forces to lay the solid foundations of the diamond industry and its world-wide interests as we know them today.

From diamonds, Barney Barnato, like Rhodes and others among the Kimberley pioneers, turned to the newly discovered goldfields on the Witwatersrand. There, too, he acquired very extensive interests and, with the experience gained in the Kimberley days, he helped to bring order into an industry which was to overshadow Kimberley. Barney Barnato's death by drowning, while on a health voyage to England, was as melodramatic as the rest of his strange history. The manner of his going could not alter the fact that this man, with all his flamboyance and theatricality, left a firm imprint on the South African scene.

The upbuilding of the mining industry—whether diamonds or gold or, in later years, coal and other mineral wealth—has not, of course, been the work of a few men. Some, among those already named, were closely associated with Barnato; others made independent contributions. As time passed, one man was to repeat the earlier story of Jewish leadership in this field. A young man of German-Jewish origin, who came to South Africa when the careers of Rhodes and Barnato had almost become a legend, was destined to assume their mantle as a mining "empire builder" in the next generation.

An Outstanding Figure

Ernest (later Sir Ernest) Oppenheimer, arriving in Kimberley early in this century to represent a firm of diamond dealers, was to be the undisputed genius of the diamond industry and in due course also the driving force behind many of the most important gold mining, base minerals and industrial developments in Southern and Central Africa.

At the time of his death in 1957, few South Africans had won such universal recognition and respect as a far-sighted leader in the national economy. Not least of his latter-day achievements were the opening up of the new Free State goldfields and the long-range deep-level developments in the Far Eastern Transvaal. Sir Ernest will also be remembered as the pioneer of the copper industry in Northern Rhodesia (now Zambia) and other undertakings outside South Africa, and as a particularly enlightened and public-spirited captain of industry.

His work has been carried on with notable ability and in the same tradition of imaginative enterprise by his son, Mr. Harry Oppenheimer.

More recently, in the direct line of succession to the men who first set their stamp upon the mining industry and made it the monument it is to South African progress, there have been men of the calibre of the late Mr. A. S. Hersov, Mr. S. G. Menell, Mr. Sidney Spiro and Mr. B. L. Bernstein. All of these hold, or have held, key positions in the upper echelons of the industry. Mr. Hersov, whose untimely death was no small loss to South Africa, and Mr. Menell were responsible for the creation of the important Anglo-Vaal group, with its widespread mining and industrial ramifications.

These men of Jewish origin have provided a conspicuous example of the fact that South Africa is still a land of opportunity for men of bold vision and enterprise. With their predecessors they have formed a significant element among those who, in Professor Houghton's words, brought a new vitality into the effective exploitation of South Africa's rich natural resources.

As the most notable embodiment of big capital in South Africa, the mining industry and its leaders, Gentile and Jewish, have had their detractors and critics. Unquestionably, however, the men who have guided the destinies of the industry and whose hands have been at the controls of this "powerhouse of modern South African enterprise"—to use Professor Herbert Frankel's phrase—have left their imprint on our national development as few others have done. That South African Jews are numbered among the pioneers and builders of this industry, as well as among its later policy-makers and leaders, is one of the Jewish community's most significant contributions to the progress and prosperity of South Africa.

In the fields of commerce and secondary industry, the part played by Jewish businessmen and entrepreneurs has naturally been spread over a wider area; but it has also, as has already been briefly mentioned, contributed no less to the strength and stability of South Africa's economic structure.

Pioneers of Commerce

Like their role in the rise and development of the mining industry, the activities of Jewish commercial men and industrialists are merged in the broad stream of national achievement, to which a multiplicity of men and interests have added their quotas. Nevertheless, as we turn the pages of South African economic history, and as we study the contemporary scene, we see ample evidence to prove how greatly individual Jews have helped to make the South African industrial and commercial system what it is today.

Only recently we have had an interesting reminder of this fact in the report that two of the oldest and largest wholesale houses in South Africa have joined hands. One of them, established well over a century ago, bears a name which for several generations has been a household word in South African commerce and industry. It is the name of the great merchant firm of Mosenthals, whose founders, Joseph and Adolph, as well as other members of the family, were among the Jewish immigrants, mainly from Central Europe, who settled in the Cape in the first half of the 19th century.

In the Jewish contribution to South Africa the Mosenthal story stands as a notable record of unbroken family continuity to this day, and of many-sided service, in commerce, banking, industry, agriculture and public life. So highly esteemed was the name that the private "banknotes" issued by the firm before the advent of regular banking were accepted as currency throughout the Cape Colony and even farther afield.

The Mosenthal brothers, and their kinsmen who joined them, typified a generation of Jewish worthies who sank their roots in the Western and Eastern Cape and the Orange Free State. They helped to build an ordered society in large parts of South Africa. Many thrived and prospered as members of the solid merchant class of Cape Town, Port Elizabeth, East London, Grahamstown and Bloemfontein. Others adventured into the interior, where they became familiar and welcome figures in remote dorps and on scattered farmsteads. This was not only for the wares they carried and as channels for bringing the farmers' products to distant markets. It was also because they represented, for many an isolated area, some of the culture and social amenities of the greater world. They lived their own lives and earned their bread; but theirs was also a civilising mission in the true sense.

A considerable number, who started as pedlars and "smouses," made their homes in outlying villages and trading stations which became the economic and financial centres of the widespread communities they served. There are innumerable examples, far too many even for an attempt at a selected list; but such families as the Friedlanders of De Aar, the Eilenbergs and Sonnenbergs of Namaqualand, and the Baumanns and Ehrlichs of the Free State were typical. An analysis of a cross-section of the Jewish population of the Cape sixty years ago shows that, while the majority were settled in the Western Province, hundreds of others were dispersed in tiny communities or as single families in some 70 villages and on farms throughout the Colony.

A Significant Contribution

It is a far cry from the days of the "smous" and the small country storekeeper, as well as of the handful of merchants in the bigger towns, to the present age of vast commercial combines, supermarkets and the highly-geared apparatus of modern commerce. Today South Africa's wholesale and retail business counts its turnover by the thousands of millions, and its contribution to the national income stands at round about 13 per cent of the total.

As in the past, Jewish businessmen at all levels, from the heads of multi-million undertakings downwards, are to be found today in the forefront of the nation's commerce. One of their outstanding contributions has been in the development of the multiple chain stores which have transformed the buying habits of the great masses of the population and introduced a new dimension into the distributive trades.

Popularly known as the "bazaars" in the beginning, these undertakings, with branches spread over all the cities and many of the smaller towns, have long ceased to cater predominantly for the type of trade suggested by that name. They have built up an imposing network of distribution to serve every section and every taste in the community. The main characteristic they have maintained throughout is that, by purchasing in bulk and cutting out many intermediate and overhead charges, they have played a strategic part in the lowering of prices and living costs and the improvement of the standards of life for wage-earners and the middle classes. They have thus rendered, and are still rendering, a valuable social service to the country.

This virtual revolution in the South African retail trade dates back over more than 40 years, but has gathered momentum more recently. It may be invidious to single out some names where so many have done so much to modernise and expand that aspect of South Africa's business life. There can be little doubt, however, that in this absorbing story a special place must be assigned to the creative energies and foresight of men such as Sam Cohen, Michael Miller, Harry Herber, Max Sonnenberg, Morris Mauerberger, Gustav Ackermann and Leon Segal. These men, who brought new concepts of departmental trading into South African commerce, must be numbered among the merchant princes of our day, worthy of a place with the pioneers of the nation's economic life.

Another side to the story is that Jewish business leaders have taken their full share of responsibility for what might be called the "government" of organised commerce, on which so much of its efficiency and smooth running depends. In its 70 years of existence the Association of Chambers of Commerce—the country's "business parliament"—has drawn several of its most distinguished presidents from the ranks of Jewish businessmen. As far back as 1894 the Cape Town merchant Ludwig Wiener, a prominent public figure in that city, was elected president; and since then the list has included such outstanding names as Wolf Ehrlich, Karl Gundelfinger, Ivan Haarburger, Harry Goldberg and Emanuel Bradlow. Besides this, Jewish businessmen have always actively participated in the work of local and regional chambers of commerce and innumerable committees—work seldom publicised but often vital to the business community and the general public.

Captains of Industry

We meet their counterparts among the leaders of manufacturing industry, that increasingly important part of the South African economy which today is responsible for a gross annual production of about R3,000-million.

In South Africa, organised secondary industry has a shorter history than commerce, mining or agriculture; but during the past 50 years it has thrown up a number of able and far-sighted personalities who have given it a commanding position in the economic life of the country.

It is a noteworthy fact that at crucial moments the central organisation in South African industry, the Federated Chamber of Industries, happened to be presided over by Jewish industrialists who, in that capacity, had to deal with novel and sometimes difficult situations. That was the case, for example, when Morris Kramer was head of the F.C.I. in 1924 and again in 1929-30, and G. B. Berlyn was president in 1938-39. In recent years the names of S. R. Back, L. Dubb, M. Bernitz, S. Goodman, H. S. Abramowitz, P. Frame, I. Philips and J. Bloom have figured among South Africa's industrial leaders at local or provincial levels.

There is hardly a branch of South African industry in which Jewish men of enterprise and initiative have not had some part, and not seldom the part of the pioneer and innovator. Even before South Africa was launched on its present industrial era, in modern terms, the Cape had seen the start of small factories for the limited market which did not turn up its nose at "colonial" products. So we find the famous name of D. H. Isaacs already linked with furniture-making, an industrialist named Isaacson trying his hand in the tanning industry, and Herman and Canard, M. Pevsner and L. Rubin helping to lay the foundations of South Africa's tobacco manufacturing industry.

Still earlier, the De Pass family made history with pioneer ventures in the fishing industry at the Cape and in the sugar industry in Natal. In Natal, also, Jonas Bergtheil, a man of restless energy and ideas, dreamt of and came near to realising the beginnings of a South African cotton industry at New Germany, where a Jewish industrialist of our time, Mr. Phillip Frame, has built up a large-scale wool and cotton textile industry today.

In the old South African Republic, enterprising men like "Sammy" Marks, Isaac Lewis and their associates, notably Alois Nellmapius, were quick to sense the possibilities of industrial development opened up by the gold mines. Assisted by generous State concessions, designed to make the Republic industrially more self-sufficient, the Lewis and Marks partnership started or planned a number of industries for the Transvaal, from the manufacture of dynamite for the mines to the processing of foodstuffs and the distilling of liquor.

War and other circumstances put an end to most of these ventures, though some were to survive and develop into permanent accessions to South Africa's economy. More than that, however, Marks and his friends proved that South Africa could "make it," and so pointed the way to later developments in more favourable conditions. Though not so spectacular as some of his "concession" undertakings, the most important contribution by Sammy Marks to South Africa's industrial progress was the role he played in proving the country's coal resources, and his first tentative efforts to create an iron and steel industry, the forerunner of Iscor.

Clothing A Nation

It is in such industries as clothing, textiles, food processing and furniture making, more than in the heavy industries, that Jewish entrepreneurs have left, and are today leaving, their most notable mark on South Africa's economic development. In many ways the most important place must be assigned in this field to the manufacture of clothing. From humble beginnings in one-man tailoring shops and backyard premises, garment making has blossomed into an industry that now provides work for about 50,000 men and women and has a gross output of some R130-million. Many hundreds of factories, from huge mass production concerns to small firms with under 25 employees, now supply between 80 to 90 per cent of the country's clothing requirements. In addition, largely through the enterprise of Jewish manufacturers and designers, the South African industry has built up a substantial export trade, with products that have won the highest praise in competitive world markets.

Protective tariffs have helped the development of the clothing industry, and war conditions during the past 50 years have also encouraged local production. This would have been of little avail, however, if there had not been people in South Africa who had the initiative and determination to make the most of the opportunities. The history of the clothing industry—and of a long line of other South African industries as well—is the story of such men as these. For the most part craftsmen or traders who had some of the know-how and the necessary business ability, they turned these to account by setting up factories and thus making a long-term contribution to the country's productive wealth.

In the Transvaal, one of the earliest pioneers in the clothing industry was H. J. Henochsberg, who came to the Rand from Durban shortly after the Anglo-Boer War and opened a small factory. Within the next few years he was followed by S. Wunsh and others. The road of progress in the various branches of the industry is signposted by the names of Braude, Beinashowitz, Jacobson, Kalmek, Kramer, Silver, Rosen, Swartz and Jaff, to mention only a few. As the industry developed, its standards of workmanship, style and efficiency grew steadily, until they could compare with some of the best in the world.

The same pattern was repeated at the Cape, in Durban and other important industrial centres. In Cape Town, Maurice Eilenberg, who is better known as a successful trader in Namaqualand, opened a factory for waterproof garments before the Anglo-Boer War and showed the way to the possibilities of the industry. Garment-making in the wider sense was launched on a modern scale at the Cape in 1907, when Simon Roy established the first factory. Thereafter the industry went ahead by leaps and bounds.

Jewish manufacturers of the stamp of Simon Roy, Bernard Shub, Reuben Back and Morris Mauerberger were in the van of every forward move. A high-water mark was reached when the factory founded by Bernard Shub little more than a quarter of a century ago was crowned with an international award for the best-designed men's clothing.

In Natal, Harry Linder and I. Philips were among the pioneers of the clothing industry; and it was in Natal, too, that Phillip Frame helped to build up a massive textile industry, thus adding his name to the record of Jewish industrialists, such as Woolf Harris and D. I. Fram, who are remembered for their contributions to that important sector of South African industrial development.

In Other Industries

While the garment and textile industries are probably the best-known fields of Jewish initiative in South Africa, the furniture industry, both on its distributive and manufacturing side, also appears to have been peculiarly well suited to Jewish enterprise. From being essentially a craftsman's trade and small home industry, furniture making has developed into a large-scale mass production unit, giving employment to roughly 20,000 workers and with a gross output of more than R50-million a year. D. H. Isaacs at the Cape has already been mentioned among the early South African pioneers in this process. Nearer to our times are familiar names like Bradlow, Goldberg, Bloch, Steele and Lubner—admittedly a very inadequate list where so many may claim legitimate credit.

Jewish industrialists have been a considerable factor in the development of the chemical industries (one thinks of Schlesinger-Delmore, Fritz Ginsberg, the Sives and Karnovskys), the tobacco industry (the Harts in the old Republican days, the Suzmans, Policanskys, and Pevsners), and the leather industry, in which Morris Kramer and Fritz Ginsberg were among the pioneers (both in the traditional home of the industry, the Eastern Province).

The vast network of the food processing industries owes a great deal to Jewish drive, business acumen and capital. Its leading personalities include the Lewis and Jaffe families, the Frankels, H. Pogorelsky, I. Albow and Abraham Shapiro, of canning fame.

There is a direct link, naturally, between the food manufacturing industries and the primary producer. It is of interest, therefore, that South African Jews, though mainly engaged in trade, secondary industry and the professions, have played their part in agriculture and kindred spheres as well.

Jews In Agriculture

A long way back in the last century the Mosenthals, already referred to, had a hand in the development of the wool and merino industries, and the De Pass family were associated with the early days of Natal sugar growing. Samuel Marks, the Hillman brothers, and the Moshals and Gevissers did much, in various ways, to encourage afforestation.

Marks is also counted among the pioneers of fruit-growing in the Transvaal; and later, in the same field, Joseph Sarembock of Ceres, in the Cape, became one of the first deciduous fruit growers in South Africa to practise advanced scientific methods of large-scale production. In the Eastern Transvaal I. W. Schlesinger developed a citrus-growing industry which is believed to be the largest single enterprise of its kind in the world today.

South Africa owes a great debt to the group of Jewish farmers in the Transvaal maize triangle who year after year contributed substantially to the nation's essential food supplies as well as to its export trade. The most remarkable figure amongst them was the late Ezrael Lazarus, nationally famous as the "Mealie King." This was partly because he was among the foremost producers, but also because he set an example of scientific farming which had a profound influence on South African maize production. His achievements had a parallel in the Free State, where the "Potato

King," the late J. B. Lurie, also proved what could be done by proper farming techniques.

Contrary to popular belief, Jews do not dominate South African banking and finance, though individual Jews have, of course, brought into the country's economic affairs a grasp of financial problems and the workings of the money and capital markets.

Pre-eminent among those who have made this type of contribution to the South African economy stands the name of I. W. Schlesinger, to whom reference has already been made as a pioneer of the citrus industry. The late Mr. Schlesinger's financial genius—some called it wizardry—showed itself not only in the world of company formation, insurance and banking. A man of creative ideas and unremitting energy, he was also responsible for the establishment of a chain of theatres and cinemas, the introduction of systematic broadcasting and of film-making in South Africa, and developments in the hotel and catering industries. Under his son and heir, Mr. John Schlesinger, his "empire" has remained a force in the South African economic system.

A Proud Record

Unfortunately, there are no recent statistics available to pinpoint the general picture of the Jewish contribution to the South African economy. An investigation by the writer many years ago indicated that the Jewish community supplied one-seventh of the South African population engaged in commerce, about 2 per cent of those engaged in primary and secondary industries, and about the same proportion of the professional and public service elements. No doubt, with the development of industries, the picture has substantially changed since then, and the conclusion drawn at the time, that Jews were taking a fair share in South Africa's new industrial upsurge, is today even more justified. That much of the initiative and industrial enterprise is provided—and over the years has been provided—from the ranks of the Jewish community is clear from what has already been said.

South African Jews are pulling their weight in the challenging task of making and sustaining a prosperous and economically progressive South African nation on this sub-continent.

Today more than ever, in the midst of world pressures and threatening dangers, a sound and dynamic South African economy is an essential condition of national survival. It is one of our most powerful weapons in the struggle to preserve the values which not one of us would wish to see sacrificed. The Jewish community can be proud of the part it has played, and will continue to play, in keeping South Africa strong and secure.

[3] The Balfour Declaration

The Balfour Declaration, cited below, so crucial to Zionist success, owed its origins in large part to General Smuts and a number of prominent South Africans. The item from the Zionist Record [3] sheds some light on this historical period. Subsequently, the Declaration received consistent official South African support [4].

Foreign Office,
November 2nd, 1917

Dear Lord Rothchild,

I have much pleasure in conveying to you, on behalf of His Majesty's Government, the following declaration of sympathy with Jewish Zionist aspirations which has been submitted to, and approved by, the Cabinet.

"His Majesty's Government view with favour the establishment in Palestine of a national home for the Jewish people and will use their best endeavours to facilitate the achievement of this object, it being clearly understood that nothing shall be done which may prejudice the civil and religious rights of existing non-Jewish communities in Palestine, or the rights and political status enjoyed by Jews in any other country."

I should be grateful if you would bring this declaration to the knowledge of the Zionist Federation.

Yours,

J.A. Balfour

[4] Latest Research Spotlights Role of South Africans in Balfour Declaration*

The main article in the first volume of the *Herzl Year Book*[1] occupying more than 100 pages, sets out to prove that the chief architect of the Balfour Declaration was Dr. Herzl, although he died 13 years before the declaration was issued and at a time when its scope and content could not have been envisaged.

*Zionist Record, May 1, 1959

Of particular interest to South Africa is the importance which the writer of the article, Dr. Oskar K. Rabinowicz, attaches to Lord Alfred Milner's part in attaining the Balfour Declaration.

With Milner are connected the names of South African Zionist leaders who at the time of Herzl and on directions from Herzl made Milner a Zionist.

In her book "The Vision Amazing," Marcia Gitlin had a good deal to say about the association between South African Zionists (Harry Solomon, Samuel Goldreich and Max Langerman) with Lord Milner at the time when he was High Commissioner in South Africa.

She mentions Herzl's letter to Goldreich in 1903 in which he said, "If you could interest Milner in our cause, it would be very valuable...."

Goldreich and others acted on Herzl's instructions. With his sound instinct for wide contacts, Herzl realized the role which Milner might be called upon to play in the attainment of the Zionist aims. South African Zionist leaders, on the other hand, also felt the need for friendship with Milner and were in close touch with him.

"Consular" Office

Milner appointed the Zionist Federation to act in a "consular" capacity on behalf of Jewish refugees from Transvaal who, after the end of the Boer War, flocking back to their Witwatersrand homes, met with various passport difficulties.

For the South African Zionist Federation to have been appointed to act as official representatives of Jewry was an event of outstanding local importance.

Marcia Gitlin described this event in her book but Dr. Oskar Rabinowicz goes further and shows that the appointment created tremendous excitement in world Zionist headquarters and was regarded as an outstanding victory for the cause. The official organ of the World Zionist Organization, *Die Welt,* of Vienna, published the news on the front and added the following postscript:

> "The recognition of the Zionist head office in Cape Town as a representative organ of Jewry is an event of far-reaching importance."

Lesson from South Africa

In a following issue, *Die Welt* published a leading article under the heading "The Lemon from South Africa."

"Friends of Zionism," the editor wrote, "see in this act a natural and gratifying progress with regard to the assessment of the Jewish problem... The English Jew does not now require a consular representation in South Africa; the whole country is his home. With regard to other countries, every Jew is free to apply to the consul of his home country. But he does not have to do so, he has now his own representation. ..."

"Jews have ceased to be a *res nullus* and have come to be regarded by the English people as an independent international individuality. ..."

"Not Zionism as a party has been recognized, but England pronounced it clearly that if the Jews have their own appropriate organization, they can exist as an independent group with all rights. Free England has given a great lesson to Jews all over the world."

Later at the sixth Zionist Congress (Rabinowicz records) the South African episode was announced from the platform by Oscar Marmorek.

"Almost every sentence he then spoke was interrupted by the applause of the delegates which turned into an oration for Lord Milner and Sam Goldreich when their names were mentioned."

In January, 1903, Sam Goldreich sent a special report to Herzl on the "Permit Commission." When in 1902 Lord Milner gave a donation of £25 for a relief fund for Rumanian refugees, *Die Welt* published a reproduction of the cheque over the whole front page and also then wrote a letter to Milner. On a subsequent occasion when Mr. Chamberlain visited South Africa *Die Welt* referred editorially to his and Lord Milner's pro-Zionist attitude.

Mysterious Ways

Miss Gitlin refers to a letter which Goldreich wrote to Dr. Wolffsohn in 1905 in which he referred to this friendship with Milner and said:

> "I wonder, will the friendship between us be of value to the Zionist cause? Providence works in mysterious ways."

Providence did work in mysterious ways, and Rabinowicz takes the story still further and shows that later, as a member of the British War Cabinet in World War I, Milner played a major role in the achievement of the Balfour Declaration. According to some authorities he was responsible for the drafting of the text.

Nevertheless, Rabinowicz complains, the role of Milner has not sufficiently been appreciated by Zionist historians of subsequent years, including Dr. Weizmann in his *Trial and Error.*

He quotes Lloyd George, who said Milner was "wholeheartedly in sympathy with the Zionist ideal" and that he, together with Balfour, were the champions who "urged the Cabinet to issue a declaration in favour of the Zionist demand."

Planted the Seed

The error of the historians has now been rectified by the illuminating essay of Dr. Rabinowicz. The most remarkable fact that emerges from his essay is that more than a decade before 1917, South African Zionists were responsible in planting the seed which helped in the attainment of the Balfour Declaration.

Readings

South Africa's part in the Balfour Declaration is therefore not restricted to Smuts and Milner. Goldreich and Langermann, the man who headed the Zionist Federation, have done a great deal to achieve it.

[1] *Herzl Year Book,* Vol. 1, Edited by Raphael Patai, with a preface by Emanuel Neumann (Herzl Press, New York).

[5] Resolution of the Cabinet of the Union of South Africa at its meeting in Pretoria on September 4, 1926.

"The Government of the Union of South Africa, which has watched for many years with interest and sympathy the endeavours of the Zionist Organization to establish a national home for the Jewish people in Palestine, an object which it regards as an important contribution to peace and civilization, wishes all success to this undertaking and is prepared through its representatives on the League of Nations and otherwise, to do whatever lies in its power to assist in the establishment of that national home."

[6] Memorandum on Africa*

As Weizmann projected a vision for future South African-Jewish cooperation [6] Ben Gurion subsequently acknowledged the importance of South African support in 1947 [7]. This support is further illustrated by the appeal in 1953 to South African Jews to assist the development of Israeli air strength [8].

[Weizmann's Note: The thesis of the following memorandum is based on the assumption that Africa will probably become the backbone of the British Colonial Empire after this war. The development scheme herein detailed is considered of great political importance and it is doubtful whether there exists any other scheme of equal importance for the future of the Empire.]

1. The development of industry, especially of the chemical industry, after this war will probably take place on lines quite different from those on which the chemical industry has developed hitherto. The sources of heavy metals required in chemical manufacturing are being depleted with ever-increasing speed and the pace at which the available petroleum wells are being exploited, have led to pessimistic predictions on the part of geologists. Schemes for the conservation of mineral oil have been developed in the United States, although they are not yet strictly en-

*Weizmann to Smuts, February 26, 1943.

forced. But in spite of that, a view is current that the American petroleum supply will not outlast the next 50 years. At any rate a shortage may be experienced before that. There is, of course, a supply of petroleum from the Middle East, from the Dutch East Indies and South America, but as petroleum will be used in ever increasing degree, not only as fuel but also as a starting point for many synthetic chemicals, it is important to realize that in using petroleum for all those purposes one draws on a capital definitely limited in quantity.

2. Apart from the general considerations mentioned in the preceding paragraph, the following remarks about the position of the British industry after this war, seem to me germaine to the subject.

During this war the British industry has centered its attention on the production of a limited number of important war materials of very high quality such as airplanes, guns, tanks, which however, will not be required after the war in the same quantities as at present. The British Government has not encouraged new enterprises even if they appeared to be of value for the further development of the industry. Quite to the contrary, the declared policy was to leave the chemical production, e.g., of aviation fuel, synthetic rubber, aromatic hydrocarbons, of plastics, to the American industry, on the ground that the raw material for such production, namely petroleum, is abundant in America and that it would be easier to import the finished goods than the raw materials. Furthermore, in the first period of the Lend-Lease transactions, the British Government has paid for supplies with the holdings which British subjects had in American enterprises. The participation [which] the British industry had in certain important parts of the American industry, has therefore entirely disappeared.

After this war the British industry will be faced with the situation that the Americans will have built up a very large and very powerful chemical and mechanical industry and the British will not be able to compete with such a well-equipped industrial power. We would certainly lose the South American markets after this war; they will come under American economic domination.

And a last not unimportant consideration: One of the greatest assets of the Empire has been the fact that practically all the natural rubber which the world required was produced within the British Empire. There can be no doubt that natural rubber after this war, will to a great extent be replaced by the synthetic product, and even the investment will have lost a great deal of its value.

3. What are the trends of development in the future chemical industry discernible now? First of all the importance of synthetic products will go on increasing and even some metals will gradually be replaced by synthetic organic products such as plastics. One must, therefore, look for a source of organic matter which can replace petroleum. Such a source is undoubtedly carbohydrates—sugar, starch, cellulose. It is practically inex-

haustible because carbohydrates are reproduced in the vegetable world ever year at least once.

By fermentation and relatively simple chemical methods of conversion, carbohydrates can be transformed into practically all the substances which the industry requires. In the case of alcohol this has been known for a long time; it has been converted on a very large scale into a number of important industrial products. But other types of fermentation appear to offer even more interesting possibilities for the synthesis of various industrial materials, than the ordinary alcohol fermentation, for instance the acetone-butyl alcohol fermentation. This process has been used on fairly large scale in many countries because of the industrial importance of acetone and butyl alcohol in themselves. During the last years, however, methods have been devised to convert these two substances into large number of chemicals, and further study will certainly open new avenues.

4. In the following lines a brief survey is given of the synthetic possibilities of acetone and butyl alcohol.

The fact that butyl alcohol is converted by a very simple process into butylene shows the potentialities of butyl alcohol. Butylene is the basis for high-octane fuel and for the synthetic rubber of the Buna type. Butylene so far has been produced from the cracking gases formed from petroleum at high temperatures; it occurs in these gases as a minor constituent, and its isolation is a cumbersome and costly procedure. Butyl alcohol gives directly chemically pure butylene and all the processes which have been based on cracking butylene are as well or better carried out with fermentation butylene. This applies specifically to the conversion into butadiene and synthetic rubber. But apart from aviation fuel and Buna rubber, other important substances can be made from butyl alcohol. Butylene can be converted by catalytic processes into aromatic hydrocarbons, which in turn lead to dyes and pharmaceutical products.

Acetone is used in large quantities in the manufacture of smokeless gun-powder. But there are manifold other uses of acetone. It has been shown, to mention only a few possibilities, that acetone can be converted into isoprene which is the basic substance of natural rubber and which is destined to play an important part in the development of synthetic rubber superior to the natural one. Acetone can be converted into a number of substances call ketones which are characterised *inter alia,* by very high-octane numbers. These ketones, therefore, may be the best solution for the problem to find a fuel for the most powerful airplanes of the future which will certainly tend to operate higher anti-knock values than the present-day 100-octane fuel. Both from acetone and butyl alcohol and also from other equally valuable fermentation products, a number of plastics can be made and undoubtedly new ones can be developed, so that it will be possible to prepare synthetic materials from fermentation products, with any desired mechanical qualities of the type which have so far been confined to metallic materials. Fatty acids like acetic acid, butyric acid and their anhydrides are made easily accessible from acetone.

5. One can indeed assume that in the not too distant future, carbohydrates will replace petroleum (and coal) as starting materials for the most vital requirements of our civilization.

If the British Empire pays attention to the possible developments as adumbrated in the preceding paragraphs, it can create for itself a position which will enable the Empire to compete with the American industry. The material basis for such a scheme exists within the confines of the British empire, where one finds an abundance of carbohydrates. The surplus production of wheat in Canada and Australia, of corn in South Africa and of cane-sugar in India and the West Indies, has been for many years past a serious economic problem in these countries. This problem will disappear at once if these commodities are looked upon not only as foodstuff, but are also considered as raw materials for a great industry. The scope of the developments sketched above is so great indeed, that it will be possible to utilize the vast quantities of carbohydrates which the African Continent produces practically without human help and which are entirely wasted today, and it will give the rise to a systematic development of agriculture in the African Continent.

6. The greater part of the scheme proposed here is based on work already done in various laboratories—in Palestine and in the United States and other parts of the world, and there is a definite prospect that the technical and economic feasibility of such a scheme will be tested first in Palestine where the conditions for the realization of such a large-scale combined agricultural-industrial project are favorable. Palestine can thus become the laboratory or the pilot-plant for the big factory into which the African Continent under this scheme might eventually develop. There is no doubt that such a scheme will give Palestine the possibility of settling a relatively large number of immigrants in a productive manner; and at the same time, the link which will be created between Africa and Palestine may strengthen Palestine's position in the Arab surroundings or may even make it feasible for Palestine to belong economically and politically to an African bloc, instead of entering the prospective Arab Federation.

[7] Sensational Facts Revealed by Ben Gurion: Official History of War of Independence.*

Jerusalem: Sensational admissions and revelations are made by Israel Prime Minister and Minister of Defense, David Ben Gurion in his personal foreword and opening chapter to the Israel Army's *Official History of the War of Independence,* which was published by the Israeli General

---

*Zionist Record, May 22, 1959.

Staff's Maarahoth Publishing Department on the eve of Israel's 11th Independence Day anniversary.

Although the War of Independence was concluded in the spring of 1949 with the signature of armistice agreements between Israel and the neighboring Arab countries (with the exception of Iraq which refused to sign the Armistice Agreement), publications of Israel Army's *Official History of the War of Independence* was postponed for 10 years.

Only now has the green light been given by the Minister of Defense and the General Staff to unveil some of the secrets of the Jewish people's epic struggle for national independence.

These are some of the revelations made by Mr. Ben Gurion:

—Israel had only 10,000 rifles and no heavy weapons when war started;

—South Africa with its relatively small Jewish community, contributed more to the Israeli war effort in terms of skilled volunteers than any other country in the world;

—Whole Israeli regiments of volunteers were trained in Germany, Austria, France and Czechoslovakia in 1948; ...

—Without foreign volunteers, the establishment of Israeli air, naval and armoured forces, as well as of weapons development and military industry, would not have been possible. Since without these forces Israel could not have achieved victory in the war, according to the official history, it can be thus agreed that the War of Independence was won thanks to foreign volunteers who comprised one-fifth of Israel's total armed strength.

[8] To the Jews of Southern Africa: An Appeal*

Five years ago many fallacies and accepted theories about the Jews were destroyed with the establishment of Israel. Israel fought with its back to the wall, surrounded on all sides by vicious enemies. But for the artery which kept supplying the heart of the Jewish People in Israel, namely air communication, we would have been lost. If not for the trickle of supplies bravely brought to the battlefront by an assortment of aircraft, the story might have been different. It was the air which liberated Israel, and it is through the air that we shall survive in any further emergency.

Realising the importance to Israel of a strong, well-trained civil aviation, Mr. Michael Comay, Deputy Director of the Israel Foreign Office, and Mr. L. A. Pincus, Managing Director of El Al Israel Airlines, brought a message to South Africa from Mr. David Ben Gurion, Prime Minister of Israel. His message was to the effect that the world to-day is in a continuous crisis, the result of which no one can foresee. Time is short and the sooner we train civil pilots to maintain and continue the civil aviation

*The Judean, September, 1953, p. 32.

system of Israel, the better it will be for Israel in times of emergency that may come. For that purpose they requested to establish a branch of the Israel Aero Association for Southern Africa in order to make the Jewish public air-minded; to give them the opportunity of participating in the training of personnel for civil aviation and to afford it an opportunity partly to shoulder the tremendous expense involved in such a scheme.

In the present uneasy state of international relations, Israel cannot afford to continue to rely upon non-Israeli personnel, as has been the case heretofore, to man its civil air communications, the life-line of the country, since they may be liable to recall to their own countries at short notice.

The qualifications required from a civil pilot capable of carrying passengers on the international routes are infinitely more exhaustive and complicated than for the military air force. It takes sometimes as long as two years to convert an air force pilot to a commander of a 4-engine aircraft like a Constellation. With the best human material at hand Israel will require at least two years in order to complement its quota of civil pilots. Both South Africa and Israel, because of climatic conditions, are not suitable for the training of pilots. Since the weather in these two countries is always clear and bright, conditions are too favourable for training exercises. This therefore has to be undertaken in countries like England and other parts of Europe where fog, snow and sleet abound, in order to familiarise the pilot with all weather conditions. Such training is costly and expensive. It will be the major duty of the members of this Association to help in the intensive programme on behalf of civil aviation in Israel.

We appeal to you to become a member of this Association, the subscription being £2 0s. 0d. annually. Members of the Association will be entitled to receive publications of Civil Aviation in Israel. They will be invited to monthly functions in the country where the messages of Israel aviation in particular and general aviation will be brought to them. Members will be further eligible to participate in the annual prize of a free return ticket to Israel which will be drawn once a year at a big public function in Johannesburg. The Committee which has been established to run the affairs of this Association on behalf of Israel, consists of very prominent and well-known personalities throughout Africa and Israel. Among the Committee are such aviation personalities as Lt.-Col. C. S. Margo, D.S.O., D.F.C., a man who distinguished himself in the South African Air Force, Mr. T. Susman, D.F.C., of the South African Air Force, and Mr. Judah, who was the Chief of Operations of the Israel Air Force.

The Association can fulfil its urgent duty, however, only if it is broad-based upon the support of the Jewish community of Southern Africa, and we confidently appeal to you to enrol as a member of this important new activity to ensure Israel's future.

Chief Rabbi Prof. L. I. Rabinowitz,
President.
William Aronsohn,
Chairman.
Yair Marshak,
Hon. Secretary.

[9] Fritz Flesch Documentation

As the official Jewish community leadership and South Africa's rabbis ceased to denounce the Government's apartheid policy after 1947, voices were raised pointing out the moral contradictions. One of the more persistent critics was Mr. Fritz Flesch, a Jewish American and former prisoner in Dachau, who has continued to accuse the South African Jewish community of acquiescence in apartheid.

a. Javits to Flesch, February 4, 1958

United States Senate

COOMMITTEE ON
RULES AND ADMINISTRATION

February 4, 1958

Mr. Fritz Flesch
8094 Whitcomb
Detroit 28, Michigan

Dear Mr. Flesch:

Thank you for your recent inquiry. I have had an opportunity to look into the matter about which you inquire and find that due to the fact that the Jewish Committee within the Union of South Africa itself is actively opposed to apartheid that it was not considered conducive to a favorable settlement if Jewish organizations outside of South Africa participated in the United Nations deliberations to which you refer.

It is indeed kind of you to have offered to send me this material, and I am sure that it will prove most helpful to me in my work here.

Sincerely,

Jacob K. Javits, U.S.S.

b. Alleged Ignorance on South Africa*

Sir. — As a visitor to this country I am surprised at the ignorance of the people I came across. I have been a citizen of South Africa for over fifty years and take a keen interest in the communal life of my country, and especially in Jewish affairs.

I have been a Deputy of the South African Jewish Board of Deputies for over thirty years and a member of committees in Johannesburg and various Jewish institutions, and have been active in connection with Zionist fund raising. We have a Government which is very friendly towards our coreligionists. The late Dr. Malan, who was Prime Minister of the Union, paid a visit to Israel, and many ministers of the church and other prominent people visited Israel and were astonished at the enormous achievement of the Jewish people during the past twelve years.

South African Jewry is well organised and the Board of Deputies, which is the sole mouthpiece of the Jews in the Union, is non-political.

A majority of us are supporting the Union Government's policy in connection with apartheid. We have nearly 13 million non-whites and only three million white people: of the non-whites about 70 per cent are illiterate and the Government is trying their utmost to compel them to send their children to school, which is free to them. In South Africa we have a Jewish population of about 120,000; we have several judges, magistrates, and many are in the Civil Service. Only recently the Union Government allowed entry into the Union of all white refugees from the Congo, among whom were about fifteen hundred Jews.

Ch. Hoppenstein.

*Jewish Chronicle, September 2, 1960

c. Fritz Flesch Rejoinders

These are not "marginal" Jews, but the TOP REPRESENTATIVES of JUDAISM in South Africa. They act like "gleichgeschaltete" "GERMAN Christians" under Hitler, but they did not get OPPOSITION in the JEWISH PRESS OF THE WORLD. They did get SUPPORT by the abstention of A L L JEWISH ORG AT UN. For this kind of Jews N.Y. Senator JAVITS, Detroit Jewish Community Council, Rabbis Dr. Eisendrath, Goldstein, Perlzweig, etc. cover-up.

(1963)

The truth is not in Senator Javits letter... but in Hoppenstein's letter.... No leader of South African Catholics, Methodists, Anglicans, etc., voiced views like the Jewish leader HOPPENSTEIN. HITLER's "GERMAN CHRISTIANS" voiced views like Hoppenstein. Inspite of the Hoppensteins, who dominate the South African Board of JEWISH Deputies, Senator Javits saw fit to send this "reply". CUI BONO?

When UN investigated the racial policies of the SA Government, ALL Jewish org. at UN (including the SA Jewish Board of Deputies) abstained from cooperation with the UN...CUI BONO? And the USA Jewish organizations don't tell why this abstention happened. CUI BONO

(1964)

d. Maurice L. Perlzweig to Mr. Fritz Flesch

WORLD JEWISH CONGRESS
Congres Juif Mondial—Congreso Judio Mundial
15 East 84th Street
New York 28, NY

April 5, 1963

Mr. Fritz Flesch
8094 Whitcomb off Tireman
Detroit 28

Dear Mr. Flesch:

The answer to the question on South Africa in your letter which I found on my recent return to New York is quite simple, and I should have thought obvious.

The Jewish non-governmental organizations have refrained from commenting on South African problems because they do not desire to worsen the already difficult situation in which the Jewish community finds itself. And they know that this restraint, whatever the arguments against it may be, is regarded as important by that community.

To put it in another way, we do not admire vicarious heroism.

The Jewish community in South Africa may be right or wrong in its attitude, but it is as entitled to formulate its attitude as you are to criticize it.

Moreover, the World Jewish Congress is precluded by its Constitution from undertaking any activity in relation to any country which has a Jewish community that can speak for itself, unless that community either requests or permits it. You may not find these considerations pleasing, but the democratic rights of Jewish communities are valid whether the results appeal to you and me or do not.

I am bound to say that I am saddened by the tone which marks much of what you have written. There is not the slightest hint of compassion for the Jews of South Africa in the position of agonizing difficulty in which they find themselves; nor do you seem to appreciate the fact that individual Jews, and rabbis, both Orthodox and Reform, have played a courageous part, out of all proportion to their numbers, in the fight against apartheid. ...

They have limited themselves to taking the community as such out of the conflict, and have done so on the ground that in South Africa this has become a matter of party political controversy. You have every right to think that this is wrong, if that is your view, but I can see no justification for the blanket condemnation of the whole community to which you have committed yourself, especially when it is conducted from the safe haven of Detroit.

Finally, I am by no means sure that these condemnations come with good grace from any country, including the United States, in which racialism, as daily incidents demonstrate, still exercises a powerful influence. The first and foremost duty of any citizen is to deal with the evil on his own doorstep before he sits in judgement on his neighbor.

Any member of the U.S. Delegation at the United Nations will tell you how heavy the burden is that he has to bear when he has to face the taunts of hostile countries, who need do no more than read stories from American newspapers and books. I take the liberty of suggesting that you might usefully turn your abundant energies to the problems of racialism at home in the knowledge that any improvement in this area will be an effective contribution to the fight elsewhere. And I conclude by reminding you of the counsel of Rabbi Hillel: "Judge not thine neighbor until thou standest in his place." Faithfully yours,

Maurice L. Perlzweig

[10] Zionism and The Union of South Africa: Fifty Years of Friendship and Understanding*

N. Kirschner

Until 1960, as N. Kirschner notes, Zionism had experienced fifty years of friendship and understanding [10]. This friendship was not affected by republic status [11] although Israel's UN vote in 1961 had some unpleasant fallout [12].

[Editor's note: "Jewish Affairs" invited Mr. N. Kirschner, veteran South African Zionist leader and former chairman of the S.A. Zionist Federation, to deal with the rise of Zionism in South Africa since Union. He has seized on a significant theme: the parallel between South Africa's development and the Jewish national renaissance.]

The story of the Zionist Movement in South Africa has, for the last fifty years, run parallel with the development of the Union of South Africa as a state, and its people as a nation. After the Anglo-Boer War, Britain sought by friendship to heal the wounds of war. So she began to take those steps which finally led to South Africa being given back to the peo-

*Jewish Affairs, May 1960, pp.42-46.

ple of the country, through the establishment of the Union in 1910. If as a result of the Anglo-Boer War, the Afrikaners lost their Republics, then, as a result of Union, both sections of the people of South Africa found the unity which binds them as a nation today.

It was because of this historic experience that South Africans have so well been able to appreciate the aims and objects of the Zionist Movement. From the beginning of Union, the leaders of the new South African nation showed a deep understanding of the great adventure of the Jewish people to build their own land. There was Botha, the first Prime Minister of the Union of South Africa: those of us who lived through the early years of Union will remember how, in a grave moment of the first World War, he expressed his support for the freedom of the Jewish people. There was Smuts, who played a part in securing the Balfour Declaration, and whose name is written imperishably into Zionist history because of all he did to help the Jewish people. There was Hertzog, that gentle soul, who gave his blessing to the Zionist Movement. There was his lieutenant, Tielman Roos, who was the chief architect of the Pro-Zionist Declaration which the Government of General Hertzog issued in 1926. There was Malan, the first Prime Minister in the Commonwealth to visit the newly established State of Israel, who came back with a message that Israel could offer inspiration to South Africa.

These men laid the tradition that there exists a bond between Jewish aspirations and the aspirations of the people of South Africa. The force of history in South Africa gave them a fellow feeling for the struggle of another people towards nationhood. Because of that tradition, all the governments of the Union of South Africa have been implicated in what Zionism has achieved—in the early years of struggle and in the results of today, when Israel stands securely as a state among the nations.

This should not be taken to mean that from its beginnings, Zionism in South Africa was a flower that was unitedly nurtured by the whole Jewish community of the Union. Far from it: it was an uphill struggle to bring the Jewish community of South Africa to a full appreciation of the vital importance of the Zionist Movement. They had grown up in comfort, and they had to be taught that there were those, outside of their comfort and ease, who had a claim to their help and support, in the struggle to rebuild the Jewish land. Those who did not wish to be disturbed in their daily lives—in their chances for advancement and wealth and ease—had to be taught the fundamental lesson that the Jewish people was entitled to a land of its own. But in this respect the Jews of South Africa were not peculiar—in every country the same fight went on in the Jewish community.

The numbers who believed were at first few. Those who could not forget Jerusalem were dotted about in the land—small groups whose hearts never ceased longing for Zion, whose minds were always occupied with thinking of the Jewish people. There were those who said *Ani*

Maamin: they believed that Jewish survival through 2,000 years gave them the right and the duty to work for the Land of Israel to be returned to the People of Israel; and that no other people could draw from the hard earth of Israel what was told in the Bible of the beauty, the glory and the richness of that land.

One strong sector was in Cape Town. There was Jacob Gitlin—foursquare he stood against all the winds that blew. He especially stands out in South African Zionism. *Lo Yonun v'Lo Yishon:* by day and by night he dreamed a dream. There wasn't a thing he was not prepared to set his hand to, in order to bring home to the Jews of South Africa the message of Zionism.

There was Lennox Loewe in Johannesburg, there was Hyman Morris, there was Samuel Goldreich. There was Leopold Kessler who afterwards settled in London and became the friend of Herzl: he led the expedition which the World Zionist Organisation sent to examine the possibilities of Jewish settlements in El Arish. They and others were active in the years before I came to South Africa, and they laid the foundations of Zionism on the Rand. There was Rev. M. I. Cohen of Bulawayo, who planted the flag of Zion firmly in Rhodesian Jewry. There were the men with whom I myself was privileged to work in the Movement. Braudo and Janower stand out immediately—but I must not add a list of names: inevitably some would be omitted who are no less worthy of inclusion than those whom memory would recall. We worked to break down indifference in the Jewish community, and to spread understanding of the problem of the Jewish people and their need for their own land. We worked against difficulties, fighting for whatever progress we made.

That was how things stood at the time of the first World War. In 1917 General Smuts left for England, to join the Imperial War Cabinet. There was a gathering of Jews in Johannesburg at which resolutions were passed asking General Smuts for his help in the cause of Zion. The climate was ripe and whether we recognised it or not, we timed our request correctly. Then came the great day when Weizmann's war work for the Allies was recognised, and the Balfour Declaration was issued. In the city on the banks of the Thames, history's answer was given to the songs Jews sang *Al Naharot Bavel*—by the rivers of Babylon.

It is not my task, nor have I the ability, to write a history. Let me say only that the Balfour Declaration revived a hope in the heart of the Jewish people which since Cyrus had not dared to rise to its full height. The Jews of the world had to face the challenge—and South African Jewry with the rest. It was a turning point for the Zionist Movement. Here in South Africa we could not but be grateful for the part played by General Smuts. By his deeds, he had written himself into the history of the smallest people, and into the hearts of all subsequent generations of Jews. And he carried his own people with him in what he did for the Jewish people. No matter what winds of change blew over this land—and there were winds that coloured some shirts grey and some shirts black—the people of South Africa remained firm friends and true.

Early in the first World War, a Jewish War Victims' Relief Fund was started in South Africa. Bernard Alexander was its president. It was the first major step of responsibility that South African Jewry assumed towards our brethren in countries where they had lost everything in the war, and where they were not wanted any more. South African Jewry undertook to care for some of the orphans from the destroyed countries, who were brought to Palestine (as it was at that time). Isaac Ochberg of Cape Town, with his warm humanitarianism, brought some of the orphans to South Africa. Some were housed in the Jewish Orphanage in Cape Town, while others were brought to Johannesburg, where the Relief Fund helped to buy Sir Lionel Philips'house, "Arcadia," and there we made a home for those children who had lost their all. And General Smuts opened that home, and the words he uttered in doing so were: "It is right that where the mighty have lived, the children shall enter."

South African Jewry became more active in the Zionist Movement: for its small numbers, it took on responsibilities which were not only of consequence to the Movement here, but became of consequence to the whole of the Jewish people, no matter where they lived. By this time the Zionist Federation had been formed, and had begun canalising South African Jewry support on a country-wide scale.

Not all was easy for those who had to shoulder the work, irrespective of what the difficulties were. Those at the head of the Zionist Movement refused to let difficulties obscure their objective. Difficulties were there to be overcome. We stumbled, we hurt our toes on the stones in the path, but we were never humbled. We carried with pride the rag that was made into a flag, because in our hearts we cherished the knowledge that the Jewish people could not be denied their historic right.

Many ardent spirits gave their help. That great and learned Jew, Dr. Landau, who in his later years became a saintly leader of South African Jewry, played an important part. Morris Alexander and subsequently Morris Kentridge, whose names are written high among South Africa's parliamentarians, lent their prestige to help the Zionist cause. Judge Greenberg stood firmly with us: from the day he said "this cause is also my concern," he was always in the centre of the Movement, advising, guiding and gladly accepting that burden which it was consonant with his eminent status for him to carry.

The years ran by, until at last we appeared before the United Nations. Whom did our leaders represent when they came before that forum? — a people broken, ground into the dust, with millions destroyed; a weather-worn remnant. But our leaders made demands for that remnant. And they awakened the conscience of those who sat round the table of the United Nations. They stirred the conscience of the nations, and there came a "Sabbath Moment"; the Jews are the people of the Sabbath to the nations of the world. And when they, the nations, stood with their souls bared before each other, they granted our request: they recognised the right of our wellnigh destroyed people to build Israel again.

The State of Israel was proclaimed on May 14th, 1948. America was first in its recognition. I understand that President Truman got up in the middle of the night to broadcast the U.S. recognition of Israel. Russia followed hot-foot... There was another recognition which followed immediately, and that was Egypt sending a plane to bomb Tel Aviv. Then, while the Arab armies descended on Israel, other nations, and South Africa among them, announced their recognition of the Jewish State.

When the War of Liberation was fought in Israel, Jewish youth in South Africa did not lack the understanding or the willingness to serve. They went gladly to fight in and for Israel. Here, again, the atmosphere in which they were reared in South Africa conduced to their understanding of the need. South Africa stands high in the history of Zionism, not only because of what Jews did, but also because those who headed the Government of South Africa gave full opportunity to the Jews to give all they could in the hard fight for freedom in Israel.

We derived rich sustenance from the leaders of Zionism who visited us from abroad. They were warmly welcomed by South Africans, as well as by the Jewish community. There came the great philosopher of Jewish life, Nahum Sokolow. There came Chaim Weizmann. Smuts used to talk of "Weizmann and Moses"—and he put Weizmann first...When Weizmann received an honorary degree from the Witwatersrand University, the Hebrew University in Jerusalem had advanced only a little way from the day when he and Lord Balfour had laid its cornerstone. He had with him, on his visit to South Africa, no more than the plans of the buildings that were to rise in Jerusalem—yet he issued an invitation to the University of the Witwatersrand to be guests in the house of learning that had not yet been built in Israel ... Since that unforgettable day, many a learned man from South Africa has indeed been the guest of the Hebrew University of Jerusalem, and has seen with his own eyes another dream of the Jewish people come true....

Before Sokolow and Weizmann, there came Shmarya Levin, that man saturated with Jewish life and lore. There isn't a village in South Africa where he is not remembered—Shmarya Levin with his stories of Jewish life, left in every Jewish home memories that never fade.

Help came to us from many quarters. There were outstanding Christian supporters of Zionism, in addition to those I have mentioned—men like Edgar Brookes, Professor Dingemans, Colin Steyn. I remember vividly a service Colin rendered. It was during the second World War. There came to us a cable from Kobe, in Japan, saying that there were some 80 refugees from Europe who had visas to go to Palestine, but they had to travel via South Africa, and they did not have transit visas for the Union. There was great difficulty, in those dangerous days, in getting transit visas. We went to Colin Steyn, and he got us the transit visas for those 80 people to reach Palestine during the war ... Such was Colin Steyn, blessed be his memory ...

There was Jan Hofmeyr. There wasn't a time throughout his public life when Hofmeyr didn't give us help, encouragement and understanding. He spoke out for the Jews, using the simile of the bush that burned but was not consumed: he said that sacred fire was the spirit which had carried the Jews through the ages; and so uplifted the hearts of the Jewish community in South Africa when things seemed dark indeed.

A bright page in South African history will always be the record that those who served South Africa best had in their hearts sympathy and understanding for another small people in their hour of need.

Now, 1960 is with us; half a century of Union in South Africa; 12 years of life for the State of Israel.

Both anniversaries take place in the same month, coinciding also with 50 years of South African Jewish effort for the Zionist cause. Today "die pad van Suid Afrika" and the road that Israel has to take are alike beset with great problems. But there is one guiding star that both peoples and both countries can follow. It shines bright and clear through the Prophet's words: "Do justly, love mercy and walk humbly with thy God." May that injunction light up our road for the generations to come.

[11] The Republic of South Africa*

A historic change will take place in the nature of the South African state on May 31st. The country which, for the past fifty-one years, has existed as the Union of South Africa will become the Republic of South Africa, and on the day it becomes a republic will cease to be a member of the Commonwealth of Nations.

It was not South Africa's wish that the Republic should fall outside the Commonwealth. When the Prime Minister went to the Commonwealth Conference in March, he went with a mandate to secure the approval of other member-states to South Africa becoming a republic within the Commonwealth. There was no objection to South Africa's converting to a republican form of government: India, Ghana and Malaya had done so before the Union decided on a similar change. Exception was taken, however, to the Republic of South Africa's continuing to follow the policy of racial separation which had hitherto been basic to the structure of the South African state. When it became clear that the application would not be approved without a vote, and that, if it came to a vote, there would be sharp division, Dr. Verwoerd withdrew the South African application. The ties of friendship between South Africa and Britain and the older Com-

*Jewish Affairs, May 1961, pp. 2-3.

monwealth members remain; but they will now have to be continued through bilateral agreements, most of which still have to be worked out; Britain has adopted a "standstill" Bill, freezing existing relations between herself and South Africa, to allow a year's period for such agreements to be formulated.

South Africa will become a republic at a time when there are wide differences among its electorate on national policies, and these differences find a reflection within, no less than between, the various political parties. There are individuals who feel that the time has arrived when South Africa can no longer resist the challenge to apply the privileges of democracy to all its races; others who feel that the position of the European must basically be protected while, at the same time, the rights of non-Europeans are progressively extended in a common society; others who feel that the solution is not a common society, but the provision of separate regions in which non-Europeans may advance to full enfranchisement and self-administration, on a basis that will conduce to a federation of European and non-European territories, each autonomous except for those respects in which the common welfare requires the umbrella of central government.

These are policies on which parties and individuals will have the same right to differ in the Republic as they have enjoyed in the Union; subject to the overriding consideration that the forms of action in which their differences are expressed shall not endanger the safety of the state. That the question of what may or may not endanger the safety of the state will itself form part of the political debate, is inevitable in South Africa's circumstances. In the governing party no less than among the opposition, it will be the duty of statesmanship to ensure that differences are expounded with as much sobriety and as little emotionalism as the difficult position of South Africa demands.

What applies to citizens in general applies in the same way to the Jewish community. South Africa's 100,000 Jews are a settled and permanent part of the European population, enjoying the same rights and subject to the same duties as other citizens, and they will accord the Republic the same loyalty as they have always accorded the Union. History offers instances aplenty of how this loyalty has been expressed in every field of South African life: we traced salient aspects of the record in these pages a year ago, when we celebrated the Union's golden jubilee. In the professions and the arts, in commerce and industry, in education, science and the social services, Jews have made a truly formidable contribution to the welfare and progress of South Africa. Exercising their right as citizens to follow their personal political convictions, without direction or interference from Jewish communal organisations (which take no part in political debate, save in such matters as directly concern the Jewish community), Jews are to be found among the members and supporters of all the country's political parties, and in some instances even in their governing councils.

That position will continue in the Republic, towards the progress of which, we are fully confident, Jews will make no less a contribution than they have made to the Union. To the Jew, loyalty to the state is a precept enjoined upon him by his Judaism. "The law of the land is the law," it is stated in the Talmud; and every Jew is directed to pray for the welfare of the state, in pursuance of that affirmation. Each Sabbath, in every synagogue, prayers are offered for divine protection and guidance to be vouchsafed to the Union and its rulers; our rabbis have made the necessary amendments to apply these prayers to the Republic. Special services will also be held in synagogues, to usher in the Republic with the heartfelt hope that God will bring South Africa safely through whatever storms may threaten, and whatever difficulties may lie ahead.

May God exalt the Republic of South Africa and lead it to new levels of national achievement, opening avenues to co-operation which will enable all races, colours and creeds to live side by side in mutual respect and trust, each helping the other to reciprocal advancement in the country which is the common fatherland of us all.

[12] Israel's Vote at UN— The Repercussions in South Africa*

Edgar Bernstein

The debate on South Africa at the United Nations this year has come as a shock to the citizens of the Republic. It has come as a shock not only for what has been said by South Africa's critics, but also for the states which have joined in voicing criticism. These have included countries which have either abstained from criticism in the past, or have been mild or reserved in their statements on our policies. Among them have been such long-standing friends of South Africa as Britain, U.S.A., Holland, Belgium and Israel.

Perhaps the most disconcerting experience for South Africa was the motion of censure moved by the Afro-Asian States against South Africa's Foreign Minister, Mr. Eric Louw, for his speech to the General Assembly defending South Africa's policy of Separate Development. The motion was carried by 67 votes against South Africa's sole opposing vote. Britain, U.S.A., the Dominions and the Western European states (with the exception of the Netherlands) abstained. Supporting the resolution were the Afro-Asian states, the Soviet bloc and Argentine, Bolivia, Brazil, Chile, Ecuador, Haiti, Honduras, Israel, Mexico, Netherlands, Panama, Peru, Uruguay and Venezuela.

*Jewish Affairs, November 1961, pp. 15-18.

Netherlands' support of the censure motion aroused strong feeling in South Africa, where the historical and cultural ties with the people and language of Holland are so extensive and profound. Bitter comments on the Netherlands attitude were made by the Prime Minister, Dr. Verwoerd, the Foreign Minister, Mr. Louw, and the Afrikaans press.

Israel's support of the motion of censure also evoked criticism. The Prime Minister, in the same speech in which he deplored the attitude of the Netherlands, made a brief but pregnant reference to it, saying: "Other nations of Europe abstained from voting, but the representation of the Netherlands Government preferred to vote. The only ally in this attitude the Netherlands Government had was the Government of Israel."

The Foreign Minister, broadcasting to South Africa from New York where he was leading the South African Delegation at the U.N. session, made more extensive reference to Israel's attitude, after sharply criticising the policy pursued by the Netherlands. He said he had not expected Israel to support South Africa, but had expected it to record an abstention, in view of the friendship and assistance which the South African Government and individual members of the Cabinet had given Israel, including special facilities for the transfer of large sums of money to Israel by South African Jews. He expressed the conviction that, "as in the case of people from the Netherlands who have made South Africa their home, so also South Africans who have racial and religious ties with Israel will disapprove of the hostile and ungrateful action of the Israeli delegation to the United Nations."

The reaction of Netherlands immigrants in South Africa to the vote of their former homeland was one of vehement criticism and protest, and the idea of sending a petition to the Netherlands Government was mooted.

Israel's support of the censure motion met with various reactions in the Jewish community. Most Jews were unhappy at finding Israel among the states which voted against South Africa. Some sought to explain or justify Israel's attitude; others were openly critical of her vote.

The *Zionist Record,* organ of the South African Zionist Federation, criticised Israel's attitude, saying it was regrettable to find Israel voting with the states supporting the censure motion, rather than abstaining with the Western group "in an instance where the right of South Africa to put its case before the United Nations Assembly was being denied." The journal added that whether or not delegates liked Mr. Louw's comments, "it is a complete betrayal of all the ideals that can bring success to the aims of the United Nations to attempt to inhibit his freedom of speech by the use of the vote as a weapon of naked force."

The *Jewish Herald,* organ of the Zionist Revisionists, was even more outspoken, critising Israel's attitude in voting against "one of Israel's first and staunchest friends" as "unwarranted, unjustified and politically unrealistic." The journal felt that too much stress was being laid on the friendship which certain Afro-Asian countries were said to be showing Israel, and in return for which, Israel was being pressed to vote with them. It acknowledged that in such a delicate situation, Israel had her own difficulties, but opined that, without minimising these difficulties, there was no valid reason why she could not have abstained from the vote. "It is precisely for such difficult situations that the right of abstention was provided."

The *S.A. Jewish Times* took a different line, arguing that Israel was struggling to detach the new African States from Nasser's sphere of influence, and that it was in the light of this struggle that Israel had reluctantly voted against South Africa. Much as this might go against the grain in South Africa, the journal felt that it would ultimately benefit South Africa as well as Israel, if the attempt to break Nasser's policy of penetration succeeded.

The *Afrikaner Yiddishe Zeitung* felt that the vote represented a clash of two rights, as between South Africa's policies and Israel's principles, and that in such a situation, Israel could not help taking the course she had followed.

The general press showed commendable restraint on this thorny issue, and refrained from any hasty expression of editorial opinion either attacking or excusing Israel. Papers did, however, give full publicity to the issue in their news columns, and approached the Board of Deputies, as the representative organisation of South African Jewry, for comment. In reply to these requests, a spokesman of the Board told the press that many South African Jews strongly criticised Israel's vote in favour of the motion of censure.

"It is recognised," said the Board's spokesman, "that Israel, in determining her international policies must take into account delicate and complex factors upon which she alone is competent to judge. Nevertheless, it is felt that this was a case in which the issue was a simple one: the question of freedom of speech in the international forum. In these circumstances, Israel should have joined other Western nations in abstaining from voting on the Afro-Asian motion of censure."

The statement went on to say that "Jewish citizens of South Africa deeply appreciate the many manifestations of goodwill shown by South Africa towards Israel, and sincerely hope that future relations between the two countries will continue on the same friendly basis."

The *Zionist Record* comment and the Board of Deputies statement, while being welcomed in South Africa, were both sharply criticised in Israel, where leading journals took up the attitude that it was improper for South African Jewry, or any other Jewish community outside Israel, to try to influence Israel Government policy: that policy, they said, had to be based on the principle of non-discrimination, even if it might not be palatable to a Jewish community like that of South Africa. Some Israeli papers, however, felt that Israel should have been more considerate of the position of South Africa and its Jewish community, after the long record of friendship between the two countries; this view was most forcefully expressed in the chief Opposition paper, *Herut*. Answering it, pro-Government papers said that Israel's vote against racial discrimination in South Africa was not a vote against South Africa as such, whose friendship was still held in high regard: Israel sought friendship with all countries, but could not sacrifice basic principles in the quest.

There next began, in the South African Jewish community, a debate on the broad issue, not merely of the vote of censure, but of Israel's general attitude to South Africa at UNO, and of the question whether South African Jews have any *locus standi* to express views on Israel's stand. This debate is still continuing, and exhibits various differences of opinion. Some Jews condemn Israel outright for her attitude, and have sent messages to Mr. Louw supporting his stand. Others, while regretting that Israel should have supported the vote against South Africa, feel that she was forced into this position by her own life-and-death struggle in the Middle East, and her imperative need to make friends among the African States and wean them away from Nasser. Yet others take the view that Israel must act on principle, even though this may discomfort South African Jewry. All these views have been expressed in letters to the press, as well as in discussion at meetings. A few Jews have threatened to stop their financial support of Zionist funds, if Israel continues to vote against South Africa; others have urged that the question of Zionist funds should not be drawn into the argument.

The motivations of those who are critical of Israel's action in voting against South Africa, whatever reservations she may have on South African policies, are readily understandable. For all their Zionist feelings, they were expressing their hurt as South Africans that Israel, after such close friendship with this country, should join the vote against it. I regard this as the natural and proper reaction of South African citizens to a situation of this kind. *Die Burger* expresses appreciation of it, in an editorial welcoming it together with the reaction of Netherlands immigrants, pertinently adding: "Do not think that this is an easy thing for the people concerned. The love for one's fatherland is born with every person. And the same Hollanders and Jews, who have just protested against the attitude of the Netherlands and Israel, out of love for their new fatherland, will stand up tomorrow and protest against no matter what world power, should the Netherlands or Israel be besmirched in the same underhand and unworthy way. And nobody would hold it against them."

At the same time, much confusion needs to be removed. The position of South African Jews is not the same as that of Netherlands immigrants who, as either citizens or former citizens of their country of origin, can claim a direct or indirect right to lodge protest with the Netherlands Government. South African Jews are neither citizens nor former citizens of Israel, and having no similar relationship with Israel to the relationship of Netherlands immigrants with the Netherlands, have no *locus standi* to take similar action. They have the same right as any other South African citizens to criticise Israel or any other country: that and no more.

Some non-Jewish friends have asked me: "Why have the Jews voted against us at UNO?" I have carefully pointed out that it was not "the Jews" who voted on the issue: it was the Government of Israel, a sovereign state which is answerable to its citizens, and to its citizens alone.

South African Jews are not citizens of Israel, and have no part in the formulation of its policies. South African Jews are citizens of South Africa, and owe their allegiance to South Africa alone. Their ties with Israel are religious and cultural; they give financial support to help the Jewish Agency settle Jews in Israel; they support religious, cultural and humanitarian institutions in Israel; but they make no financial contribution to the Government of Israel, nor are they involved in anything the Israeli Government does. This applies equally to Jews all over the world. Israel's Prime Minister, Mr. Ben Gurion, defined the position clearly when, several years ago, in reply to questions about the position of American Jewry in relation to Israel, he said that American Jews were citizens of the United States and not of Israel; they owed their allegiance as citizens entirely to the United States, and owed no allegiance to Israel.

These considerations apply no less to the question of Israel's support of the motion of sanctions against South Africa in the U.N. Special Political Committee (which is awaiting consideration by the General Assembly as I write). However much South Africans may feel hurt (and in my opinion justifiably so) that Israel should have supported the sanctions resolution (albeit with reservations: she opposed the expulsion clause and abstained on the petrol and arms clauses), it must be clearly understood that Israel's attitude at the United Nations is decided by the Israeli Government, which neither asks nor would entertain guidance from South African Jewry. Conversely, South African Jewry frames its attitudes and policies without dictation from Israel, which scrupulously respects the community's position as a separate entity, owing its citizenship loyalty unequivocally to South Africa, whatever the intercommunication of ideas, religion and culture between South African Jewry and Israel may be.

[13] Hendrik Frensch Verwoerd*

The assassination of Dr. Verwoerd in 1966 gave the Jewish Board of Deputies opportunity to proclaim appreciation of his positive approach to apartheid [13]. The following year, despite the persistence of some official discord, South Africa showed its sympathy for Israel in the June 1967 war [14, 15, 16].

That the Republic of South Africa passed through the experiences in

*Jewish Affairs, September 1966, pp. 4-5.

the last few weeks with so much outward calm is a tribute to its basic stability and to the good sense and goodwill of all sections of its population. The tragedy which befell the country in the brutal murder of the Prime Minister, Dr. Verwoerd, in the very heart of the precincts of Parliament, plunged the whole population, without regard to political division or race, into mourning, and revealed an impressive unity of spirit. The new Prime Minister, Mr. B. J. Vorster, taking office in these unforeseen circumstances has been greeted with widespread expressions of goodwill which augur well for the future.

The outpouring of grief over Dr. Verwoerd's tragic death and the warmth of the tributes paid to him, revealed to what extent his image had changed from that of party politician to national leader and statesman. His removal from the helm was indeed a major national tragedy. He had steered the ship of state through critical years with a firm hand and a clear vision and had inspired confidence through his integrity, sincerity and complete dedication to his high office. Many people felt that he was about to open a new chapter in South Africa's development, holding out the promise of better relations with neighbouring African states and widening freedoms for the Republic's non-white peoples.

A Controversial Period

It was a measure of the enhanced status which Dr. Verwoerd had achieved also within the Jewish community that, when paying tribute to him, speakers and the press did not gloss over the fact that, at an earlier period in his career, he had been a controversial figure in Jewish eyes. Retrospectively, we can see that he reflected in that period the prevailing attitudes of his Party, which was passing through a major ideological crisis. When the Party eventually purged itself of foreign influences and returned to the traditional South African path of religious tolerance, Dr. Verwoerd fully honoured the Party's pledge to keep public life free of anti-Jewish policies.

It is true that a few years ago, when Israel sided with the Afro-Asian nations in denouncing South Africa's racial policies and advocated sanctions of various sorts, Dr. Verwoerd did not conceal his sense of disappointment and resentment. However, in due course, he gave the country a clear lead by insisting that Israel's policies should not be permitted to arouse hostile feelings against the Jewish community in this country. "The Jews," he said, "were citizens of South Africa and in numerous ways had shown their patriotism to South Africa. No anti-Jewish feeling should be permitted to arise in South Africa ... The Government certainly would never adopt any such attitude against the South African Jewish population."

A Challenging Vision

Dr. Verwoerd played a major part in giving to the concept of *apartheid* (which rightly or wrongly had acquired overtones of unjust discrimination), a new, challenging and positive interpretation. He proclaimed his vision in ringing tones in his last major address at the celebration of the 5th anniversary of the Republic earlier this year, in these words: —

> "We are not insensitive to the ambitions of others. On the contrary, we who as a nation had to fight for what we have and who have achieved this freedom, cannot but understand similar ambitions in the breasts of others. Those who believe in their own nation and its separate existence are best capable of understanding the desires of others to achieve the same.
>
> "We understand the nationalism of each of the separate states of Africa. We understand the similar ambitions of various nations and national groups at present within our own boundaries. And because of our own experience, we not only understand their aspirations, but also wish to help lead them to fulfilment in the right way. Freedom must be an achievement not only for a selected few, a dictator or two, but for the masses, for their progress and their happiness."

This was Dr. Verwoerd's vision. He was prevented by the hand of an assassin from demonstrating whether he could bring it to reality.

Mr. Vorster's Opportunity

Mr. Vorster, who has succeeded to the Premiership by the unanimous vote of his Party caucus accompanied also by the good wishes of the Republic as a whole, has declared his intention of strictly adhering to his predecessor's policies. His task is a formidable one at a time when the Republic is under attack from so many quarters. His new role demands more than strict adherence to the declared principles of the National Party. He is called upon not only to safeguard the security and internal stability of the Republic, but also to prove to the world that its attacks upon the Republic's racial policies are without justification.

The challenge which faces this country is to convince the world that separate development is indeed an equitable and just policy holding out prospect for greater opportunities and wider freedoms for all who inhabit this land. May it be Mr. Vorster's privilege and good fortune to help bring that about.

[14] An Inspiration To Men Everywhere: How the South African Press Reacted*

"Observer"

The striking feature of the manner in which the South African press

---

*Jewish Affairs, June 1967, pp. 12-17.

handled the Middle East crisis was the strong sense of involvement displayed both by the English and (perhaps more emotionally) by the Afrikaans papers.

The events unfolded in the headlines as inevitably as tragedy or as rapidly as nightmare. Day by day, tension visibly increased, hope waxed and waned across the front pages, as the point next to catastrophe was reached with the withdrawal of the UN forces, the closing of the Gulf of Aqaba and Nasser's challenge to Israel's very existence.

A major concern of the South African press naturally was that escalation might tumble the entire world into war. It found vent not only in direct expression of this worry but also in estimates of relative strengths, the willingness of, and degree to which, America and Russia could contain the conflict, the extent to which Nasser was prepared to go, the extent to which Israel could let him go.

The United Nations became a target for many papers. They contrasted its retreat in the face of Middle East belligerence with readiness to intervene in a peaceful South West Africa. Thus, bitingly observed *The Volksblad,* U Thant had acceded to Nasser's request, "no doubt to be rid of the burden of keeping the peace in the Near East while the General Assembly deliberates on how to disturb the peace in South West Africa." Not that the UN was without its defenders. *The Star* pointed out that the Secretary-General had had to accede or break the Charter. *Die Burger* noted that the organization could still serve as an instrument to save the prestige of the disputants. Nevertheless, as the crisis developed to its culmination, there was constant criticism particularly in the Government-supporting press, of the role of the world organisation.

Sympathy For Israel

A feature of the course of development was the powerful current of sympathy for Israel which displayed itself only the more strongly as the crisis moved into war, although there was always the fear of the hostilities spreading. On the brink of war, not all newspapers were confident of Israel's chances, and most apparently believed she would have a hard row to hoe. A typical item was the London report which was featured in most papers. It appeared in *Pretoria News* under these telling headlines: "Many Changes Since 1956—No Walk-over Victory For Israel This Time." The *Rand Daily Mail* was gloomier than this: "If Israel took the initiative and launched an offensive, these divisons (among the Arab states) would temporarily heal and Israel would find herself fighting on all fronts against far more numerous, though less militarily adept, enemies. It would be a war Israel could scarcely hope to win." Even more pessimistic was *Die Oosterlig* which was fervently pro-Israel from beginning to end: "No matter how prepared and courageous, it can scarcely be expected of small Israel to hold her own against such a massive, fanatically religious attack."

With the outbreak of war, the front pages were all monopolised by reports of the fighting, and the papers burgeoned with photographs of battle scenes, feature articles on various aspects of the conflict and profiles of leaders. General Dayan was undoubtedly the main figure of interest and many articles of his career, as well as anedcotes, were published.

On the question of who was the aggressor, the South African press did not disguise where its sympathies lay. The tendency was to suggest that Israel was the technical aggressor but President Nasser with his provocative behaviour was the real aggressor. Quite clearly, it was felt that if Israel had launched the first attacks, she was justified. "Israel's need to act for its own salvation became real and urgent," declared the *Star*. By closing the Gulf of Aqaba and blockading Eilat, Nasser had committed "a blatant act of aggression which Israel found impossible to ignore." There was general agreement on the need to keep the conflict localised and for the big Powers to use their influence to ensure a speedy end to the fighting. "Nothing, nothing whatever, is more important than keeping the war a local one," emphasised the *Cape Argus*. The immediate task, said the *Natal Witness,* was to "drive sense into Egypt and Israel and bring about a cease-fire."

As it became apparent that Israel was on the road to a rapid victory, attention began to focus more on the aftermath. For the West, "a rapid Israeli triumph will come as a relief: their embarrassing posture of neutrality will seem to have been justified by events," said the *Rand Daily Mail*. The lessons of the crisis and of the war now began to be drawn — many points of identification between Israel's position and that of South Africa were found.

Republic's Identification with Israel

What gave the war particular interest to the South African press was not only the presence of an involved local Jewish community, but also the feeling that Israel was engaged in combat with countries which had been among the main attackers of the Republic. The reaction of the South African Jews provided an immediate point of contact, and it soon became clear that non-Jews were identifying themselves with this reaction as never before. "South Africa's Jews have particularly strong ties with Israel which they have supported generously with both money and men — and women — and if the situation does explode into war there will be many South African-born soldiers in action," observed the *Evening Post*. When the situation did explode into war, the paper referred to the response of local Jewry and added that "many non-Jews will wish to have an opportunity to make a contribution too."

The activities of Jews throughout the land in raising funds, donating blood, and sending volunteers to Israel was extensively publicised and lavishly illustrated by photographs. There were also reports of non-Jews who had spontaneously come to the fore and were offering aid in all forms for Israel. Particularly warm and friendly was the description given by Rykie van Reenen in her feature, "Op die Randakker," in the *Beeld*, of the manner in which Johannesburg Jewish women rallied to the aid of Israel. She wrote: "Leave the ants, King Solomon. Here, indeed, is the modern parable for unequalled industry. As an Afrikaner I watched with frank admiration. Oh, I said softly to myself, for a cause big and crystal-clear enough to swallow in one mighty gulp all the personal clashes, the private fueds, the ambitions, misunderstandings and differences of opinion! It's a dangerous business, I do know, always to look for parallels in history. But it's difficult not to see in the zeal and concern of South African Jewish women for Israel something similar to the activities of Afrikaans (and Pro-Boer English speaking) women in the Cape when the Boer War broke out in the Republic. The same, the same attachment to own flesh and blood fighting for the right of independent survival! And who, never let us forget, was a more ardent spokesman for that freedom than the Jewish woman Olive Schreiner?"

Financial Aid

However, there was a brief period in which the issue of aid for Israel gave cause for speculation. In general, it seemed to be taken for granted that this aid would be permitted, but in several papers, there were suggestions that there would be limits to the amount of financial aid which the Government would authorise. The *Daily News*, for instance, reported that millions of rand were accumulating throughout the country, but it was not clear whether the Government would allow this to be transferred to Israel.

The *Transvaler* suggested that extraordinarily large sums would not be allowed to leave the country. The paper recalled the preferential treatment accorded funds for Israel in the past and the withdrawal of this concession after Israel voted against the Republic at the United Nations.... The Republic had no interests in the region, it said, adding that both parties in the conflict had competed with each other in adopting an unfriendly attitude towards the Republic. South Africa expected all citizens to place her interests "first."

However, this was soon followed by the official announcement that the Government would allow transfer of funds for purely humanitarian purposes "within limits." The funds were to be "used by charitable non-government organisations in Israel solely for humanitarian purposes." The amounts authorised from time to time would be "determined in the light of South Africa's economic position and interests."

The *Transvaler* was virtually alone among Government-supporting papers in adopting this critical line (although its general reporting of the Middle East situation, was imbued with a more sympathetic tone). The *Vaderland* took the Government decision to be evidence of its irreproachable attitude. "On this principled basis we Afrikaans-speaking people were also allowed to demonstrate our sympathy for Rhodesia in her fight. We welcome the decision. Thus does a Nationalist Government, uniting principle and humanity, maintain the national balance in our own country and in its relations with the outside world."

Die Beeld wrote: "The reaction of the overwhelming sympathy with Israel, which was evident in South Africa during the past week, is good and right and human. But how much stronger would it have been had Israel not to a significant degree taken sides with the enemies of South Africa?"

Pro-Israel Sympathies

Die Vaderland, although neutralist, qualified this position by admission of its sympathy for Israel, "The fundamental principle of South African foreign policy is too well-known to justify any further repetition—respect for the inviolability of the integrity and sovereignty of free nations." The paper went on to express a reproach for Israel's recent attitude to the Republic—this too has been a consistent theme in Government-supporting papers, although not heavily stressed. "South Africa has for years consistently opposed the threat to Israel's territorial sovereignty, and we did not get back much from Israel in return. Nevertheless this does not in any way alter our attitude on principle. It is unnecessary to ask with whom our sympathies lie, but in our country we also have groups belonging to other nations, like the Moslems of the Cape, ..."

In contrast to the somewhat reserved attitude of these papers was the cordial and open sympathy evinced by the organs of the Nasionale Pers group. "The present-day White South African sees striking similarities between the history of his own country and that of the restored Jewish homeland," said the *Burger.* Even Israel's participation in anti-South African gestures at UN because of its interests in Black Africa was understood in South Africa and "does not detract from the anxiety with which the present crisis is being followed in our country. Israel, like South Africa, is a stronghold and point of support for the West, whether the West always likes it or not."

Israel's Vote at U.N.

The reservations in sympathy were evidently due not only to the official policy of neutrality but also in some measure to Israel's behavior in regard to South Africa at the U.N. In the view of Government-supporting papers the futility had been shown of courting the Afro-Asian nations—Israel, like the rest of the West, should have learnt a lesson now. "For years, Israel, although under exactly the same or an even greater external threat to its national sovereignty from hostile neighbour states as the Republic, estranged itself from South Africa by its eager, anxious wooing of the free African states as a support against Arab pressure," noted the *Vaderland.* Now, in the hour of crisis, the African members of the Security

Council had ranged themselves against the West. "We can justly ask Israel, if it manages to struggle out of the present trouble, whether it will revise its former attitude."

Israel's refusal to accept the U.N. as an intermediary and insistence on direct peace negotiations with the Arabs was commended by *Dagbreek* which said: "This is also our standpoint on South West Africa. We trust that henceforth the Israeli Government will have a more realistic outlook on world affairs. Hitherto it has even adopted a strong position against South Africa in the U.N. in order to appease Arab hostility. It is now the duty of the local Jewish leadership to remind the Eshkol Government of the former unfriendliness."

Benefits to the Republic

At the same time, there was general recognition that Israel's stand in the Middle East had brought the Republic many benefits. Most obviously of course, it had brought to the fore the importance of the Cape sea route. "The ill wind in the Middle East has blown South Africa some good, driving away the doctrinaire fog and showing South West Africa in all its insignificance *[sic]* and the importance of the sea route around the Cape of Good Hope," declared the *Cape Argus*. The point was driven home harder by papers like the *Transvaler*. "The Republic has an important task because the Suez Canal has lost its importance. It is important for the big Powers now to have a power at the southern point of Africa which makes its harbours available to their ships and, if the war should spread, will guard the security of the Cape sea route. It is ironical that some of the leading Powers for whom the Cape sea route is so important will not supply the Republic with weapons."

But there were other benefits. Even before the outbreak of hostilities, Dawie asked in his *Burgur* column: "How much does South Africa owe to the sharpness of the conflict between Jew and Arab since 1948? This is difficult to assess, but it is evident that Nasser's Israel problem had a braking effect on his drive towards mischief in the south. He was a ringleader in the movement against the white man in Africa but dangers nearer home prevented him from playing the role he undoubtedly desired. Next to South Africa and Algeria, Egypt is the most formidable military power in Africa. Israel has the means—propagandistic, economic and military—which help to pin down what otherwise would have been more available for the anti-South African campaign of the Pan-Africanists."

As victory drew nearer, the sense of identification grew more overt and there was a spirit of thanksgiving. "The solid Israeli victory can make international politics and relations much more bearable for South Africa in a number of respects," declared the *Volksblad*. "The invasion of South Africa would now have to be indefinitely postponed. "The strongest ally of the Blacks, Egypt, lies wounded." A subsequent editorial warned those who wanted to eliminate the Whites in Southern Africa to "think hard about what happened to the Arabs who wanted to devastate Israel ... we, like Israel, are prepared to defend our territory—and that includes South West Africa—with equal determination."

A more succinct—and more dramatic—expression of this sense of identification were the victory headlines in the *Natal Mercury*: "They're Licked."

Significant too was an article in the *Beeld* with the heading: "Jews taught us a lesson." This told how Nationalist M.P.'s were saying that "We Boers are now very much in the debt of the Jews and that Israel's lightning victory has given the Republic another five years to strengthen herself and to prove the good intentions of her policy."

Senior Government representatives showed an appreciation of a number of "fringe benefits" accruing to South Africa, according to an article in the *Star*. One was turning away the world spotlight from South West Africa, another was the demonstration of the value of the Cape route and also the ineffectuality of the United Nations as a peace-keeping instrument. In defence circles there was pleasure at the way Israel's French equipment stood up in the ground and air battles.

A political survey published in the *Cape Times* and other papers described how the Middle East crisis had absorbed the attention of M.P.'s and Senators whose sympathies lay "overwhelmingly with embattled Israel."

Admiration

The general reaction to Israel's successes was one of admiration and in many cases of amazed wonderment at the speed and completeness of the victories. The world was astounded at the blitzkrieg which had destroyed the myth of Arab power and Communist illusions within a few days, observed the *Vaderland*. For the *Volksblad,* it recalled the struggle of the Boers who gained "imperishable glory with their bravery, courage and persistence." The paper urged South Africa to become as prepared as "the Jews of Israel who gripped the imagination of the world with their success last week." The *Oosterlig* said Israel had dumbfounded the world with her achievements and highlighted this with the contrast: "And this while millions almost literally shut their eyes and ears to avoid watching the annihilation of the tiny country and the total extermination of the Jewish people."

The feature, Van Alle Kante, in the *Burger* was headlined "Martial Spirit of the Jews Amazed the World." People had not known the Jew like this, wrote the columnist. "In the days of the Bible he was the party who was often shoved around by others. With the coming of the state of Israel, his own, the modern Jew proceeded to active resistance to his attackers. For even before 1956, with the bloody clashes of 1947-48 which preceded the coming of the state, the Jews amazed the world; they were suddenly completely different from the anonymous, shuffling mass who subjected themselves strangely will-lessly and without much visible reaction to the slaughterers during the Second World War." On the latest performance, one could almost believe that this martial spirit had become a permanent national trait.

What was representative of much of the feeling was expressed by Laurence Gandar in the *Rand Daily Mail* when he suggested that it could be argued that "Israel, by her single-handed action, saved the West from a massive diplomatic defeat by Russia and her Arab proteges." He concluded: "Israel's unhesitating defence of her rights and the retribution she visited upon those who sought war with her have been an inspiration to men everywhere. She has made it feel good to be alive in such stirring times when right has triumphed so decisively over what looked very much like might."

[15] 25th National Congress, November 23-26, 1967
The Role of the Board Today*

Maurice Porter

Introduction

The title of this talk, "The Role of the Board Today," immediately brings to mind that the South African Jewish Board of Deputies has a long history—it was established in the Transvaal over 64 years ago and as a national body over 55 years ago. It also serves as a reminder that, while the functions and objects of the Board have remained basically the same during all these years, the specific problems with which it has been concerned have changed from time to time. ...

Israel-South Africa Relations

In quite another sphere, international forces have had a very direct, and a continuing, impact upon Jewish public relations in the Republic. I refer to the State of Israel—its very existence, its influence, its policies. Israel-South Africa relations are too vast a subject to be dealt with adequately in a few minutes, but a few points of importance should be stressed, even in summary form.

1. South Africa has a long and admirable record of sympathy and support for Jewish national aspirations in the Holy Land. This goodwill has similarly been displayed towards the State of Israel in many ways and is much appreciated.

2. The State of Israel has done much to raise the status of Jews the world over and to create a favourable image of the Jewish people.

3. The Jewish community in this country has appreciated and valued

*Jewish Affairs, November 1967, pp. 7-9.

South Africa's friendship towards Israel and is most anxious that it should continue.

4. The religious, historical and cultural bonds which bind us to Israel do not in any way impair or weaken our unqualified loyalty to the Republic of South Africa. I am indeed sorry to see that the bogey of "dual loyalties" has again been resuscitated by some people.

These bonds with Israel are independent of the policies of whatever particular group or party may be in power in Israel at a given time. In any event, the Government and people of Israel alone determine the policies of their Land, over which the Jews of the Diaspora cannot have any sway.

5. All of us—Jews and non-Jews alike—should endeavour not to exaggerate recent differences between Israel and South Africa, which arise from the different perspectives from which the two countries view their respective problems and situations. We should rather aim at reducing these differences, by keeping in mind the many points of common interest and mutual understanding which exist between the two countries.

Local Sympathy for Israel

If proof were required of how deep is the reservoir of goodwill in this country towards the national aspirations of the Jewish people, it was notably demonstrated in the days of May and June, when the very existence of the State of Israel was threatened. South African Jews were deeply moved by the numerous expressions of sympathy and support which came from all sections of the people, and most notably by the friendly gesture of the South African Government which, despite past differences and without attaching any strings, authorized the transmission of the substantial sums which had been contributed by the South African Jewish community (and also by many non-Jews).

I have no doubt that in Israel, too, this demonstration of goodwill and friendliness has been appreciated. However, it is only realistic to recognize that, in the complex world of today, Israel and South Africa have to pursue their own policies in the light of their own specific complex situations.

Inter-Group Relations

Jewish life continues a normal course in South Africa, the Jewish community is well integrated, and the Jewish citizen enjoys full opportunities in all spheres.

As an integral part of the population we face the same dilemmas and problems that confront all who live in this country. We participate in the political life of the Republic, not as a group, but as individuals, and it is as individuals that our role should be adjudged. I am glad that this is now more generally understood.

Jews and Race Policies

However, we do still find, periodically, that from some quarters the demand is made that the Jewish community, as a group, declare where it stands, particularly in regard to the race policies of the Republic. This demand reveals a basic misconception regarding the way Jews think and act politically. It reflects the traditional stereotype of the Jewish community as a closed, tight entity, a stereotype which dies very hard.

Anyone who knows the situation in South Africa—or for that matter in any other country—must be aware that there is no uniformity of political viewpoint among Jews, and that they include in their ranks supporters of all the political parties. In consequence there is not, and there cannot be, a uniform or collective Jewish attitude on such a major political issue as the principle of separate development, or its implementation in practice. I believe that there is as much diversity of opinion on these matters among the Jewish community as among the South African population as a whole.

[16] South Africa-Israel Relations*
Louis Hotz

Two South African Members of Parliament who recently visited Israel, both belonging to the National Party, have been describing their impressions in South African newspapers, and both have had much to say in praise of the country and the people, more particularly their spirit of dedication and their fantastic will to work and create. Not that the two observers were uncritical, but this only added to the value of what they found to admire.

On one point both men—Mr. M. J. van den Berg and Dr. Jack Loock—were emphatic. It is a point on which a good many South Africans will strongly agree with them. The M.P.'s deplored the fact that South Africa has no official representation at Government level in Israel. The result is, they pointed out, that there is no one there with authority to speak on behalf of South Africa or to keep responsible opinion in South Africa informed about the conditions and, even more important, about the psychological temper and climate in Israel.

There is no one to state the case for South Africa from the standpoint of the South African powers-that-be. Nor is there anyone to correct misapprehensions such as are inevitable, or almost so, with countries far apart and living under different conditions, but in many ways sharing common problems without the mass of the people on either side being aware of the fact.

Mr. van den Berg and Dr. Loock believe that some of the difficulties which have arisen between South Africa and Israel in recent years would

*Jewish Affairs, January 1968, pp. 6-7.

have been avoided with closer contacts and a recognised South African voice in Israel. It would have of course have been a two-way traffic, because an official observer in Israel, with continuous first-hand knowledge of what people were saying and thinking there, would also have been able to enlighten South Africa. This could probably have helped to clear up misconceptions which have soured relations between the two countries.

Mr. van den Berg in particular has stressed this view, though he may perhaps have gained a rather exaggerated idea of the extent of Israeli unawareness and misunderstanding of South Africa's serious human problems. After all, there are plenty of unofficial spokesmen of and "ambassadors" for South Africa in Israel. Most of them have a pretty good knowledge of the situation here and are able to impart it within the circles in which they move. Still, Mr. van den Berg was perfectly right in underlining the view that there was more need for South African diplomatic or consular representation in Israel than in many other countries, certainly in the Middle East.

The Need for Diplomatic Representation in Israel

South Africans of all shades of opinion have made no secret of the fact that they regard Israel as a vital element in the over-all requirements of South African international security. This was made abundantly clear in the general South African reactions to the recent Middle East conflict and its aftermath of continuous tensions. The point has been further emphasised by the changed strategic position likely to follow Britain's withdrawal East of Suez. This can only assist in reinforcing the importance of Israel for the whole of Africa and the countries abutting on the Indian Ocean.

In a spirited reply to anonymous criticisms of his belief in the necessity for an official South African "presence" in Israel, Mr. van den Berg remarked with regret that there had never been "the slightest form" of official South African representation in the Holy Land. For the record it may be recalled that in fact South Africa many years ago did have some sort of official representation in Israel (or Palestine, as it was then known). That was when Mr. M. Haskell was an honorary trade commissioner cum-consul for South Africa there. Undoubtedly this did help to some extent to encourage trade and other relations between the two countries. But other times, other manners...

Presumably there were reasons why, even in happier days, no regular diplomatic relations were established by South Africa with the new State of Israel on the customary reciprocal basis and that representation remained a unilateral affair. At one stage a former South African Foreign Minister, when questioned on the subject in Parliament, expressed the view that the circumstances—the volume of trade and so on—did not justify the stationing of a South African representative in Israel, though at that time such representation actually existed in Cairo. But whatever the position may have been then, as it appeared in Pretoria, conditions have changed materially as the years have passed. More and more South Africans, not only from the Jewish community, visit Israel and the volume of trade and financial relations has increased considerably.

In short, despite latter-day developments—and possibly because of them—there seems to be a decided case for a South African official presence in Israel, even if it is only at consular level, as Mr. van den Berg and Dr. Loock have urged. Bearing in mind a recent South African consular appointment in the Middle East, we might fairly ask why Beirut and not Jerusalem? ...

[17] South Africa and Israel Meet in Africa*
Louis Hotz

By the late 1960's it was noted that Dr. Vorster's "outward" African policy coincided with Israeli interest in the continent [17]. This convergence was also supplemented by the growth of the diamond trade, a trade generally not included in official statistics [18].

In an attempt to win support for their cause at the United Nations, we are told, Arab propagandists have been trying to exploit anti-South African feeling among certain African states by suggesting that Israel and South Africa are linked in an "unholy alliance" in the service of Western imperialism. The two countries, they say, help each other materially and morally and have a common purpose in the struggle in the Middle East which, it is alleged, is also the struggle for domination in Africa. The intention behind the allegations is obvious: to stir up Black African governments against Israel in order to gain reinforcements in the United Nations council chambers, in spite of the fact that many of those governments have good reason to be on friendly terms with the Jewish state.

How far this move will succeed is doubtful, and it is even more so in the light of the clear evidence in recent weeks that responsible African opinion is beginning to display greater goodwill towards South Africa. Twisted though it is, however, to suit the Arab propaganda aims, the argument that South Africa and Israel have a basic community of interest in the Middle East and farther south has more than a grain of truth.

There is nothing secret or sinister about it. The strong ties between the two countries, closer than ever since the 1967 war, are inseparable from their geographical and strategic position from their anti-Communist outlook, and from all the realities of their national existence. For South Africa the Middle East—with Israel standing guard as the small but irreplaceable sentinel for the free world—is stationed in the very first line of her

*Jewish Affairs, November 1970, pp. 6-7.

security. Or, to put it in another form, Israel safeguards the corridor which must be defended as long as possible if it is not to become the highway of potential aggression by a common enemy. The future of the passage between the Mediterranean and the Indian Ocean, which is crucial for Israel, is no less essential to South Africa than the protection of the Cape sea route. Should it fall into hostile hands, hostile both to Israel and to South Africa, the Cape sea route would be practically outflanked and the problems of South African security would become vastly more formidable.

For Israel a friendly, well-earned and economically strong nation at the southern end of Africa, while she herself holds the key to the northern end, can only be a valuable strategic asset at her back door.

In short, the destinies of the two countries, so different in many ways but so alike in the fundamental conditions of their survival, are interwoven in a much more meaningful sense than any enemy propagandist could conceive or, for that matter, would be happy to see. But that is not the whole story either. Israeli and South African interests converge not just on the eastern fringe of the African continent but still more positively in the heart of the continent itself.

Both share an interest in the material and social development of those among the 200-million Africans who wish to seek their help and cooperation. Both countries, in their different ways, have something substantial to contribute to under-developed Africa in its progress towards the 20th century. In some of the newly independent states, notably in West Africa and parts of East and Central Africa, as well as in former British colonial territories, Israel has already made appreciable contributions. These have been not so much in the shape of capital investment, which Israel can ill afford these days, as in the form of expert advice, training and the fruits of her own unique experience in the best use of limited natural resources.

South Africa's relations with her fellow-African states have followed somewhat similar lines, although in her case there have been practical problems to resolve from which Israel has been spared. Where Israel's assistance has, on the whole, been warmly welcomed, South Africa has for many years come up against ideological, political and economic barriers which are only now being gradually breached here and there. These are practical difficulties; but the main point is that for South Africa the road to Africa is a vital part of her destiny, much more so, of course, than is the case with Israel.

Complementary Roles

Though the stakes involved are different in the two cases, it is on African soil that the paths of Israel and South Africa are certain to cross in the seventies and, to an increasing extent, in the more distant future. It is not, and never has been, a question of rivalry but rather of the one complementing the other where they do happen to meet. In those parts of the continent where South Africa is not barred by long-standing antipathies she will inevitably play a greater role than Israel ever could. She is nearer the scene of action, her stake will be greater, and her material resources will give her a status which Israel could not hope to achieve. Nevertheless, Israel will have the opportunity—an opportunity she has already to some extent grasped—to peg out for herself a well-defined place in the African sun.

Ultimately, the contribution which Israel as well as South Africa can make in Africa will depend on the settlement of their own special problems of co-existence in the international community. Israel must have peace and security and, with these, the lifting of the political and physical obstacles which have hemmed her in from the beginning. While not by a long way her only natural outlet, Africa is certainly an important one. Israel's hopes of building a permanent and developing sphere of influence and friendship in Africa will only be fulfilled, however, when her present long and wasteful struggle for survival and recognition by her Arab neighbours is finally over. A more considerable and normal flow of Israeli know-how and technical leadership into large areas of Africa south of the Sahara would be possible if it were not stemmed at the source by the constant diversion of precious assets to meet the needs of security. Directly or indirectly, Arab enmity blocks the way.

South Africa, untiringly seeking contact and fruitful co-operation with the rest of Africa, has come up against similar problems in a different guise. Here, too, we have a picture of active hostility or passive rejection, of chronic attempts at isolation which are only partly explained by the spirit of self-isolation, the traditional laager mentality inherited from another age. But whatever may have been the case in the past, there are plenty of indications that South Africa is endeavouring to find her way, not on sufferance but of right, into the new Africa.

Homecoming for S.A.

Historically, we may remind ourselves, it would be more of a homecoming than the coming of a stranger to a strange land. South Africa has been there before, very much so, in two world wars, in the journeyings of missionaries and explorers, and in the prestige won for South Africa in colonial and semi-colonial days by statesmen like General Smuts, who today is being recognised as the pioneer of our outward policies. That was, however, the old Africa, which was an appendage of Europe more than anything else. In the second half of this century Africa has changed beyond recognition and a new kind of South Africa has become necessary to gain an accepted place there.

Though much more peaceful but perhaps not much easier, this process of adaptation does not differ very much from the experience of Israel in her own particular circumstances. It may not be without significance that the lull in the shooting war where the Middle East meets North Africa has coincided with the signs of a positive swing away from the cold war by

Black Africa against the White-controlled South.

Perhaps it is only fortuitous; but the deeper historical and human forces at work at both ends of the continent might well be the groundswell of a movement which will profoundly affect the future of the two problem-nations in this vast area. The new Arab-African federation of Egypt, Libya and the Sudan, formed to confront Israel, pin-points the fact that Israel's and South Africa's interests are finding common ground in Africa. There the confrontation of the Black States with South Africa, through the O.A.U., has long been a fact of life.

[18] Diamonds

a. Israel Seeks Diamond-Trade Lead*

Israel is striving to become the international leader in polished diamond exports and the president of the country's diamond industry predicts this should happen by 1975.

The forecast was made by Moshe Schnitzer, who also is the president of the World Association of Diamond Bourses.

In an interview, Mr. Schnitzer said Israel's sales in four years should reach at least $250 million annually and enable the country to overtake Belgium as the world leader.

Mr. Schnitzer said the goal would be accomplished by attracting more foreign Jewish diamond entreprenuers, expanding the selection of Israeli gems, introducing new technology into the industry, and developing new markets.

Diamonds are Israel's best foreign-currency earner.

The international industry had a bad year in 1970 because of the recession in the big United States market. But Israel's 6.4 percent drop in sales from a record-breaking year in 1969 was a smaller setback than other major diamond exporting nations.

Israel had a turnover of $202 million last year compared with $215 million in 1969. The general decrease internationally was about 27 percent.

"Considering what went on in the States and what other producers suffered," Mr. Schnitzer said, "1970 was a big achievement for us."

Israel's salvation appears to have been due to its specialization in medium-size stones. Sales held up fairly well in this popular size but big stone producers were hit hard because of the stock-market sag and tight money of the depressed American economy. According to Mr. Schnitzer, Israel produces 85 percent of the world's medium size polished diamonds—stones ranging from one-thirtieth to one-half carat.

*Christian Science Monitor, January 6, 1971.

b. 47th Street: Where Diamonds Are for Now*

It is a grimy block in mid-Manhattan, distinguished mainly by the crowds gaping at tacky displays in the dusty store windows and the murmur of intense men bargaining endlessly on the sidewalk. Sleek young hustlers in flashy suits and star sapphire pinky rings brush past solemn-faced older men, many of them clad in the shapeless black coats and hats of the Hassidic Jews. Everywhere there is clamor and motion; messenger boys push their way through clusters of men gesturing vigorously in a time-honored ritual of *hondling* (haggling). The customers move from window to window, but more to look than to buy—for this stretch of West 47th Street between Fifth and Sixth Avenues is a street of expensive dreams.

The block is New York's diamond row and it handles fully 80 per cent of the U.S. diamond traffic, which itself is more than 60 per cent of the total world market. Here, with business methods honed by time and tradition, 800 dealers and more than 1,500 cutters, setters, jewelers, appraisers, gem lawyers and insurance men service some 23,000 American retail stores, which annually sell more than $700 million in diamond jewelry.

Nazis: Unlike other diamond centers, such as Antwerp or Bombay, New York had no real diamond-processing facilities before World War II. "In those days," one dealer recalls, "it was just a place for traveling salesmen." But as Nazi troops swept through Europe, diamond merchants—nearly all of them Jewish—snatched up their stocks and fled. (Indeed, it has long been 47th Street lore that some of the men now doing business there bought their way out of concentration camps with diamonds they had managed to hide on their persons.)

The result is one of the most colorful anachronisms in American commerce: a close-knit community steeped in tradition and rich with the self-ridicule and cosmic absurdity of Jewish humor. Like many other such relics, the world of 47th Street is slowly giving way to supermarket merchandising and the impersonal economies of scale. But meanwhile, as *Newsweek*'s Jane Friedman found in a week-long round of the block, the diamond community endures—mainly on absolute trust.

"If the law of the jungle prevailed," Zale Corporation's International Diamond Division president Allen Ginsberg explained, "we wouldn't be able to do business. So it's important for us to trust each other." A dealer may have thousands of dollars worth of stones out for inspection with only a memo from a customer to show for them. When the stones are returned, the customer simply assumes his memo will be voided; he trusts the dealer that much.

The system works well, as does the ancient way of concluding diamond deals. Typically, buyer and seller sit opposite each other, in a room chosen

Newsweek, May 8, 1972.

for the brightness of its northern exposure. The buyer opens a paper parcel of finished diamonds, picks out one stone at a time with a pair of tweezers and examines it carefully from all angles with a jeweler's loupe so he can see the finest details. Buyer constantly criticizes the quality of the stones; seller insists they are beautiful and worth the price. Finally, buyer might admit that while they're not the best stones in the world, at such and such a price he *might* consider them. Seller heaves a deep sigh and, with a shrug of resignation, agrees to sell. All this has been transacted in any number of languages. Albert J. Lubin, executive secretary of the Diamond Dealers Club, says: "You can start dealing in Yiddish, switch to French, Polish, Russian and Flemish ... and then finally end up in Yiddish again."

At the conclusion of every deal, Yiddish is the language that binds. To cement a deal, the seller must give the buyer what is called *mazel und broche*—or luck and blessings. "It's a custom and the law," says Albert Lubin. "It's the end of things—and they never back out."

Africa: In most cases, the diamonds on 47th Street begin their journey from the African mines of De Beers, the enormously rich and powerful cartel that controls 90 per cent of the world's supply of rough diamonds. With its virtual monopoly, De Beers can pick and choose customers through its Central Selling Organization (CSO), which imperiously maintains: "To be a client of the CSO is deemed a privilege by the worldwide trade." Every five weeks, some two dozen *diamantaires*—the aristocrats of 47th Street—fly to London to attend the CSO's "sights," or sales. With some 200 other dealers from around the world, the American dealers view stones at the CSO office and buy, on a take-it-or-leave-it basis, basic "boxes" of diamonds containing stones weighing about 1,200 carats and costing at least $250,000.

Back in New York, most diamantaires turn their stones over to contractors for cutting and polishing. A typical contractor is Max Roisen, who fled Belgium in 1940 and began his career as a cutter. Roisen's operation is crowded into a dimly lit room, sooty and gray from the years, and filled with the sound of whirring drills. One of Roisen's employees is Puerto Rican; a few are Belgian, Dutch or German. Most, however, are lookalikes in their beards and black yarmulkes (skull caps) . . . .

c. Western Alliance Thrives on Diamond Spoils*

South Africa is the world's biggest producer of gem diamonds. Israel is the world's largest diamond polishing center. And the United States is the world's largest gem diamond market.

South Africa's diamond industry, which is dominated by the De Beers Group of E.F. Oppenheimer, produced over $140 million in exports in

*Contrast, October 20, 1972.

1969. In that year, Israeli exports of polished gem diamonds exceeded $200 million, the largest foreign currency earner of the Jewish state. The diamond industry is the second largest enterprise in Israel, employing over 15,000 primarily skilled European Jews.

The United States accounts for 60 percent of the world's consumption of gem diamonds. There are over 23,000 retail stores in the United States who sell over $700 million annually in diamond jewelry. Sales have been on the down-trend as American youth, particularly the new breed of liberated women, have become disenchanted with traditional commercialization of marriage customs, particularly the purchase of a diamond.

The international diamond production and trade is practically monopolized by the DeBeers Group through its Central Selling Organization (CSO) in London. The CSO maintains control over the fragile diamond price structure by its iron grip on the sales of South African, Namibian (South West African) and Angolan gem diamonds. Zionists fear the exposure of Israeli complicity in South African *apartheid*.

Many of the major contributors to the United Jewish Appeal and purchasers of Israeli Bonds are big diamond dealers and financiers who have heavily invested in the Israeli and South African economies.

At the recent Black National Convention held in Gary, Indiana, a resolution was adopted calling for the dismantling of the Zionist state of Israel and supporting the African and Palestine liberation movements. Israeli sympathizers later forced some members of the Congressional Black Caucus to water down the text of the resolution.

[19] Strange Nonalliance*
C.L. Sulzberger

The strange "non-alliance," noted by C. L. Sulzberger in 1971 [19] blossomed prominently during and in the wake of the October 1973 war [20].

Johannesburg, South Africa—There is a remarkably close if little known partnership between Israel and South Africa. This relationship between the nation controlling Africa's southern tip and the nation still holding the gate to its northern tip affects political, economic and military affairs.

Above all, from this country's right-wing viewpoint, it has psychological importance. Among foreign critics of South African policy there are many Jewish voices, especially in the United States and Britain. South Africa therefore feels that if Israel is sympathetic this will help its own international standing.

---

*New York Times, April 28, 1971.

Moreover, the fact that Israel has closed the Suez Canal gives this country incidental benefits. Some twenty thousand ships passed Capetown last year as compared to eight thousand annually before the canal was blocked. Finally, the Suez closure enhances South Africa's strategic standing by focusing attention on it as global pivot and southern hemisphere bastion.

Afrikaner South Africa and Jewish Israel both began in 1948 when the Nationalist party gained control of this country and Palestine was partitioned. South Africa was one of the first states to recognize Israel. Its Prime Minister, D. F. Malan, was the first foreign chief of government to visit it.

The Afrikaner sees Israel as another small nation, surrounded by enemies, where the Bible and a revived language are vital factors. As Jannie Kruger, former editor of *Die Transvaler* wrote: "The Afrikaners...are *par excellence* the nation of the Book." The fundamentalist Boers trekked northward with gun in one hand and Bible in the other.

Both South Africa and Israel feel isolated in the U.N. but regard this as no final judgment of history. South Africa feels that Israel, like itself, is an outpost of the West. Moreover, it sees Israel as today facing the kind of Soviet pressure in the Mediterranean and Red Sea area that may be expected here tomorrow when Russia has consolidated its Indian Ocean position. South Africa believes that Israel delays the Soviet's southward push.

Like Israel, South Africa feels the role of language and religion are important to national survival. Prime Minister Vorster even goes so far as to say Israel is now faced with an *apartheid* problem—how to handle its Arab inhabitants. Neither nation wants to place its future entirely in the hands of a surrounding majority and would prefer to fight.

Both South Africa and Israel are in a sense intruded states. They were built by pioneers originating abroad and settling in partially inhabited areas. The only people here when the first Dutch arrived were Bushmen and Hottentots but the Zulus would be living in Johannesburg were it not for the Boers' northward trek.

Vorster says: "We view Israel's position and problems with understanding and sympathy. Like us they have to deal with terrorist infiltration across the border; and like us they have enemies bent on their destruction."

For diplomatic reasons, neither overstresses the bond in public. Nor is the economic tie fundamental although Israel trades with South Africa and receives substantial contributions from the Jewish colony here.

But there is, in addition to everything else, consideralbe military understanding. The only two battles given major attention in this country's maneuver schools are Tobruk, where a South African unit was defeated in World War II, and Israel's Six Day War in 1967.

South Africa manufactures the Uzi submachine gun under license; the

Uzi is an Israeli invention and the license was granted through Belgium. I have been told unofficially but cannot confirm officially that a South African mission flew to Israel during the Six Day War to study tactics and use of weapons.

Likewise, wholly unconfirmable rumors float around that after the Israelis secured plans of the French Mirage fighter engine through agents in Switzerland, they improved it and made blueprints available here. But all such reports are unconfirmable and wholly blanketed by security.

The basic truth remains that this country, which has few friends abroad, regards Israel as one of them. For some time Israel's policy of cultivating black African nations was resented. Now this has been forgotten in the belief that Israel's stand against Russia and Russian proxies at this continent's extreme north helps prepare a position for a similar stand, if need be, when the day for such comes to the extreme south.

[20] October 1973 War

a. Moral Support for Israel*

The Minister of Defence, Mr. P.W. Botha, said in George, Cape Province, that South Africa would give moral support to Israel in the Middle East war, and that he did not doubt but that ways and means of showing the Republic's sympathy in a practical way short of war would be found, reports the South African Press Association.

There existed a deep feeling of sympathy in South Africa with Israel in its struggle against forces supported by "Communistic militarism," said Mr. Botha.

"Although we pray that this war will not set the world on fire, I have no doubt that we shall find ways and means of showing our goodwill towards Israel," declared the Minister.

Israel, now engaged in a life and death struggle, guarded the Suez Canal. South Africa guarded the sea freedom of the Western world around the Cape of Good Hope, said Mr. Botha.

Speaking at Keetmanshoop, the Prime Minister, Mr. B. J. Vorster, said that the war in the Middle East was basically being waged against Israel not by Syria and Egypt, but by Russia, and if the Communists got their way it could hold important consequences for South Africa.

"Terrorist activities are not primarily aimed at Rhodesia or the Portuguese territories. They are aimed at exhausting South Africa so that they (the Communists) can control the Cape sea route. This has always been their chief aim and strategy," declared the Premier.

---

*South African Digest, Week Ended October 19, 1973.

b. South African Jet Downed Over Egypt*

A South African jet was shot down over the Suez Canal by Egyptian forces, according to the conservative British newspaper, *The Daily Telegraph.*

Richard Cox, the *Telegraph*'s defense correspondent, cites what he calls "reliable reports" that an unidentified Mirage [Meer-Azh'] jet shot down by the Egyptians in late October was one of the several planes sent to Israel from the South African Air Force. French-built Mirage aricraft are sophisticated fighter planes, similar to the American F-105 and the Soviet MIG.

The presence of the South African aircraft over Egypt puzzled observers, says the *Telegraph,* since Israel has relied on its modern American-built Phantoms and Skyhawks during the Suez fighting. The 35 Mirage jets in the Israeli Air Force are among the oldest aircraft it has.

South Africa, by contrast, owns more than 40 Mirage Jets, some of them newer models than those the Israelis have, and they form the backbone of its Air Force. France sold the jets to South Africa in spite of a United Nations embargo against arms to that country's white government.

The *Daily Telegraph* conjectures that South Africa sent a number of volunteer pilots and their planes to Israel so that they could gain some vitally-needed battle experience. The South African Government fears that one day the South African Air Force may have to contend with Soviet-built aircraft and Soviet-trained pilots much closer to home.

The *Daily Telegraph* report helps explain Egyptian president Sadat's [Sah-Daht'] recent warning that his country will only grant prisoner-of-war status to captives who are Israeli citizens. Thus, any South African pilot captured by the Egyptians would not be eligible for release under a prisoner exchange program.

Although Israel has never agreed to full diplomatic relations with South Africa, ties between the two countries have grown steadily colser. The South African Prime Minister Vorster [Foss-Ter] expressed these sentiments when he said, "Like us they have to deal with terrorist infiltration across the border; and like us, they have enemies bent on their destruction."

Increasingly, South Africa sees Israel as an ally with not only similar problems, but similar enemies as well. South Africa's white government which is outnumbered five to one by the blacks it rules, is the object of intense criticism from black-ruled African nations.

And Black Africa is almost totally united behind the Arab cause. In the last two years, 26 African countries have broken diplomatic relations with Israel, 18 of these since the recent fighting began.

Africa News, Volume 1, Number 39, Thursday, November 8, 1973

The *Daily Telegraph* report speculates that the route followed by the South African jets was up the West Coast of Africa, with refueling stops at Portuguese bases in Angola and Guinea Bissau. From there they are thought to have joined with American aircraft flying replacement equipment to Israel from the Azores, Portuguese islands in the Atlantic Ocean.

In an interview with the British Broadcasting Corporation, Richard Cox, author of the *Telegraph* article, insisted that his source for the story was reliable. He predicted, however, that South Africa would deny it.

They did. Prime Minister Vorster said Cox's story was "devoid of all truth." He said his government was taking no part in the Middle East fighting.

c. South African Sympathy for Israel*

Louis Hotz

In the massive South African demonstration of goodwill towards Israel in her latest ordeal—and few countries outside of Israel herself could have followed her fortunes of war with greater sympathy than South Africa—there was one recurring theme which found expression in most newspapers, on the radio, and from public platforms. It was the acute awareness among people of all shades of opinion that Israel's fight for life and security was a fight which directly or indirectly also affected the future of this country.

Admiration for Israel's stand and passionate concern for her success were coupled with the sense of a vital common interest between the two peoples. In normal times each has its own problems to contend with and its own way of life. But in a period of crisis any such differences were forgotten in the realisation, deeply felt in South Africa particularly, that what was at stake in the Middle East struggle was not only their personal fate but also, it may be, the peace of the world.

South Africans who shared this view—and above all those whose business it is to think and plan ahead in terms of strategy and national safety—saw in Israel the northern bastion against a potential aggressor more dangerous than the Arabs, while South Africa herself was seen as the southern bastion against the same enemy.

Israel at the junction of Asia and North Africa and South Africa at the meeting place of two oceans in the far south of Africa are geographically placed to command vitally important world routes. It has become an accepted part of South African thinking that the two countries are interdependent on that score. Again and again, during the weeks of tension and fluctuating battle, we heard the statement echoed that if Israel fell or if her position was seriously impaired, Southern Africa might well be next on the list, at any rate not a long way down the list.

Jewish Affairs, November 1973, pp. 14-15.

Possibly these fears were exaggerated and possibly, too, Israel is less concerned to play the role of policeman in her part of the world, except in so far as her own security is imperilled, than South Africa is as the guardian of the Cape sea route. Nor is Israel troubled by quite the same ideological considerations as South Africa.

In the emotional atmosphere of this struggle these are some of the realities to remember, just as we must remember that South Africa, not immediately threatened physically, looks at the dangers ahead from a rather different angle than Israel. South Africa's everpresent concern is the dread of gradual Communist infiltration deep into the heart of Africa, eventually striking at South Africa herself from within. This fear, too, may be exaggerated and in any event the risks of a direct attack such as Israel has suffered may be very remote at this stage, though this is no reason for relaxing preparedness and vigilance.

In spite of all that, however, it is still the case that close bonds of common concern exist between South Africa and Israel and that the future of South Africa, in one way or another, does hinge to a large extent on the outcome of the struggle in the Middle East and the ultimate settlement reached. The fate of the Suez Canal alone represents an issue linking South Africa and Israel, as has been clearly proved since the closure of the waterway.

But South African attitudes on the war have not been solely conditioned by the military aspect or even by the larger strategic implications. Thoughtful South Africans who hailed Israel as an effective obstacle to Communist ambitions, also drew an important conclusion from that situation in a rather different sense.

In Israel's stand against a powerful enemy, with all the odds apparently against her, now as in the past, they found a plain warning that South Africa needed a greater sense of national unity. It was also an implied warning that South Africa was living on borrowed time. South Africans had, in other words, been given a breathing space, for how long they could not know, but they could permit themselves to hope, long enough to close their ranks and put an end to divisions they could not afford to perpetuate in a dangerous world.

That was one conclusion which impressed itself on responsible South Africans, as they looked at the Middle East picture. It was summed up in a statement, often heard these days, that military preparedness, though essential in itself, was only half the battle. What was equally essential was to have behind the armed forces the moral strength that comes from the kind of solidarity and spirit of sacrifice which is one of Israel's most formidable weapons.

Another conclusion from the events in the Middle East, related to the first, was that South Africa had to put her house in order if she was not to be overtaken by the forces building up elsewhere in Africa with the help of the same power which constituted the ultimate threat to Israel. Perhaps this was the point that came through most clearly in the more preceptive South African reflections on the war.

The Russian-backed onslaught on Israel, fought partly, it should be remembered, on African soil, and followed by the lightning shock of America's brief but ominous confrontation with Moscow, flashed a danger signal which South Africans could not ignore.

[21]   Bantustans and South African Foreign Policy

South Africa's decision to utilize the Bantustan concept as an approach to foreign relations [21], although denounced vigorously by Blacks, was increasingly viewed with sympathy by the Israeli government at a practical level [a, b, c, d].

a. Bantustans as Instruments of Foreign Policy*

As indicated above, the transformation of the bantustan programme in the early 1960s from one of limited local self-government to a programme aiming at eventual independence was forced upon the South African Government by its new isolation in the period of decolonization. The precipitate rush to realize this programme in the 1970s has manifested itself in, and as a result of, a period of increased isolation for the *apartheid* regime stemming from its intransigence not only in regard to domestic racial policies, but also in respect of its illegal occupation of Namibia and the extension of the bantustan programme to Namibia, and its support for the illegal rebel regime in Rhodesia (Zimbabwe).

In an attempt to break out of its isolation on the African continent, the South African Government has in recent years sought to "normalize" its relations with independent African countries as a first step to gaining African acquiescence to the perpetuation of its *apartheid* policies. At the same time, the Vorster Government has sought to deepen the involvement of the major Western Powers in the *apartheid* economy and to draw closer to them in strategic relations, thereby overcoming the political restraints which make it difficult for the Western Powers to enter into the closest and most open alliance with South Africa of the sort the *apartheid* regime would undoubtedly prefer. In both the African and Western spheres of its foreign policy, the South African Government has projected the bantustan programme as its alternative to the policies advocated by the liberation movements, by the Organization of African Unity (OAU), by the United Nations and by anti-*apartheid* movements and other progressive organizations throughout the world.

*The South African Bantustan Programme: Its Domestic and International Implications, reprinted from *Objective Justice* (Vol. 8, No. 1, Spring 1976) pp. 9-10.

In doing so, Pretoria has found its traditional allies actively willing to help—not least by giving official recognition and publicity to the persons installed by Pretoria in positions of authority in the bantustans. In recent years, the first significant exercise of this kind appears to have been the invitation by the United States Government for Chief Buthelezi to conduct a two-month tour of the United States from April to June 1971, barely a year after Chief Buthelezi's installation as chief executive officer of the Zulu "territorial authority." In October of the same year, Chiefs Mantanzima, Buthelezi and Mangope spent three and a half weeks in Britain as guests of the British Government, and thereafter two weeks in West Germany as guests of the Federal Government. Since then, most of the bantustan leaders have spent at least two to three months each year visiting the United States, the Federal Republic of Germany, Britain, Switzerland, Holland and other Western countries. In additon, Chief Buthelezi has visited several African countries, including those most directly involved in the southern African conflict and some of those most sympathetic to the Vorster regime's policies of dialogue and detente.

The availability of the bantustan leaders as free-ranging emissaries of the South African Government's bantustan programme has created a new dimension to South Africa's foreign policy. The importance of this new dimension lies not so much in the fact that for the first time black spokesmen are traveling abroad to advocate the racial policies of the *apartheid* regime as in the fact that these spokesmen are able to gain admittance to, and achieve acceptability in, influential circles in the West—Christian, financial and commercial, and intellectual—where the South African Government itself has long been unable to achieve any credibility for its policies by conventional diplomatic means.

Furthermore, in these important opinion-making circles, these spokesmen are now able to solicit participation in the economic development of their "homelands" and to oppose policies directed at the isolation of *apartheid* South Africa on the grounds that such policies will harm those whom they are intended to help. In such circles there is often no, or insufficient, awareness that the bantustans are not and cannot ever become independent nation-states comparable even with independent African countries like Botswana, Lesotho and Swaziland (with which they are sometimes misleadingly compared). The fact that the bantustans are themselves only notionally-linked fragments of land, all comprising part of the territory of South Africa and closely enmeshed in the economy of that country, is often lost sight of. Consequently, the problem of the socio-economic development of these areas is often seen as being similar in its essentials to general development needs in the third world, whereas the reality is that South Africa is an industrialized country and that the backwardness of the "homeland" areas is directly attributable to the *apartheid* policies of successive South African Governments.

As we have seen, the backwardness of the reserves is due to grossly unfair and unilateral land apportionment on a racial basis; to the exclusion of all main industrial and mining centres from them; to the resettlement in them of millions of African men, women and children from "white South Africa"—in short, to their well-established function as reservoirs of cheap labour in the *apartheid* economy. Against that background it is blatantly hypocritical of the Vorster regime to present itself—as it does—as being engaged in the largest development programme in the third world, if not in the whole world. And it is more than hypocritical of it to be pretending to seek to engage governmental and nongovernmental resources from the developed world in this farcical development programme. The overnight conversion of the South African Government to enthusiasm for this policy stems from its realization that the projection of the bantustans internationally would provide it with an important new means of legitimizing the foreign capital inflows which have been so crucial to South Africa, both economically and politically, in the past decade. This was the main strategic consideration which prompted the South African Government in 1973 to overturn a longstanding detail of policy and to open the "Bantu homelands" to foreign investment.

Faced with this new development, the international community needs to inform itself of the realities of the bantustans and to exercise great vigilance so as not to accept in the light in which it is now presented a racist policy which in its former manifestations has been overwhelmingly repudiated by world public opinion. In particular, organizations and bodies which feel a special moral responsibility towards oppressed Africans and which seek practical ways of relieving their sufferings need to avoid taking steps which might encourage the South African Government to continue in its present line of approach to the "homeland" areas and relieve it of the over-all responsibility it has assumed for the welfare of South Africans of all races. Moreover, at governmental level it is becoming imperative for the United Nations to respond to the demand of the African States, made at the extraordinary session of the Council of Ministers of the OAU in Dar es Salaam in April 1975 and reiterated at the Kampala summit in August, for the rejection of the whole bantustan programme. The relevant part of the resolution on South Africa adopted then called on all United Nations Member States to desist from establishing any contacts with the homeland "leaders."

Only this approach, carried out as part of the wider campaign for the isolation of the *apartheid* system in all spheres—political, military, economic, cultural and scientific, and sporting—provides a realistic and meaningful basis for a solution to the problem of *apartheid* and for solidarity with the struggle of the people of South Africa against it.

b. Praise from General Dayan*

General Moshe Dyan said on his departure by air from Jan Smuts Air-

**South African Digest*, September 15, 1974.

port, Johannesburg, to Tel Aviv after an extended visit to the Republic: "South Africa belongs to the free world. Israel is very interested in maintaining close relationship with the Government of South Africa.

"South Africa is a developed country; there are most impressive development schemes under way here, but it must take its military problems seriously."

General Dayan said: "I'm sure that you people not only don't need advisers, but also feel like me when other people give me advice about what to do in Israel."

He had had a long and fruitful discussion with the Prime Minister, Mr. B. J. Vorster, and he had also talked with Chief Gatsha Buthelezi of KwaZulu.

c. Natal's Rich Tapioca Dish*

Lawrence Morgan

New confirmation of the huge economic potential of Natal's Makatini Flats area has come from an internationally-known Israeli organization of agricultural development consultants.

After exhaustive studies at Makatini it has reported a vast possibility for crop production, including cassava—"tapioca".

The Israeli group was commissioned at high cost by the Tiger Oats group to investigate large-scale cassava production at Makatini—up to 20,000 ha.

Tiger Oats is also looking at the possibility of creating bulk handling facilities at Richards Bay to handle large exports of the crop. A German company, foremost in the rapidly expanding international cassava trade, is interested in the scheme.

But a big hold-up has occurred. No Government decision has yet been made, and it is unlikely that this will be made before the complete consolidation plans for KwaZulu are placed before Parliament, possibly later this year.

Until then, there is doubt about who exactly will own or occupy the land.

Tiger Oats is now one of several big organizations which have been studying Makatini and KwaZulu generally with the prospect of participating in homeland development on the official agency basis.

*South Africa Financial Gazette, May 17, 1974.

d. Israeli Aid for Homelands?*

Israel could help to develop the South African homelands, *Ha'aretz*, the

*South African Digest, April 30, 1976.

influential Israeli newpaper, suggests in a special article.

The assistant editor, Mr. A. Schweizer, says Israel could teach the people of the homelands modern agricultural techniques and how to combat erosion.

Israel has successfully helped other Black states in the past, Schweizer writes, and mentions Transkei among others, which will shortly become independent and where such aid could be given. He even foresees Israel's ties with South Africa enhancing its standing with Black Africa. He says that in the light of improved relations it is accepted that South Africa will allow Israel to take part in its development projects.

The writer adds that Israel rejects outside criticism of Mr. Vorster's and Dr. Muller's visit to Israel since an independent country can invite whoever it wishes. Whoever wants to condemn South Africa on moral grounds must have "clean hands" themselves. Few countries can produce such testimonials about themselves and their guests, Mr. Schweizer says.

[22] Military Collaboration and the "Black Peril"*

In the aftermath of the 1973 war and Israel's isolation in Africa, both countries turned more openly to each other. [22], [23].

The past month has seen a new stepping up of links between Israel and South Africa, in the political, military and commercial fields. Officially, both sides continue to play down the importance of the ties, but they are now becoming of increasing importance in all ways to both sides.

In early September, it was revealed in a London newspaper that the South African Navy was to buy Gabriel missiles from Israel. Specially developed in Israel, the missile, which is sea-to-sea, has a range of about twenty miles, and proved its effectiveness during the October War last year, when it was used against the Syrian navy, and in attacks on the port of Latakia. It has been of considerable interest to a number of Western navies. For South Africa, it will mark an important addition to her missile strength. This is the first time that hard proof of military links between the two countries has surfaced for some time, although during the October War, the Egyptian military high command reported that they had shot down a South African Mirage jet along the Suez front, while in March this year, President Kaunda of Zambia accused Israel of sending a major general to South Africa to train her forces in counter-insurgency.

Meanwhile, at the end of August and beginning of September, two important Israeli visitors went to South Africa. One was General Meir Amit, formerly second in command to Moshe Dayan when the latter was chief

---

**Third World Reports,* Vol. 5, No. 7, September 1974.

of staff in 1953, and the second was Dayan himself. Amit is now boss of Koor, the industrial holding company owned by the Histadrut, the Israeli trade union federation. Koor has formed a joint company with the South African para-statal steel giant, ISCOR, for the import and distribution of steel in Israel, and earlier this year announced a new deal with the South African company Adcock Ingram for the joint financing of a major factory near East London, in South Africa. Koor is now emerging as a major part of the burgeoning economic undergrowth linking the two countries, and Amit's visit raised some speculation that a new deal might be under preparation.

Dayan, meanwhile, who was accompanied by his wife, was in South Africa as a guest of the South Africa Foundation, the businessmen's group formed specifically to improve South Africa's image abroad. Israeli politicians who visit South Africa usually go as guests of one or other of the various Zionist groupings among the South African Jewish community, which provides at least a fig-leaf for the embarrassing fact of their presence. Dayan, however, chose to accept the Foundation's invitation, and most of his stay was based around an arranged programme. His wife went a few days earlier for medical treatment in a Johannesburg clinic. Why the Foundation picked Dayan as a guest is not absolutely clear, but it may be a little more than a coincidence that Dr. Shlomo Peer, an Israeli who helped Dayan, and Ben Gurion, to form the Rafi party in the early sixties, subsequently emigrated to South Africa, where he emerged not only as one of the prime movers of the Israel—South Africa Trade Association, but also as a member of the Committee of the Foundation.

While in South Africa, Dayan addressed the annual conference of the South African Zionist Federation. He told them that Israel's biggest problem at present lay not in the military or economic fields, but in the fact that Oriental Jewish immigrants outnumbered immigrants of European origin, and urged more South African Jews to consider immigration. His evocation of the 'black peril,' albeit a Jewish one, struck a responsive chord in the hearts of his South African audience, many of whom are devout supporters of *apartheid.*

[23] The Israeli Link With South Africa*

Stanley Uys

Cape Town—Senior Israeli military officers visit South Africa regularly to lecture South African officers on modern warfare and counterinsurgency techniques.

This is one of several important military and industrial links that have been established between Israel and South Africa.

*New York Post, July 14, 1975.

Two other projects are participation by the state-owned South African Railways in construction of a railway in Israel, and construction of an Israeli plant in South Africa to desalinate seawater for drinking and irrigation.

Confirmation of these two projects was given in Johannesburg earlier this week by Gen. Meir Amit, formerly Israel's intelligence chief and currently head of the giant Koor Industries.

Koor Industries comprises 150 independent companies, 75 of them major manufacturers, and has links with ISCOR (the state-owned Iron and Steel Corp. in South Africa) and five other major South African industrial concerns.

When it was put to Amit in an interview that apart from major industrial projects Israel and South Africa enjoyed good military relations, he replied, "That is an understatement."

Referring to the rail and desalinization projects, Amit said, "The finer points of the scheme are still being discussed at top government level. There are also security and political considerations against publicizing the full details at this time."

Amit disclosed that a joint Israeli-South African venture in the manufacture of agricultural chemicals, including insecticides, would come into operation in Cape Province next year.

Amit disclosed further that a tank farm for the storage of oil under tight security conditions was being built in Israel and that this was a "partnership venture" with South Africa. The oil tank units, made by a South African company, are being assembled in Israel, he said.

According to a report from London, a $2.3 million collection of valuable oil books about South Africa has been offered to an Israeli university on condition that it establish a department devoted to the promotion of closer historical, cultural and political relations between Israelis and Afrikaners.

Former Afrikaner Prime Minister Dr. Daniel Malan visited Israel shortly after the present national government came to power. Afrikaners often have stressed their affinity for Israel, drawing a parallel between Israel and South Africa as small nations struggling to survive among hostile neighbors.

[24] UN Anti-Zionist Resolution

The South African white minority and its leadership showed a great deal of sympathy for the Zionist ideal and Zionist settlement activities as legitimate expressions of "Jewish nationhood" in Palestine, quite similar to their own efforts at maintaining their own "white nationhood" in Africa. The UN resolution con-

demning Zionism as a form of racism provided another context for underscoring the same point.

a. The UN crisis*

Decades of Western permissiveness and spinelessness at the UN have culminated in the unavoidable moment of truth.

The majority resolution of the General Assembly declaring Zionism—Jewish nationalism—to be racism, puts the existence of the organisation at stake.

The Arabian enemies of Israel have succeeded in elevating their anti-Semitism to the status of "world opinion." Likewise through South Africa's persecutors our ideal to maintain a free White nationhood in Africa, was given the international stamp of satanic evil.

The ball is with the Western countries, who must now weigh their fear of Arabian reprisal against conscience and decency. It is especially the United States which held out the prospect of more than just verbal protest.

South African prophets since General Smuts have never stopped warning that the UN with its illegal action against us, was planting a time bomb in its own stomach; for customs become habits now. The bomb has exploded.

It is obviously the beginning of a new chapter in the history of the UN. It may also be the last.

**Die Burger,* November 12, 1975

b. UN and Zionism*

No-one can blame South Africa if it regards the wild reaction to the decision of the UN General Assembly to equate Zionism with racialism with a certain amount of malicious joy.

For years the Republic was a voice crying in the wilderness. Its message that the witch-hunt of the communists and the Third World against South Africa's ethnic policy—supported by Western liberal-leftist elements—may still lead to the downfall of the world body, continued to fall on deaf ears.

South Africa, however, does not want to find justification for her policy in negative criticism of Israel. All we hope for is that the West will finally realise that the first step on the road to self-destruction is inevitably followed by a second, and that the end of the road comes much quicker than one ever expects.

**Die Transvaler,* November 12, 1975

c. Racism*

Looking at the flood of indignant reaction to the latest decision of the United Nations, namely, to brand Zionism as a form of racism, one has to regard comment from top officials of the world body as being the most significant. Short and to the point was the reaction of Dr. Waldheim, the United Nations is in a critical condition. The comment from the Chairman of the General Assembly, Mr. Gaston Thorn, was that this time, the extremists had gone too far.

For quite some time now, observers have felt that the United Nations has lost its real purpose as an instrument for solving differences between countries and for promoting mutual interests. In the political field, it has simply become—in the words of the American Ambassador—the instrument by which the built-in majority of tyrannical dictatorships are forcing their will on the rest of the world.

Through the years, South Africa has been the country which has had to bear the brunt of this. And because the Republic was unable to bring any significant international power to bear, even friendly Western countries tacitly accepted the twisting of the United Nations manifesto to misinterpret South Africa's policies and get a dig in. Only recently, the Political Committee decided not to recognise the independence of the Homelands, and to declare the South African Government illegitimate.

A convenient stick with which to beat South Africa, was the accusation of racism. It was an emotional creed which made honest reasoning and an acceptance of the true facts unnecessary ... and gave the critics the automatic sympathy they desired. To try and hit at Israel—another target in the power struggle with the West, with tactics shown to be successful, was only natural.

This time however, they bit off more than they could chew. The attack on Zionism is something which cannot be accepted by any Western country. This is why there is now talk of a turning point at the United Nations, while there is even talk in the American Congress of terminating the country's membership.

There are advantages in the situation for South Africa. The UN Action Programme against Racism has now been exposed as nothing more than a political campaign which has virtually nothing to do with racism, and the West no longer supports it. However for the United Nations, the prospect of disintegration has never been so real.

SABC News Commentary, November 12, 1975

d. The Wheel Wants to Begin Turning*

It could just be that the about-turn by intelligent and worried UN

Die Volksblad, November 13, 1975

members, which South Africa has hoped for so long, is beginning to set in with the stand of those members against the anti-Semitism drive of the majority. When the Scandinavian countries, Canada, Australia and New Zealand join the United States, Britain and countries of the European Continent in voting against proposals aimed at "racism" in South Africa, then it seems as if the wheel wants to begin turning. And the split over Zionism runs right through Black Africa as evidenced by the voting in the General Assembly.

It also appears that there are growing doubts about the purity of the motives of the anti-*apartheid* countries which have now gone so far as to damn Zionism as racialistic. It is only logical for the disillusioned UN members to pay attention to the similarities of and differences between Zionism, which they do not want touched, and separate development, which they themselves have for so many years condemned to the extent that they, together with the rest, have declared it racialistic and damnable.

Then they will find that there are more similarities than differences. Basically Zionism is also concerned with the right of a nation to its own territory, its own homeland, state and independence. Such a home for the Jews was created with the blessings of the UN. Arabs and others now wish to destroy this state and are using the selfsame UN for their purposes. As a founder member, South Africa enjoyed full membership of the UN. Communists and others wish to destroy it and want to use the UN for this.

In the case of South Africa the West condoned interference in the internal affairs of the country, against the UN Charter, because the West wanted to retain the goodwill of the Third World, and therefore also began talking of racism in South Africa. With the precedent of interference well established, the next objective, Israel, was tackled. And now many UN members can see where they are being led.

Hopefully they will now also realise that the campaign against South Africa is not only against an individual "homeland" for the Whites, but also against individual independent states for the Blacks—namely that it is not "racism" in South Africa that bothers the UN majority, but that the most influential agitators among them wish to take it from the West, cause chaos and internal strife here, just as in Angola, so that the riches and strategic position of the territory can be used in the global battle against the free West.

[25] UN Security Council Admits PLO

The South African press considered the admission of the PLO to the UN Security Council debate, with the status of a full-fledged member state, a very dangerous precedent. The Friend *draws the analogy between the PLO and the guerrilla and liberation movements in southern Africa.*

a. Appeasement*

On the one hand the Western countries are considering joint action against terrorism in the shape of kidnappings, bomb attacks and highjackings which shook the world in 1975. On the other hand the appeasement of terrorists or at least their soul-mates continues enthusiastically.

During the debate of the Security Council on the future of the Middle East, the Palestine Liberation Organisation has been allowed to take part in the discussions. A more accurate description of this movement is "terrorist organisation." Many of the terrible deeds committed in 1975 were the work of Palestinian terrorist groups of which the Liberation Organisation was the organising body as it were.

The latest example of appeasement is that in Paris a meeting of Unesco (the UN's educational, scientific and cultural organisation) was postponed to avoid an expected confrontation about the General Assembly's decision which equated Zionism with racism—this in what is supposed to be a non-political organisation.

A resolve to stop the appeasement of terrorists and those who support them is evidently not one of the strongest New Year resolutions of the Western countries.

Beeld, January 16, 1976

b. An Extremely Dangerous Precedent*

The General Assembly of the United Nations has recently lost much of its esteem in the world as a result of the irresponsible behaviour of the developing countries and the violation of its own rules and conventions. The Security Council, the world organisation's most important body, is now being threatened by a similar danger. The course and result of the 10-day debate on the Middle East—the world's most dangerous powderkeg—could irreparably damage the Security Council.

One blunder led to another. The first mistake was that the leader of the Palestine Liberation Organisation, Yasser Arafat, was received like a hero in 1974 by the UN and even permitted to address the General Assembly. For Israel—a state accorded full recognition by the UN—it was obviously offensive that a terrorist movement that had taken an oath to destory Israel was accorded so much recognition and status.

Arab persecution of Israel increased within the UN. Attempts to expel Israel from the organisation never amounted to much, but it was driven

Die Burger, January 14, 1976

Readings 159

out of organisations like Unesco and the International Labour Organisation. The climax came last year in November when the General Assembly decided that Zionism was equal to racism. This was scornfully rejected by Israel and most Western countries, and moved a furious Israeli Prime Minister, Mr. Yitzak Rabin, to declare that by it the UN was "stripped of all moral and political power."

Despite strong opposition from Israel and the United States, the Security Council, at the insistence of the Russian ambassador to the UN, came to an "understanding" that representatives of the Palestine Liberation Organisation be allowed to attend the session on the Middle East. Israel promptly announced that it would boycott the meeting.

On Monday, the first day of the discussion, only the United States voted against the admission of the Palestine Liberation Organisation. Three other Western countries—Britain, France and Italy—abstained. The British ambassador, Mr. Ivor Richard, did condemn sharply a speech made by the Russian ambassador, but maintained that he did not want to vote on a question of mere procedure.

If the Security Council wishes to destroy its own esteem and authority, it should continue to ignore wise words such as those of Mr. Daniel Moynihan. He warned that recognition of the Palestine Liberation Movement, which represents no state, could lead to the UN later having to welcome resistance movements from "half of the world."

The precedent set holds great dangers for almost every country that has had dealings with resistance or terror groups, or will still have dealings with them.

c. Double-edged Sword*

In the past few days two events have occurred which illustrate the capacity of people to create booby traps which contain the potential for their own disaster.

Earlier this week the Palestine Liberation Organisation won admission to a United Nations Security Council debate—giving it the status and powers of a fully fledged member country—by an 11 to one vote. The lone opponent (Israel is boycotting the session) was the United States.

But three member countries, Britain, France and Italy, abstained, thus giving tacit approval to this blatant and utterly one-sided distortion of United Nations procedures. They also thereby gave tacit approval to the recognition of a group whose tactics of terror are the very antithesis of what the United Nations was designed to achieve.

(It is perhaps not surprising that the United Nations building in New York is at this very moment under heavy guard to prevent a repetition of the terror bomb incidents there earlier in the week.)

*The Friend, January 15, 1976

And today we report the payment by the ruling Labour Party in Britain of sums of money to "guerrilla and liberation movements" in Southern Africa. This is, of course, in fulfillment of an earlier pledge by the Prime Minister, Mr. Wilson. Recipients and intended recipients of funds include the South West Africa People's Organisation and "liberation movements in Rhodesia."

The mischievousness of these payments, small as they may be, cannot be strongly enough condemned. In both Rhodesia and South West Africa negotiations are taking place aimed at achieving a non-violent constitutional solution to the separate problems.

Nothing can be more calculated to sabotage these negotiations and lend encouragement to the violent alternative than the Labour Party's gesture.

The United Kingdom has already lost more than 1400 men, women and children to terrorism in Northern Ireland in the past six years.

How many more hundred deaths will it take to bring home the message that terrorism is indivisible?

[26] Prime Minister Vorster's Visit to Israel, April 1976

a. A Very Welcome Visit*

A red carpet welcome awaited the South African Premier, Mr. B. J. Vorster, when his El Al aircraft touched down last week on Ben Gurion Airport near Jerusalem.

From the aircraft door he was escorted to the apron where his host for the four-day visit, the Israeli Premier, Mr. Yitzhak Rabin, with Mrs. Rabin and other VIPs, were waiting to greet him.

Mr. Vorster was accompanied by Mrs. Vorster, the Minister of Foreign Affairs, Dr. Hilgard Muller, Mrs. Muller and the Secretary for Foreign Affairs, Mr. Brand Fourie. A party of 12 South African pressmen travelled with him.

The South African Premier started his first day in Israel with visits to the country's shrines and holy places. He laid a wreath at the Yad Vashem Museum and Memorial.

Later, Mr. Vorster held talks with Mr. Rabin and some of his ministers. The talks included a working lunch which was also attended by the Israeli Foreign Minister, Mr. Yigal Allon, Dr. Muller and Mr. Fourie. He also paid a courtesy call on the President of Israel, Prof. Ephraim Katzir. That evening he was the guest of the Mayor of Jerusalem, Mr. Teddy Kollek.

In four hectic days he made personal contact with many influential

---
*South African Digest, April 16, 1976

Israelis throughout the country.

The three main Israeli newspapers all carried editorials welcoming the news that Mr. Vorster would be arriving. One carried its comments under the heading "a very welcome visit." The influential *Jerusalem Post* said: "He has proved himself to be that very rare creature—a political leader who has educated himself to the need of recharting his country's racial and foreign policy in response to a changing reality."

Mr. Vorster is the second South African Prime Minister to pay an official visit to Israel. The late Dr. D. F. Malan was there in 1953—the first foreign Prime Minister to visit Israel since its establishment in 1948.

The two countries are involved in a number of joint projects and trade is being expanded. Diplomatic relations were raised to ambassadorial level in January.

Mr. Vorster has visited ten other countries in Africa, Europe and South America on six publicised visits since 1970. His policy is to seek to normalise relations between South Africa and all non-communist and anti-communist states.

The South African and Israeli premiers, Mr. B. J. Vorster and Mr. Yitzhak Rabin, have committed themselves to peace in their areas, reports Ormande Pollok.

The leaders were speaking at a banquet given in Jerusalem on the eve of the South African Prime Minister's departure after his successful four-day visit to Israel as guest of Mr. Rabin.

The banquet was attended by about half of the Israeli Cabinet. Mr. Rabin said South Africans could understand the historic and spiritual meaning of Israel's battle for independence. However the battle for peace had not yet been won. Israel would never give up.

Mr. Vorster, replying said: "Peace is what we all seek ... I have dedicated myself to work for peace in Africa. There might be temporary setbacks but in the end I have no doubt that those who desire peace will do the utmost to try to bring it about."

Mr. Rabin praised the contribution of South African Jews to Israel and said that Israel had always, from the time of General Smuts (a former Premier), found sympathy in South Africa for the return of the people to Zion.

b. Hands Across Africa*

The Prime Minister, Mr. B. J. Vorster, last week announced an economic, scientific and industrial pact with Israel through the establishment of a joint Cabinet committee of the two countries.

Making the announcement at a press conference in Jerusalem at the end of his four-day visit to Israel, as guest of the Israeli Premier, Mr.

South African Digest, April 23, 1976.

Yitzhak Rabin, Mr. Vorster said: "We have decided to establish a ministerial joint committee comprising Ministers of South Africa and Israel."

He added that the committee would meet at least once a year to make an overall review of economic relations between the two countries and would discuss ways and means of expanding economic co-operation and trade.

A steering group would be established to regulate the exchange of information and ideas.

Among the aims of the committee would be an expansion of investments, development of trade, scientific and industrial co-operation and joint projects using South African raw material and Israeli manpower, he said.

The formation of the committee at Cabinet level to strengthen the ties between the two countries is seen in Jerusalem as setting the seal on a visit which is viewed as a success from every angle, reports Sapa.

South African exports of iron and steel to Israel are rising rapidly. They have increased from 30,000 tons in 1973 to an estimated 170,000 tons, and Israel aims to boost this to 200,000 tons annually, reports Sapa.

Industrial links are also being forged between the two countries. The South African Railways is participating in a multi-million rand railway project in Israel, while Israel is building a seawater desalination project in South Africa.

The Israeli export drive led to the arrival in Cape Town in February this year of the first consignment of Jaffa citrus. The Israeli citrus exchange representative said at the time that the fruit would supplement the local supply and help improve existing trade relations between South Africa and Israel.

c. Vorster Visits Southern Sinai*

Masada, Israel, April 10 (UPI) — Prime Minister John Vorster of South Africa toured the mountain fortress of Masada today, ascending by cablecar and wooden steps to the last Jewish stronghold in the uprising against Roman rule in A.D. 66 to 73.

Earlier in the day, Mr. Vorster visited the southern tip of the occupied Sinai Desert and said the area was strategically important to Israel. He is combining sightseeing and official talks during his four-day visit to Israel and toured the town of Ophir at Sharm el-Sheik and a nearby naval base guarding the Strait of Tiran.

"Vorster told newsmen relations between South Africa and Israel have never been so good," an Israeli broadcast said. "He did not think this would harm South Africa's relations with its Arab oil suppliers."

*New York Times, April 11, 1976.

d. Vorster Visit to Israel Arouses Criticism*

Terence Smith

Jerusalem, April 17—The visit here this week by Prime Minister John Vorster of South Africa produced a spate of headlines, four days of speeches about Israeli-South African friendship and, at its conclusion, a sweeping new economic-cooperation pact.

But the visit also raised some questions, both among Israelis and abroad, as to the wisdom and desirability of the burgeoning relationship between Jerusalem and Pretoria. It was challenged at home on both moral and pragmatic grounds, and abroad by friendly Western countries such as the Netherlands, which expressed official concern at the visit.

According to diplomatic sources, the Dutch Government advised Israel that the visit would complicate the efforts of Israel's friends abroad to persuade the world that there is no connection between Zionism and racism.

Predictably, the visit was attacked by the Organization of African States and a spokesman for the Arab League in Cairo. The criticism was echoed by a commentary in the Soviet party paper *Pravda* denouncing the "racist-Zionist alliance against the African and Arab liberation movements."

Despite the negative reactions, Israeli officials seemed largely satisfied by the visit and the improved relations called for under the new pact. The agreement is expected to result in an immediate expansion of two-way trade, utilization of South African raw materials and skilled Israeli manpower in joint projects, and the stepping up of already cordial scientific relations.

It may also involve a major expansion of the arms supply relationship, although both Governments denied that this was discussed. There were persistent reports that South Africa was prepared to finance an expansion of Israel's arms-producing capacity and was interested in purchasing the Israeli-built Kfir jet fighter.

Mr. Vorster described such reports as "utter nonsense," but his lengthy visit to the Kfir factory served to increase speculation that a major deal was in the making.

There was also speculation, again unconfirmed, that South Africa had agreed to provide Israel with supplies of uranium as part of the exchange agreement.

Whatever the actual details of the agreement, the visit underscored the deepening relationship between two countries that find themselves isolated diplomatically and surrounded by hostile states. It is a relationship built on both the similarity of their respective situations and practical economic, military and political considerations.

The formal link between the two countries dates back to 1948, when

*New York Times, April 18, 1976.

South Africa was among the first to recognize Israel's independence. The relationship remained cool through the 1950's and 1960's, however, when Israel spoke out strongly against *apartheid* and built up close contact with the black African states.

All this changed after the 1973 war. All the black African states but three—Malawi, Swaziland and Lesotho—severed diplomatic relations with Israel and began to vote against it in the United Nations. South Africa became Israel's sole substantive supporter on the continent and one of the few governments anywhere not calling for her withdrawal from occupied Arab territory.

At the same time, Israel served a practical purpose for South Africa. It provided a nondiscriminatory market for South African goods and occasionally served to hide the South Africa label. "South African textiles destined for sale in black African countries, for example, were shipped to Israel, finished here, then marketed with a "Made in Israel" label.

e. Mount of Olives and Sharm E-Sheikh: Rabin lauds South Africa's Detente Bid*

Pretoria's efforts for African detente and prosperous coexistence without interference were lauded by Prime Minister Rabin at a dinner in Jerusalem Sunday night in honor of visiting South African Prime Minister John Vorster.

After voicing "South Africa's long support of Israel as a free and independent Jewish State," Mr. Rabin said: "I believe both our countries share the problem of how to build regional dialogue, coexistence and stability in face of foreign-inspired instability and recklessness."

"This is why," he went on, addressing Mr. Vorster, "We here follow with sympathy your own historic efforts to achieve detente on your continent, to build bridges for a secure and better future, to create coexistence that will guarantee a prosperous atmosphere of cooperation for all the African peoples, without outside interference and threat."

Earlier, officials in Jerusalem firmly denied that Vorster was here to buy arms or to set up an "anti-Communist alliance." There has been speculation to this effect in some press reports from Pretoria.

Mr. Vorster himself told newsmen on Friday that talk of an impending arms deal was "utter nonsense." Israel's ambassador to Pretoria, Yitzhak Unna, who is here for the visit, told a radio interviewer that Israel's and South Africa's defense needs were quite different.

Mr. Unna said the visit had no "specific diplomatic goal." It signified the improving relations between the two countries. South Africa had been one of the few countries that had not turned its back on Israel after the

*The Jerusalem Post Weekly, 13 April 1976.

Yom Kippur War, the envoy noted, and relations had become increasingly normalized since the two countries had raised the level of their representations to full embassies following the war.

He said South Africans regarded Israel as frontline bulwark against Soviet expansionism. The invitation to Mr. Vorster by no means implied approval for South Africa's *apartheid* system, Mr. Unna added. Israel maintained normal relations with many states whose internal systems it did not approve of—and vice versa.

Mr. Vorster was quoted by Israel Radio as commenting during a tour to Sharm e-Sheikh Saturday that "relations with Israel have never been so good." He did not think, the radio said, that his visit here would harm South Africa's relations with its Arab oil suppliers.

The visit to Sharm e-Sheikh was the first by a visiting head of government. Mr. Vorster commented to his Israeli guides that he could well understand the strategic significance of the place.

Accompanied by the commander of the Navy, Aluf Binyamin Telem, Mr. Vorster visited the nearby naval base and toured a Reshef class missile boat.

Mr. Vorster and his party flew to Sharm in an Arkia Herald, flying low over the Santa Katarina monastery en route. From Sharm, they flew to Masada, where they heard an account of the Zealots' last stand from archaeologist Gideon Ferster.

Mr. Vorster, who flew into Israel late Thursday night with his Foregin Minister, Hilgard Muller, their wives, 12 officials and 14 newsmen, began his visit on Friday morning with a service at the Yad Vashem Holocaust Memorial. "Remarkable," he commented in a low voice, as Memorial director Yitzhak Arad explained the exhibits.

Vorster himself had opposed his country's participation on the side of the Allies in World War Two, and was interned for anti-Allies activities.

He listened with bowed head as South African clergyman intoned psalms in Afrikaans, and a cantor sang the El Male Rahanim prayer for the dead. Then he laid a wreath in his country's national colors and kindled the "eternal flame."

From Yad Vashem the motorcade headed for the Israel Museum where South African-born curator, Mrs. Hadassah Levin, guided Vorster and his party around the Shrine of the Book. The visiting Premier, who was plainly fascinated by the ancient Isaiah manuscript, swapped Biblical verses in Afrikaans with Mrs. Levin.

The party then toured Bethlehem as guest of Mayor Elias Freij. On Friday afternoon Mr. Vorster paid a courtesy call on President Katzir. He spent the evening with Mayor Teddy Kollek and guests at the mayor's home.

Mr. and Mrs. Vorster spent Palm Sunday visiting Christian sites in Jerusalem and Galilee.

They first attended prayers at the Garden Tomb in Nablus Road, then visited the Mount of Olives.

As the Vorsters stood viewing the panorama below them, a group of tourists from South Africa's Natal provinces drove up in a minibus, spotted their Prime Minister and began singing the South African national anthem, in Afrikaans.

The Prime Minister turned to the tourists, took off his hat and stood silently.

He then walked over to the dozen tourists and started shaking hands. "This is a very emotional moment for me," he was quoted as saying in Afrikaans. "I appreciate it very much."

A member of his party told *The Jerusalem Post* afterwards that Vorster's party had been very impressed by the beauty of the holy places, and the very good condition in which they are kept.

They were due to leave Israel yesterday, after visiting an Air Force base and the Israel Aircraft Industries.

f. Israel's South African Ties*

Benjamin Pogrund

[Benjamin Pogrund reports from South Africa of the speculation and surprise that accompanied Prime Minister John Vorster's recent visit to Israel and the Israeli-South African accord that concluded his visit.]

South Africans have been astonished by the Israel-South Africa pact agreed to during Prime Minister John Vorster's visit. Widely welcomed in public comment, the details and far-ranging nature of the pact far exceed anything which had been thought might result from the visit.

Some anxiety is, however, being expressed as to whether the "enigmatic embrace," as one newspaper has termed it, might lead to an escalation of attacks on both South Africa and Israel.

The very fact that Mr. Vorster went to Israel came as a surprise. Not many countries in the world have been willing to have South African leaders pay official visits; the last one by Mr. Vorster was just over a year ago, to Paraguay.

The Israeli visit, when it became known, received support here as being desirable from South Africa's point of view, in helping the country to break out still further from its international isolation and in giving Mr. Vorster the opportunity to hear new views and to see new places.

Afrikaaners were especially enthusiastic. A Calvinist, deeply religious people, their view of Israel is that of the Land of the Bible. Still more, they identify closely with Israel, seeing a similarity of interest in two "White" nations, at the head and foot of the African continent, waging lonely

---

*Jerusalem Post, April 20, 1976.

fights for survival against overwhelming Black numbers supported by international Communism. They believe that they—and Israel—are misunderstood by the world and are the victims of betrayal by those who should be their friends.

With all this, the announcement of the economic, scientific and industrial pact and the creation of an inter-Cabinet committee, revealing an undreamt-of degree of cooperation and friendship, was startling.

Among whites, there has been a warm response cutting across political and language lines. Predictably, the Government-supporting newspapers have been more lyrical in their acceptance and praise than their English-language counterparts, paying full tribute to Mr. Vorster for his "personal triumph."

Even while congratulating Mr. Vorster on the pact, the English papers have tended to voice their concern that it could backfire, inflaming the enemies of both South Africa and Israel to greater efforts against them. It is noted that the deal between the two countries helps to "whitewash" *apartheid,* and it is wondered what powerful incentives encouraged the association when so many ostensible disadvantages, particularly to Israel, could flow from it.

The answers seen here are, on the one hand, that the common desire for survival has dictated the course of action followed by both South Africa and Israel, and on the other hand, the hope is expressed that Israel will use the economic leverage offered by the pact to seek to persuade South Africa to change its racially discriminatory ways.

The worries about the troubles the pact could trigger off have also been considered by some Afrikaans papers. But the conclusion is that both South Africa and Israel will gain from their association, will become stronger, and hence will be in a better position to stand up to their respective enemies.

The South African Jewish community, speaking through its leaders, has no reservations about the matter. A headline in one newpaper sums it up: "Jews Hail Vorster." It cannot be said whether the irony of the headline was deliberate or accidental. In any event, it has been greeted as "a most imaginative act of statesmanship on the part of both countries," with the point also being made that South African Jews "would obviously have an extremely positive attitude to the agreement because of their ties with both countries."

It must be accepted, however, that even though not stated in public, there are South African Whites of Liberal persuasion, whether Jewish or non-Jewish, who have a somewhat different view. For the opinion expressed by such people is that they are stunned by Israel giving *apartheid* South Africa a degree of acceptance, for whatever reason, which no other country in the world has up to now been willing to do.

It is equally certain that among the country's Black population, much of the opinion will be even more antagonistic towards Israel for its support of the South African system. This view, naturally, will be fully shared in independent Black Africa and is presumably a factor taken into account by the Israeli Government in deciding to have such close relations with South Africa.

Without a doubt, Mr. Vorster has pulled off a major triumph. His seeking out of friendly relations with Israel also reflects his disillusionment with the West, and with the U.S. in particular, because of the lack of support for South Africa in its Angolan involvement.

In a way, by flying in the face of world opinion through teaming up with Israel, Mr. Voster is trying to assert his own independence and non-reliance on the West.

g. Israel's Shortsighted Policy on South Africa*

Naomi Chazan

Israel's South African connection has been one of the most sensitive issues in Israeli foreign policy. Two major schools of thought have evolved.

The first, the ethical one, opposes relations with South Africa on moral grounds. Its proponents claim that links with a white supremacist regime are abhorrent to the fundamental humanitarian principle on which Israel was founded. The second approach justifies Israel's ties with South Africa in national-interest terms.

Supporters of the current policy of rapprochement state that practical military, political, and economic concerns outweigh other considerations at this point. They bolster their argument by pointing to the unprofitable returns resulting from the Israeli effort in Black Africa, and suggest that stronger ties with South Africa are a natural by-product of Black Africa's wholesale rupture of relations with Israel.

A closer look at the substance and the repercussions of Israeli relations with South Africa raises serious doubts about the extent to which these ties further Israel's national interests. In fact, the long term consequences of the present policy may yet prove positively detrimental to Israeli foreign and domestic concerns.

A number of short-term Israeli interests are said to lie at the core of the South African connection. The first is economic. South Africa is a major producer of certain raw materials, notably diamonds, that are in demand in Israel. It has also been said that South Africa offers a ready-made market for Israeli manufactured goods. The trade record, however, is nothing short of dismal. Trade with South Africa accounts for but 3 per cent of Israel's overall trade. Israel has consistently had a negative trade

*Interchange, Vol. 1, No. 9, May 1976.

balance with South Africa, importing about three times as much as it exports. Moreover, the volume of trade with Black Africa, even after the break in diplomatic relations, has been greater, in absolute terms, than that with South Africa.

A second Israeli interest raised in connection with South Africa concerns the Jewish community there. Israel has always viewed the condition of the 120,000 Jews of South Africa as a matter of interest to it. This concern is not merely fraternal. The South African Jewish community is the wealthiest, per capita, in the world. Its Zionist Federation is well organized and active. Its contributions to Israel have always been generous. The supply of funds from South Africa's Jews (except for a short period in 1971 when the flow of contributions to Israel was temporarily halted by the South African Government in reaction to an Israeli donation to African liberation movements), has been steady despite shifts in the state of formal relations between the two countries.

While the significance of the South African Jewish community should not be belittled, there is room to question whether Israel must, or indeed can, act as a guardian of South African Jewry. There are many instances of Israeli non-support for regimes of countries in which Jews reside; South Africa need not be an exception.

A third component in Israel-South African relations is the military one. Although details on this factor are necessarily sketchy, there are indications that it is more weighty than the minimal benefits accruing to Israel from her other linkages with South Africa.

In the past few years cultural and political ties with South Africa have been added to the network of Israeli relations with that country. Whatever the immediate benefits Israel has derived from these links, the implications for Israel of her pragmatic policy have been nothing short of negative. The strengthening of relations with South Africa has become a very real obstacle in Israeli attempts to revive diplomatic relations with Black Africa. The South African connection has further alienated Israel from the Third World and made the possibility of rapprochement with these countries remote.

Moreover, the South African alliance has linked Israel, even if wrongly, with the most conservative and reactionary forces in the international arena. Such an image, pragmatists may suggest, need not in itself be a cause for concern. But this argument can hold only if backed by tangible political returns. These do not exist in this case. South Africa has been effectively ostracized from the United Nations and other international forums, and it has no political clout in global gatherings. The resolution of the General Assembly, condemning Zionism as a form of racism and racial discrimination akin to *apartheid,* is the most serious result to date of the general tendency to juxtapose Israel with South Africa.

There is thus very real danger that the few Afro-Asian states that have not voted against Israel in the UN will be driven to do so because of the

South African link just as many African states recognized the MPLA in Angola as a reaction to South Africa's intervention on behalf of UNITA.

h. Israel Takes On An Odd New Ally*

Felix Kessler

Jerusalem—"What do we have in common with South Africa?" says the young Israeli secretary. "Well, their neighbors want to throw them into the sea, too."

The question of what Israel seeks in promoting closer ties with South Africa increasingly is being asked here, following South African Prime Minister John Vorster's recent visit and the announcement that both countries envisage greater cooperation and trade links.

It is a question that troubles many Israelis, on moral and practical grounds. One high government official provides an emotional glimpse into some of these self-doubts when he sputters about the "hypocrisy" and "moral ambivalence" of many other nations, particularly European, on such issues.

"Here are the British, the French and now even the Italians falling over themselves trying to sell more arms to the Arabs," he says, "and then they lecture us about Vorster."

Yet there's no denying that he, like many Israelis, is troubled by some implications of Israel's deepening South African connection. South Africa's racial policies aren't "morally right," he says. "We don't approve of *apartheid* and are absolutely appalled" at its social implications. There's a political background to his indignation. He's particularly incensed over an American television program that recently depicted Israel's treatment of its large Arab minority as a form of "unofficial *apartheid.*"

Israel doesn't, of course, have an official (or even unofficial) policy remotely resembling South Africa's stringent racial laws and customs.

Legally, Israel's Arab citizens are entitled to the same rights as Jews. In practice, however, this Jewish-oriented society has provided Arabs with more limited educational, economic and political opportunities.

Most Israelis acknowledge this, though their consciences aren't necessarily troubled by this development. One view, as stated by a writer in *The Jerusalem Post,* holds that "Israel's Arabs should remember that they have no less than 20 states of all conceivable political shades dedicated to Arab nationalist goals. The Jews have only one state in which to express their national identity." In other words, Israel is a Jewish state—love it or leave it.

This isn't, of course, the only Israeli viewpoint. Others find it self-destructive for Israel, surrounded by hostile neighboring states, to alienate

---

*Wall Street Journal, April 23, 1976.

these Arab citizens who seek the benefits of fuller integration *within* the Jewish state, not its annihilation. "It's our luck that they want to share the advantage of being Israelis," says Mattityahu Peled, a former Israeli general and a dovish critic of government policy.

Mr. Peled is sardonic about the "sudden love for South Africa" exhibited by many Israelis and apparently the government. In the past, he recalls, Israel had consistently voted in the United Nations to condemn South African racial policies. Today, he says, many Israelis tend to exaggerate the similarities between the countries, perhaps because each appears increasingly besieged and friendless.

Much criticism voiced here of the government's new-found kinship with South Africa is based on fears that it helps paint Israel deeper into its political corner. Some critics find such friendship as a form of political bravado, perhaps an outgrowth of Israel's siege mentality, to embark on this alliance with its predictable adverse consequences, and then to rail against international criticism.

The terms of the new economic cooperation pact between Israel and South Africa haven't been spelled out. Although Mr. Vorster toured Israeli aircraft and naval facilities, he denied reports that the visit heralded a major arms-supply relationship. There also were rumors that South Africa was preparing to supply Israel with uranium, and that Israel was training South Africans in security techniques.

"Israel is in the survival business," says an American-born Israeli. "Survival is harsh. Not everybody is our friend, and we're kind of isolated. Now we're in a tight corner and that kind of cuts your priorities."

Those Israelis who justify the growing South African links do so in long-term, pragmatic terms. Yet the benefits of South African trade haven't been visibly great in the past. At least 14 other nations—including Switzerland, Sweden, Denmark and Rumania—in recent years have been more important trading partners than South Africa, which accounts for only 3% of Israel's overall trade. (It should be pointed out, however, that Israel does provide South Africa with a market such as in textile-finishing, where goods frequently have been re-exported to black African nations. Arms sales also aren't computed in the trade figures.)

The South African connection is particularly ironic following the public rage displayed by the government (and most Israelis) when the UN condemned Zionism as a form of racism akin to *apartheid*. In this light, the political blurring of the two policies today could be seen benefiting only South Africa at the expense of Israel.

Mr. Vorster tried to emphasize this point by noting at a press conference—at which he evaded most questions—that Israel and South Africa enjoyed "similarities in many, many instances, from climatic conditions upwards."

For some reason, Prime Minister Yitzhak Rabin went even further in discovering the two countries' similarities in a toast to Mr. Vorster at the

South African's farewell dinner here. Mr. Rabin said Israel was following "with sympathy your own historic efforts to achieve detente on your own continent, to build bridges for a secure and better future, to create coexistence that will guarantee a prosperous atmosphere of cooperation for all the African peoples, without outside interference and threat."

Perhaps some of Israel's attachment to South Africa is a reaction to the worsening relations with the U.S. Israeli politicians are hardly playing down rifts with America these days or de-emphasizing their displeasure over President Ford's slicing of $550 million of U.S. aid. Critics of the government, however, say that this would represent a pointless show of political pique, with temporary benefits at best.

An Israeli government official, whose outrage over the UN's anti-Zionism vote is recalled by a visitor, responds that this nation has been forced into its ambivalent stance in recent months. "We've been driven into an unhappy frame of mind," he says.

i. "Middle-Level" Power Alliance*

For South Africa, the benefits derived from Vorster's visit to Israel seem increasingly significant. The *apartheid* regime anticipates that the Economic, Industrial, and Scientific Pact signed with Israel will give South African goods duty free access to the European Common Market and the US. Israel has agreements with the Common Market and the US Government which give Israel "most favored nation" status. Under the new agreement, the *apartheid* regime can send its "semi-finished" goods to Israel, where they would be "finished," stamped with a "made-in-Israel" label, and then sold to European and American consumers. Thus, this agreement will allow South Africa to circumvent any economic boycott campaigns. Additionally, the South African Council for Scientific and Industrial Research announced that there will be joint South African-Israeli conferences on scientific topics to be held annually. *(Star,* Johannesburg, Apr. 17, June 5, 1976).

Meanwhile South Africa's much declared admiration for Israel's military tactics against the Palestinian liberation groups has produced a lot of speculation that the Israeli Army is providing counter-insurgency training to the South African military. A member of the Knesset (the Israeli Parliament) from the Independent Socialist Movement, Ms. Marcia Friedman, has charged that hundreds of Israeli soldiers were attached to important units and major bases in South Africa and have participated in training maneuvers with the South African army. The African National Congress stated that "the cooperation between Israel and South Africa [has as its] design a war of aggression against their neighboring states and the

---

*Southern Africa, Vol. IX, No. 7, August 1976.

liberation movements." *(New York Times,* June 1, 1976; *Noticias,* Maputo, Apr. 14, 1976).

This success on economic, political, and military affairs produced by the visit to Israel has propelled the *apartheid* regime to advance a new strategy to maintain itself in power. It will now seek alliances with "middle-level" world powers. On April 22, in Parliament, Vorster stated that he believed "non-communistic and anti-communistic [*sic*] countries can work happily together economically, in spite of differences in internal policies and differences in outlook" and it was necessary for "middle-level" powers to cooperate. Besides the states of Central Europe, the *apartheid* regime will probably seek a formal alliance between the right-wing police state regimes (supported by U.S. military assistance) that exist in the Middle East, Latin America, and Asia. In fact, such regimes have a lot in common with South Africa's *apartheid* regime; they all use violence to eliminate the democratic opposition and to prevent a redistribution of the wealth to the people. One such "middle-level" power, Taiwan, has upgraded its diplomatic ties with South Africa to the ambassadorial level. A possible European candidate for the new alliance, Austria, has recently expressed its interest in exchanging South African iron ore for Austrian technical expertize. Last April, a group of 70 Austrian professors, researchers, and students affiliated to the University of Graz's technical school toured ISCOR projects. As a result of the tour, the group's leader— Professor Waldenmarfied, who is a leading Austrian industrialist—announced that Austria wants to participate in the Saldanha-Sighen project. Meanwhile Finland, another European country South Africa would want to include in its projected alliance, has stated that it is re-examining its trade ties with South Africa. *(Star,* Johannesburg, Apr. 24, 26, May 15, 22, 1976).

j. Protest Against the Open Alliance with the Racist South African Regime*

Dear Prime Minister Rabin—The undersigned members and friends of Givat Haviva Educational Foundation in the United States express their shock and dismay at the news of Prime Minister Vorster's visit to Israel for the reported purpose of arranging a major sale of Israel arms to the South African government. Nothing would contribute more to heightening the damage done by the reprehensible UN resolutions on Zionism than for Israel to emerge in open alliance with the racist South African regime. As Zionists, we strongly urge you to reconsider—telegram sent April 4, 1976, signed by sixteen supports of Givat Haviva.

*Interchange, Vol. 1, No. 9, May 1976.

[27] African Response

Despite African protests [27] the consolidation of Israeli-South African links remained the order of the day [28].

a. Kaunda, Machel Warn of Conflict*

Lusaka—The Presidents of Zambia and Mozambique have jointly condemned the new ties between South Africa and Israel as "a racist-fascist alliance directed at continued domination and oppression of the people of South Africa and Palestine."

In a joint communique issued at the end of the five-day state visit to Mozambique by President Kaunda of Zambia, the two leaders declared their continued opposition to *apartheid* as "a racist and fascist system" condemned by the entire world.

The two Presidents said the victories of Frelimo, the MPLA and the PAIGC had "smashed the myth that an oppressed African people cannot successfully take up arms and inflict humiliating defeats on colonialist, imperialist, racist and fascist forces."

President Machel, said the communique, "stressed that the unity of the progressive and revolutionary forces constituted a solid and indestructible base to launch sharp demolishing strikes against the common enemy."

The Presidents reiterated their decision to establish a permanent joint commission to foster economic and other cooperation between Zambia and Mozambique.

In a speech at Beira over the weekend, President Kaunda warned that Southern Africa was about to be enveloped in a conflagration in which many lives would be lost.

According to a report in the *Sunday Times* of Zambia he said Black Africans would not be to blame for this racial conflict, because it was not their choice.

b. Statement of the African National Congress of South Africa to the International Forum on Zionism and Racism Held in Tripoli—24th to 27th July, 1976

This international forum on Zionism and Racism is taking place at a time when the racist South African regime of Vorster has demonstrated to the world its true fascist nature by its brutal massacre of unarmed people, many of whom were children of ages ranging from 13 to about 16 years. This forum is also taking place at a time when the heroic people of Palestine, under the leadership of the PLO, are in the grips of a struggle

---

*Star, May 1, 1976.

against their enemy and that of mankind i.e. Zionism. It is taking place at a time when the zionists and racists are trying to weaken the liberation movements at all costs. ...

As you may be aware, the people of South Africa have for many years now, been waging a relentless struggle against the successive white racist regimes of that country, a relentless struggle for the seizure of political power which the racists have made their exclusive possession, in the same way that the zionists have done in Palestine. The successive white minority regimes of South Africa have deprived our people of their land and today have created what they call Bantustans or homelands. Thousands of our people, because of their opposition to the racist policies of the regimes, have been forced to leave their fatherland to live in foreign lands as refugees or second class citizens. This is what the zionists have done to our Palestinian brothers and sisters. This is a clear attempt by the racists to weaken the liberation through the creation of tribal Bantustans.

In order to make the majority of the population forever dependent on the white minority whilst they themselves remain divided the racist regime has created the so-called Bantustans which comprise about 13% of the total land area of the country and are supposed to be occupied by over 70% of the population of the country. These Bantustans are barren, unproductive and scattered pieces of land which have already failed to maintain the 7 million people that have been forcibly removed to those areas. There is no work for the people in these areas and thus they are forced to return to the so-called white South Africa to sell their labour at extremely sub-human salaries and while there, to be treated as temporary sojourners in the country of their birth. In the Bantustans themselves, the so-called leaders have been chosen by the racist white regime and not by the people themselves and are today doing the dirty work for the racists. The African National Congress condemned the creation of these Bantustans as a fraud, an attempt to fragment and balkanise our country for the comfort of the white minority and international monopolies who reap huge profits from the super-exploitation of our people.

The political and economic power in the country is completely in their hands, while the majority of the population, the black people, are treated as tools of labour in the white-owned factories, mines, farms and homes. Since 1960, the political organizations of the black people have been outlawed and many of their leaders like Nelson Mandela, Walter Sisula and Govan Mbeki have been sentenced to life imprisonment on the infamous Robben Island, merely because they dared to oppose the inhuman racist policies of the regime whereby a white skin means superiority and privilege and a black or brown skin means inferiority, oppression and deprivation. This banning of the peoples organization has however not destroyed them but has made them to become even more militant and more determined to achieve their goal—the liberation of their people and country.

Like the PLO, the African National Congress is fighting for the birthright of the oppressed, super-exploited and landless people of South Africa. We say that our country is large enough to accommodate all the people, black and white, who live in it. It would be racialistic of us if we aimed at driving the whites into the sea, this is why we say let us live together as equals and forming one solid nation.

This the racist regime has refused, and is determined to use all its military hardware to safeguard the interests of the white minority and international monopolies, as they have lately done in Soweto and other townships.

Only a few months ago, Vorster, the so-called Prime Minister of South Africa, a known fascist, paid a visit to Israel accompanied by his military and state security chiefs, revealing the close ties between zionism and racism. The results of this visit are already visible: while the Zionists invaded Uganda, the racists invaded the People's Republic of Angola and Zambia. While the zionists were breeding squabbles among the natural allies and supporters of the PLO in order to weaken the latter, the racists are doing the same in Africa. It is the duty of the progressive and democratic forces of the world to be extremely vigilant and to give all their support to the liberation movements, just as the imperialist forces such as the USA, Britain, France and West Germany are giving support in the form of weapons to the South African racists and to the zionists, weapons that are not only used against the liberation forces but also against independent and sovereign States.

As we are meeting here today, the Convention that declares *apartheid* a punishable crime against humanity, has been ratified, yet the French are helping South Africa to develop into a nuclear power the same as the USA is giving that possibility to the Zionists. The two evils, racism as represented by Pretoria and Zionism by Tel-Aviv will soon pose a real threat to both African and Arab States. This then calls for even closer Afro-Arab unity, for more support to the PLO and the liberation movements in Southern Africa so as to allow them to destroy the Zionist and the racist regimes before they become nuclear powers.

The ANC of South Africa calls, through this international forum, on the world not to recognise the independence of the so-called Bantustans and to endorse the OAU resolution that maintains that recognition of the Bantustans will be treachery not only to the people and the liberation movement of South Africa but to Africa as a whole. ...

[28] Consolidation of Relations

a. South African Link to Israel Grows (Closer Relations Reported to Include the Delivery of Military Material)*

William E. Farrell

Jerusalem, Aug. 17—Israel's diplomatic and commercial ties to South Africa have increased dramatically in recent months in a strengthened relationship between the two countries that reportedly includes the sales of Israeli-manufactured military equipment.

While there is little hesitance on the part of Israeli officials to discuss the growing commercial trade between the two nations, these officials are reluctant to discuss the military transactions. Nevertheless, information has been seeping out in various quarters, including the foreign press and the Israeli radio. These disclosures include the following:

—An Israeli radio report that Israel is building at its Haifa shipyard two long-range gunboats armed with sea-to-sea missiles for the South African navy. Other accounts place the number of boats at six. The 420-ton boats cost about $6 million without armaments. With missiles the cost is estimated at $18 million a boat.

—Reports that about 50 South African naval personnel, on temporary civilian status, are training in the Tel Aviv area to man the missile boats, with the expectation that the first of the vessels will be ready in January.

—Unconfirmed reports that the sales agreement with South Africa includes delivery of up to two dozen Israeli-built Kfir jet planes.

—Reports that in exchange for South African raw materials, including an estimated one million tons of coal a year to buoy the Israeli steel industry, the Israelis would provide South Africa with advanced military electronic equipment.

Criticism Is Feared

Israeli officials are loath to discuss the reported military aspects of the exchanges between the two countries because of South Africa's pariah status among many nations and particularly because of criticism expected in the United States from such quarters as the black Congressional caucus and from liberal American-Jewish groups.

The Israeli Government has long opposed Prime Minister John Vorster's racial policies and any inquiries concerning Israel's current dealings with South Africa elicit a re-affirmation of that opposition.

Mr. Vorster visited Israel in April, the first such visit by a South African Prime Minister in 24 years. During his stay, Mr. Vorster told re-

---

New York Times, August 18, 1976.

porters that he had discussions with Prime Minister Yitzhak Rabin and Foreign Minister Yigal Allon dealing with "ways to expand trade, encourage investments, the setting up of joint scientific and cultural ventures and loans for the joint utilization of South African raw materials." At the time, he denied reports of an arms deal.

Such reports grew in intensity after Mr. Vorster had toured an Israeli missile boat at a naval base near Sharm El Sheik and after he had visited the Israeli Aircraft Industries plant near Tel Aviv, which manufactures Kfir fighter planes.

Foreign Policy Justified

Government officials here justify Israel's stepped-up dealings with South Africa in a number of ways, including:

—A contention that such dealings are consistent with a foreign policy that sanctions diplomacy with any nation wishing to pursue diplomatic relations with Israel.

—A pragmatic rationale based on the country's inflation rate, estimated this year at about 30 percent, and its strong need for foreign currency and raw materials.

—The fact that Arab pressure forced many black African nations into severing diplomatic relations with Israel in 1973, including countries in which Israel had made major "good neighbor" gestures over the years. Israeli opponents of the Government's increased dealings with South Africa say the policy is a shortsighted one that will seriously impede Israel's efforts to restore the severed relations with black Africa.

—A contention that declining South Africa's offer of amity might have an adverse affect on that country's small, generally wealthy, and mostly Zionist community of 120,000 Jews.

A number of Israeli Government officials are irked by what they consider to be the special attention being given to the country's dealings with South Africa. They contend that they are being subjected to a double standard since many other countries, not necessarily enamored to South Africa's racial policies, also have dealings there.

b. South Africans Training in Israel*

Tel Aviv, Aug. 9 (JTA) — A group of 50 South African navy personnel are in Israel training to operate Israeli-built missile boats, Kol Israel reported last night. The Israeli radio station said Israel is building for South Africa two of the boats which are of the Reshef class, the same type that participated in New York's Operation Sail July 4. The first boat, equipped with Israeli Gabriel sea-to-sea missiles, is expected to be delivered early next year, according to the radio. The radio also reported that an Israeli-designed coastal patrol boat will be built under license in South Africa.

*Jewish Telegraphic Agency, Daily News Bulletin, August 10, 1976.

c. Israel and Africa*

Despite efforts by both sides to play it down, a major expansion of Israeli-South African relations is under way following recent visits to Jerusalem by Prime Minister John Vorster and Labor and Mining Minister Stephanus Botha. South Africa has bought two of Israel's 415-ton Reshef missile ships and will get four more. South African crews reportedly are training in Haifa. (Reports of purchases of Israel's new Kfir jet fighters are denied but persist.) The two countries will also team up in Israel to build a railroad, a steel-rolling mill and a hydro-electric plant that will use Mediterranean water diverted into the Dead Sea valley. Israel has placed a major order for South African coal and the Vorster government is showing keen interest in Israeli electronic and control equipment.

*Newsweek, August 23, 1976.

d. Israeli Soldiers 'In Namibia'

John Borrell

Lusaka—The South-west Africa People's Organisation (SWAPO) claims that South Africa is employing Israelis and British mercenaries to help it control a 20-mile wide buffer zone being created along Namibia's borders with Angola and Zambia.

The movement's president, Mr. Sam Nujoma, said in an interview here today that SWAPO had proof of the presence of Israeli counter insurgency experts and British mercenaries in the buffer zone.

[An Israeli Defence Ministry spokesman said in Tel-Aviv today he had no information about Israelis helping to control the Namibian border. The spokesman said: "I do not know about any Israelis doing this sort of job in South Africa or any other part of Africa."]

Mr. Nujoma said that the British mercenaries had been working for the South African Government for nearly four years and were engaged in the installation of electronic devices to detect guerrillas trying to cross the buffer zone. The South Africans, he went on, had recently started using Israelis in the buffer zone because, as he put it, they acknowledge them as experts in desert warfare.

When asked what proof he had of Israeli involvement in Namibia, Mr. Nujoma replied: "Our guerrilla forces have evidence that there are Israelis there." Pressed further, he said that people living in villages along the border had seen the Israelis wearing South African Army uniforms.

"Our people identified them by their facial features and by the fact that they spoke Hebrew among themselves and appeared to have no

*Guardian, August 23, 1976.

knowledge of Afrikaans," Mr. Nujoma said.

The SWAPO leader pointed out that South Africa's Prime Minister, Mr. Vorster, had recently visited Israel where, according to Mr. Nujoma, he reached agreement on setting up joint military operations. "That's clear evidence that there are joint Israeli-South African actions," he said.

Commenting on last week's announcement from Windhoek that the target date for Namibia's independence was December 31, 1978, Mr. Nujoma said his movement would not recognise any South African moves on the territory.

"SWAPO will therefore continue to intensity the armed struggle. We will continue with the fight until genuine democratic freedom and independence is achieved in our country." he said. "We will wage the armed struggle against any puppet regime Vorster installs in Namibia. We will crush it."

Mr. Nujoma denounced the Turnhalle talks in Winhoek as "a mockery of democracy." He said that suggestions Turnhalle delegates should meet with SWAPO in either Zambia or Tanzania were pointless.

"SWAPO is not prepared to talk to the puppet chiefs. They are useless. But we are ready to talk with the South African Government at any time and place with the exception of Namibia. Of course, we will talk only to them on the basis of how and when they withdraw their administration," he said.

e. South-West Africa Group Says Israelis Fight There*

Lusaka, Zambia, Aug. 22 (AP) — The militant South-West Africa People's Organization asserts that Israel is helping South Africa in military operations in South-West Africa, or Namibia, and says it is expecting help from both Cuba and the Soviet Union to step up the guerrilla war there.

The group's leader, Sam Nujoma, charged today that the Israelis were engaged in military operations along the border between South-West Africa and Angola.

"Recently the South Africans began employing Israelis to help them control the buffer zone they have cleared along the Angolan-Namibian border," Mr. Nujoma said here.

South Africa's white minority Government has long ignored United Nations demands that it give up South-West Africa, a former German colony, but a multiracial committee backed by the South African Government recently set Dec. 31, 1978, as the date for independence.

---

*New York Times, August 23, 1976.

[29] Zionist South African/Jewish-American Relationship—Implications for the Future

The "fallout" of Israeli-South African relations on Black Americans and groups concerned about apartheid *brought a Zionist-South African offensive in Jewish visits [29] and in American Jewish Congress statement.*

a. U.S. Editors Tour *Apartheid* State: Zionist-S. African Relations Promoted*

Israel's Ambassador to South Africa Yitzhak Unna told the editors of twelve major U.S. Jewish newspapers who toured South Africa in May that by presenting a positive view of South Africa in their papers they would "be doing South Africa/Israel relations a service" and would also "be doing South Africa a service." Conditions in South Africa are actually much better "than the anti-South Africa propaganda slant tends to make out," Unna told the editors. The Ambassador made this assessment just a month before the South African government's brutal repression of the anti-*apartheid* resistance which broke out in Soweto in June and soon spread elsewhere in South Africa.

The editors' trip was paid for by the South African Tourist Organization, a semi-governmental agency, and Pan American Airlines. The editors were escorted by William Evans of Pan Am's Special Projects and by the general manager of the South African Tourist Organization's New York office. Billed as a visit to the Jewish community in South Africa, the tour was designed to promote Pan Am's new New York-Rio-Johannesburg flight, and tourism to South Africa.

The intentions of the trip's sponsors were outlined in the May 27 issue of *Jewish Weekly* by Philip Hochstein, editor and publisher of that paper and a participant in the tour. "Pan Am's introduction of a new New York to Johannesburg route via Rio de Janeiro has signalled public relations efforts to attract the Jewish tourist. The invitation to the Jewish editors is part of that effort.... South Africa especially wants Jewish tourism because of its potential volume and also because of the hope that a common interest in Israel's survival and in resisting Russian imperial domination may spread understanding abroad of South Africa's uniquely complex race problem and its strategic world role. Confronted by the suggestion that the Russians may undermine South Africa by championing equal rights for Blacks, both could more easily manipulate a prematurely racially integrated South Africa because the whites would then be rendered help-

*Palestine!, July - August 1976.

less by inexperienced Black majority rule."

The official leadership of South Africa's Jewish community, the South African Jewish Board of Deputies, has worked for many years, with uneven success, to win support for or neutrality on *apartheid* from international and U.S. Jewish organizations.

Despite the controversial nature of the tour, no editor declined the free trip for ethical or political reasons, Pan Am's Evans, who selected the editors on the basis of the size of circulation of their papers and geographical distribution, told a writer for *Palestine!*

Jesse Lurie, executive editor of *Hadassah,* said that he had supported the Zionist tourism boycott of Mexico last year because of the Mexican Government's vote for a U.N. resolution denouncing Zionism, along with South African *apartheid,* as a form of racism but said that he had no qualms about encouraging visits to South Africa. Lurie commented, "South Africa is a beautiful country, a fascinating one. There is no reason to boycott it." Lurie added that he had told the South African Minister of Tourism, "You have a beautiful country. It reminds me very much of Israel. It has insoluble problems."

According to Lurie the group had met members of the Jewish Board of Deputies and numerous government officials, but he himself had met only one black South African, a millionaire.

The trip was in line with recent official government measures to strengthen relations between South Africa and Israel. The editors' trip was made shortly after South African Prime Minister Johannes Vorster visited Israel, where he concluded a major trade pact. Vorster, who was jailed during World War II as a general in the South African Nazi organization "Osserwebrandwag," and a member of its military wing, the "Stormjaers," was received warmly by the Israeli government. At a state dinner in Israel, Prime Minister Yitzhak Rabin toasted Vorster, saying, "I believe both our countries share the problem of how to build a regional dialogue, coexistence and stability in the face of foreign-inspired instability and recklessness."

Evans of Pan Am arranged an interview for the twelve editors with Unna, Israel's Ambassador to South Africa, who outlined, according to the *Jewish Press,* "some of the underlying philosophies and reasons behind the unusual closeness that has developed between Israel and South Africa." The interview has since been printed in Jewish newspapers in the U.S.

b. Israel And South Africa: Closeness In A Hostile World*

In an exclusive interview granted to a small group of American Jewish newspaper editors including the *Jewish Press,* Israel's Ambassador to

---

**Jewish Press,* June 18, 1976.

South Africa, Yitzchak Unna, outlined some of the underlying philosophies and reasons behind the unusual closeness that has developed betweeen Israel and South Africa.

In the course of his opening remarks, Ambassador Unna pointed to the sharp increase in trade between South Africa and Israel. In 1969 there was $3 million in trade between the two countries, which in the last seven years has grown to over $80 million. The main imports from South Africa to Israel are steel, iron and other metals; and the major items being shipped from Israel to South Africa are chemical fertilizers, electronic equipment, general machinery as well as fabrics, fashion wear and citrus products. Following are some of the excerpts of that interview:

Question: What are the primary factors in bringing Israel and South Africa together?

Answer: I would say if you ask a South African and in particular an Afrikaner, he will give you three reasons for this closeness. He will say first of all we have a common Biblical heritage, and I would not underrate this feeling. The Afrikaners are a devout Christian Calvinist people, who know the Bible perhaps even better than we do, including the Old Testament, and they make a comparison. You find this very often they make a comparison between the Great Trek of the Afrikaners away from the British to the Transvaal and the Exodus of the Jews from Egypt. And, as I have just said to some friends, as they treked north they would give to the towns and villages where they settled Biblical names like Bethlehem, Bethal which is in Hebrew Bethel, Benoni and so on. So there is a common Biblical heritage which they respect tremendously in Israel. Then there is a feeling which is perhaps a slight oversimplification which the South Africans feel that South Africa and Israel are in the same boat. A small community surrounded by preponderance of hostile neighbors which has to survive. There is a Jewish community here of roughly 117,000 people, Jews who really have an unblemished record of fidelity to Israel, who feel very strongly about Israel, who participate both financially and culturally and spiritually in the upbuilding of Israel who have a very good *aliyah* from here to Israel thanks to the good relations existing between the government of South Africa and Israel. The Jews are really in a way in a privileged position inasmuch as they are able to send funds to Israel, they are able to invest in Israel. All these things, well you can't do it to any other country, you cannot transfer funds to England, you can't transfer funds to the United States, you can invest in Israel so there is a certain privileged position here to which we give recognition in terms of our relations with South Africa, and as I said the growing trade relationship, and also there is over the last two years to three years a growing scientific relationship. South Africa and Israel have many problems in common such as soil conservation, desalination, and more and more scientists from both countries tend to visit the other country, identify areas of mutual interest, work on joint projects and so on and so on. So it is a relationship which is growing progressively closer despite the inherent political difference, which obviously exists between the two countries.

Question: Mr. Ambassador, what do you think of the unusual reaction around the world to the visit to Israel by South Africa's Prime Minister, Mr. Vorster?

Answer: Well, I think too much has been made of the South African Prime Minister's visit to Israel, perhaps I should even say that to certain extent a dual standard has been applied too, because after all a number of years ago, we had the Prime Minister of Roumania in Israel, and when Mrs. Golda Meir visited Roumania and there was no outcry anywhere in the world that Israel is going Communist because we entertained the Roumaniam Prime Minister and the Israel Prime Minister visited Roumania. We have had all kind of heads of states from third world countries in Israel, who are not precisely torchbearers of progressive libertarian thought, and nobody has suggested that Israel is letting down on its liberalism. I think that there is here a tendency, because of the South African Prime Minister has visited Israel, to apply what I would call a dual standard here. The South African Prime Minister himself has said after his visit, that the cooperation between the two countries is an example of two countries cooperating in the economic, industrial and scientific field despite their political differences, we don't mix in South Africa's affairs, South Africa does not tell us what to do, in fact just the other day, Mr. Vorster went so far as to say and South Africa feels free to develop ties with countries which are unfriendly to Israel just as Israel obviously is free to develop ties of friendship with countries which may feel unfriendly towards South Africa. So it is a pragmatic relationship, which I believe, I believe that in the wake of the Prime Minister's visits, the benefits accruing to Israel will increase in terms of, in the economic field especially. Also in the fields of the facilities which will be placed at the disposal of the South African Jewish community to participate more actively than in the past, through investments and other methods in settling or helping Israel to consolidate her economic question. We obviously bore in mind that there would be adverse repercussions in other countries to this visit, but I believe that one has, in a complexed life as one has today, one has to weigh up the pros and cons, there are no solutions which are wholly ideal or are wholly negative, and I think on balance, the South African Prime Minister's visit to Israel will produce something on the profit side of the balance sheet as far as Israel is concerned.

Question: Mr. Ambassador, is it your view that because of the special relationship between South Africa and Israel, that it is the obligation of the Jewish communities in America, Israel or for that matter anywhere, to look favorably upon South Africa?

Answer: Look, I would take my guide line from what the Minister of Tourism — Mr. Marias Steyn said to you last night. South Africa is not a Utopia, in fact very few countries are, even Israel is not a Utopia, we all have our shortcomings, nobody doubts, including the South Africans, that South Africa has its shortcomings, but I do believe that such a visit as yours here, as the guests of the South African Tourist Organization and Pan Am, will enable you to have an honest look at South Africa, you will be able to, I think, divorce hostile propaganda from the reality of the situation, which I believe is far more sanguine than the propaganda the anti-South African propaganda slant tends to make out, and if you in your various papers present an accurate and sincere picture as you see it of South Africa, and I have no doubt that this is what you will be doing, you will be doing South African/Israel relations a service, you will be doing South Africa a service, and I think you will be doing your own intellectual integrity a service. This is as far as I can go.

Question: Mr. Ambassador, in view of the relationship of South Africa with the oil exporting nations how does your position here fit with the geo-politics of this situation?

Answer: Now, of course, South Africa like Israel is dependent on oil imports. Both lean heavily on Iran with whom both South Africa and Israel have very cordial relations. South Africa in addition just had some contacts with some of the Arab countries. There were reports last year that South African Ambassador in London had paid visits to Saudi Arabia, Kuwait, and other rich oil sheikdoms and I think one would be correct in speculating that he did not go there for his health alone. And if one bears in mind that South Africa has gold, which perhaps is attractive to the Arab mentality rather than paper money, there are certain suggestions which might fit the picture.

Question: Mr. Ambassador, could you comment on the military aspects, if any, of Israel's agreements with South Africa?

Answer: Well obviously, when I was with Mr. Vorster in Israel, he was very keenly interested in our army and our navy and our air force and he saw an aerial display, but you know these are, in a political sense, like tourist attractions like the Western Wall, and Mount Zion. One likes to show the military muscle one has. South Africa has a supply line to France, her air force is built on a weapon system supplied by the French. Even assuming Israel were prepared to supply weapon systems to South Africa, which it is not, the French would see to it that nobody else muscles into the market, and they are very effective in keeping other people out. There was no exchange of military deal of any kind, whatsoever, in fact there was no agreement! There has been a slight exaggeration. What happened was that towards the end of the visit, one of the talks between ministers, a suggestion was made that Ministers meet periodically, possibly once a year, to discuss current economic, industrial and scientific cooperation, and in fact we do have such an agreement with the U.S., we have a joint ministerial committe in which Secretary Simon represents the United States and the Minister of Finance Robinowitz represents Israel. They meet every so often, once or twice and sometimes in Israel and sometimes in the United States, but this is purely an *ad hoc* arrangement to deal with current matters, and this is what has been decided on when the South African party was in Israel, that we would establish a machinery to deal with current economic, industrial and scientific matters, and the machinery has not yet been put into motion.

Question: Mr. Ambassador, what of these realistic prospects for Israel's improving relations with the black nations of Africa, how could you assess them, what has been done as far as its prospects?

Answer: Well we do get signals from some of the Black African countries to say that they are rather sorry that they surrendered to Arab blackmail and they feel that they've made a mistake and given the right conditions and right opportunities they would like to resume relations with Israel, and it is interesting here in a South African/Israeli context, see that there is no contradiction because the very same countries which do send out these signals about a willingness in principle, to resume relations with Israel, are also the African countries which do conduct a dialogue policy with South Africa, and I particularly refer to countries like the Ivory Coast, Liberia, the Central African Republic and so on. Plus the few who are prepared to resume relations with us, but not necessarily talk to the South Africans, but on the whole those countries which talk to South Africa are also sort of making noises towards us, in fact our trade again, trades and Israeli exports to Black Africa in 1974 which is the year after the rupture of diplomatic relations with the Black African countries, grew by 65% over 1973. So trade goes on and we are represented commercially in most of the African countries, in fact I would say all African countries except Uganda. Israeli companies continue to function there, and business in many respects goes on as before.

c. Columnist Impressed with *Apartheid**

Just one month after the 12 Jewish newspaper editors visited South Africa, militant protests by black students broke out against aspects of the *aparthied* policies of the regime. According to U.N. reports, up to 1000 demonstrators were killed by South African security forces in repressing the uprising.

The international outrage at the brutal repression was derided by Phineas Stone, the lead columnist for the *Jewish Week,* whose editor Philip Hochstein had just returned from the editors' trip to South Africa. The newspaper has a circulation of over 100,000 in the U.S.

In a column filled with racist slanders, Stone criticizes the "liberals" who suggest that South Africa "turn to 'gradual' equality." Equality between "a primitive but overwhelming Black majority" and "an advanced white ruling minority" would lead first to expulsion of the whites and

---

Palestine!, July, August 1972.

then to "years, and perhaps decades of mutual slaughter" by the country's "rival Black tribes," Stone argues.

Stone writes that the "group of Jewish editors [who] visited South Africa just some weeks ago ... were, on the whole, impressed with the logic and sincerity of the 'Separate Development' [*apartheid*] program" of the regime.

d. Defend Israel On S. Africa*

A national Jewish organization has released a study claiming that Arab and black African states are maintaining "thriving trade relations" with South Africa, while those same countries attack expanded economic relations between South Africa and Israel.

The report, prepared by the American Jewish Congress, said that "while black African countries have loudly condemned South Africa's racial policies in public, privately they recognize that they must trade with the *apartheid* regime if their economies are to survive and grow."

Nineteen African states trade with South Africa, the AJC said, many of whom have condemned the recent visit to Israel by South African Prime Minister John Vorster which led to growing Israeli-South African ties.

South Africa's most expensive business dealings in Africa are with the socialist government of Mozambique. According to the report, South Africa provided almost half of Mozambique's total foreign imports last year.

South African exports to the rest of Africa totaled $493 million during 1975, while imports amounted to $266 million, according to the study. In addition, the report claims, Saudi Arabia has "purchased large quantities of food-stuffs from South Africa and sent a ... mission to Johannesburg to discuss the purchase of several million dollars worth of prefabricated building materials."

"For the sake of economic survival even profound political differences are often shunted aside," said Rabbi Arthur Hertzberg, president of the AJC. "So it is with black Africa. So it is with Israel."

Civil rights leader Bayard Rustin, who heads a committee called "Black Americans to Support Israel," had written Hertzberg to express his "chagrin" at growing Israeli-African trade relations. After reading the AJC report, Rustin said, he had "modified" his thinking.

"I am grieved when Israel expands trade to South Africa," Rustin said. "But I am even more grieved when Africans do likewise. I denounce the hypocrisy on the part of Africans who attack this trade when they are doing it themselves."

However, added Rustin, "I will continue to be distressed with any nation that trades with a country in which black children are being shot down."

*New York Post, September 3, 1976.

[30] Further Collaboration on All Fronts

In the face of mounting criticism and international condemnation of the Israel-South Africa link, some Israeli and Zionist spokesmen insinuated that the Zionist state might re-examine its position. But later developments proved the opposite. The Zionist state, far from reconsidering its position, has indeed strengthened its economic, political and military relations with South Africa.

a. Israel May Re-Examine Its Relations with South Africa*

Israel might re-examine its relations with The Republic of South Africa in view of increasing criticism against Israel throughout the world, according to a newspaper report yesterday. *Maariv* reported in an exclusive story that consultations among high level Foreign Ministry officials, to be followed by consultations with Premier Yitzhak Rabin and Foreign Minister Yigal Allon will take place soon, to reassess all aspects of the present ties between Israel and South Africa.

According to *Maariv*, some officials in Jerusalem feel that such a reassessment would be made in view of a new administration coming to Washington. In any case, the paper concluded, Israel would maintain a "low profile" in its relations with South Africa. The paper also mentioned that two ministerial visits to South Africa were recently cancelled by Finance Minister Yehoshua Rabinowitz and Commerce Minister Haim Bar Lev.

Jewish Telegraphic Agency, Daily News Bulletin, November 26, 1976.

b. Israeli Arms Grow, Sales to South Africa Increase*

Israel, which in recent years has been the largest recipient of United States military aid—to the tune of $2.2 billion in 1976—has in turn sprouted a booming arms export industry.

Israel exported an estimated $500 million worth of sophisticated arms to over 20 countries in 1976. *Aviation Week*, citing U.S. sources, expects that the figure will rise over the $1 billion mark in 1977. This represents a percentage of the Israeli gross national product that exceeds the arms export percentage of the United States' GNP, the world's leading arms exporter.

The arms industry provides Israel with badly needed foreign exchange revenues, and in addition provides Israel with a way to expand its arms producing facilities, thereby lessening its dependence on the United States for armaments.

Liberation News Service, No. 843, January 19, 1977.

Much of the Israeli arms trade is surrounded by secrecy—as an Israeli Defense Ministry official explained to a *New York Times* reporter: "We never discuss who the countries are. Our customers have the privilege of anonymity."

Finds Lucrative Market

However, according to press disclosures, Israel has found a lucrative world market, especially among countries which the United States supports as part of its foreign policy, but which in some instance it finds difficult to send arms to directly.

South Africa has been the most prominent and controversial example of this practice. In a recently negotiated deal, Israel sold South Africa six long-range gunboats equipped with surface-to-surface missiles worth $150 million altogether. Two dozen Israeli-built Kfir jet fighter planes are also reported slated for possible future delivery.

Israeli supporters claim that Israel's arms trade with South Africa is small compared to arms sales to the *apartheid* regime by European countries.

However the sale of Israeli gunboats worth a total of $150 million and scheduled for delivery in coming years, comes close to rivaling the total French arms sale to South Africa from 1965 to 1974, which totalled $224 million. France has been South Africa's largest arms supplier.

Jennifer Davis, a researcher at the American Committee on Africa, explains that at a time of increasing isolation of South Africa internationally, Israel has rapidly expanded its trade ties with South Africa, allowing South Africa access to sophisticated technology from a new source. Trade between the countries could potentially include Israeli nuclear technology. South Africa has indicated it will supply Israel with uranium in the future.

Israel has also sent army advisors to South Africa to give instruction in counterinsurgency techniques. An Israeli arms producer recently opened a subsidiary in South Africa, and South Africa last year indicated that it will invest in the expansion of the arms industry in Israel.

Chile, another repressive regime which has been the target of international public protest, recently negotiated the purchase of Israeli Shafir air-to-air missiles.

South America on the whole is developing into a prime area for Israeli sales, since, to the anger of U.S. arms producers, U.S. foreign policy has in general prohibited the sale of sophisticated U.S. arms that could fuel an arms race in the neighboring Southern Hemisphere. *The Military Balance*, a London publication, identifies Israel as a primary arms supplier to Bolivia, Ecuador, El Salvador, Mexico and Nicaragua.

Among other countries to which Israel has reportedly sold arms recently are Kenya, Taiwan, Iran and Greece.

Sophisticated Arms

The arms Israel exports are generally high technology weapons, often with sophisticated electronics, precise machining and aerospace metals. At a recent electronic warfare equipment show in Europe, 25% of the systems displayed were produced in Israel.

Designs and parts for Israeli weapons often originate in the United States. The Shafir missile headed for Chile, for example, is described by *Aviation Week* as "a copy of the Raytheon AIM-9D/G with solid state components packaged in Israel. One third of Israel's Shafir missile production is slated for eventual export, according to *Aviation Week*.

Weapons manufactured under American license or containing American components technically require U.S. government approval before a country can export them.

In many cases, as with the Shafir missiles, Israel makes minor modifications in the design and claims it is not a U.S. weapons system. Sale of weapons such as the Kfir, however, which uses GE engines, does require U.S. approval.

Interestingly, the mushrooming Israeli export industry has generated fears even among some U.S. weapons producers. They worry that the U.S. military assistance may create Israeli industries "that could eventually compete with U.S.-built hardware in other markets," according to *Aviation Week*. . . .

c. Israelis Look at Homeland Investment*

JERUSALEM — Two representatives of the Bantu Investment Corporation (BIC) are currently in Israel in an attempt to promote investment in homeland industries among Israeli businessmen and manufacturers.

An advertisement in the local press called on all Israelis interested to contact the commercial section of the South African Embassy in Tel Aviv.

Apparently the telephone virtually did not cease ringing from the moment the notice appeared.

Attracted

Many Israeli companies and individuals are attracted by the idea of investing money, know-how, or both, in the Bantu Investment Corporation which was established in 1959 to promote economic

---

The Star (Johannesburg), February 26, 1977.

development in the black homelands.

No names or exact figures are being made public but there appears to be a large amount of Israeli plastics industries interested in the scheme.

A possible plan would be for Israeli manufacturers to utilise the low cost semi-skilled labour available in the Republic and then import the goods back to Israel, either completed, or with the necessary finishing being handled here and then exported elsewhere, possibly to the European Economic Community (EEC) with which Israel has excellent ties.

Safari

The two officials in Israel are Mr. M. du Toit and Mr. Mynhardt. They are on the final leg of a European safari drumming up investments in the corporation.

Over the past four years the corporation's industrial development scheme has reportedly doubled its investment yearly. In the past six years it has constructed about 200 factories employing about 200,000 black workers. The investment, so far, is about R140-million, half provided by the Government-backed corporation and half by private investors. The private sector includes companies from the US, Britain, Canada, West Germany, Switzerland, Italy and the Netherlands.

d. Studies Indicate South Africa and Israel Increase Cooperation*

John K. Cooley

ATHENS — Israel is strengthening its economic and military cooperation with the white-supremacy regime in South Africa, according to information studied at the recent African-Arab summit conference in Cairo.

South Africa has long been purchasing arms from Israel, supplying it with diamonds and other raw materials, and sharing technology in such areas as railroads, development of gas energy from coal, and arms manufacture. And now—Israeli newspapers and other published sources report—South Africa operates with Israel a large plant to manufacture electronic devices for counterinsurgency and other sensitive fields denied to South Africa by Western governments.

The Israeli newspaper *Maariv* reported last December 9 that Israel's Tadiran electronics firm, a subsidiary of Israel Aircraft

Christian Science Monitor, March 15, 1977

Industries, has built a plant at Rosalene, near Pretoria, in partnership with a South African group under the name Consolidated Power.

During his four-day visit to Israel last April, South African Premier John Vorster visited Israel Aircraft Industries. He reportedly expressed interest in purchasing Israel's Kfir fighter-bomber, which the United States recently refused to permit Israel to sell to Ecuador. If any Kfirs offered to South Africa were powered by the U.S.-based General Electric J-79 engine, like those offered to Ecuador, logically they, too, would fall under the U.S. embargo.

After Mr. Vorster's departure from Israel, Israel radio reported South African purchase of two of Israel's fast 420-ton Reshef class gunboats and orders for four more. The gunboats are equipped with Israel's Gabriel Missile.

Oil industry sources reported last year a major Israeli order for South African coal and supply to Israel of the technology for a coal-gasification process developed in South Africa.

Published figures show that Israel-South Africa trade has risen 400 percent since 1972 and was worth about $100 million last year.

The Cairo conference earlier this month heard allegations, originally from Sam Nujoma, president of the South-West African People's Organization (SWAPO) which fights South African rule in that territory, that Israeli counterguerrilla experts are involved in operations against SWAPO guerrillas in northern Namibia (the African name for South-West Africa). There have been many reports of Israeli aid to Ethiopia against guerrillas in Eritrea, but the status of this help under the new Marxist-leaning Ethiopian military regime, which has lost U.S. military aid, is uncertain.

e.   Israel May Be Iscor's Link with Common Market*

Peter Allen-Frost

JERUSALEM — Israel will represent the South African steel industry in the Common Market, according to Mr. Hillel Seidel, a Knesset (Parliament) member for the Israeli opposition "Likud" faction.

In a letter to Minister of Commerce, Mr. Haim Bar Lev, sent last month, Mr. Seidel asked whether it was true that the giant industrial conglomerate Koor will act as South Africa's steel agents since the boycott of the EEC prevents South Africa from direct dealings. Israel is an associate member of the EEC with preferential trade tariffs.

*The Star (Johannesburg), March 19, 1977.

Mr. Seidel said that since Minister Bar Lev had so far not replied he assumed there was no secret involved. The MP said his facts came from four different sources which he refused to name.

Minister Bar Lev told me that, so far, he had not received Mr. Seidel's letter and when he did, he would "examine the situation."

Asked to comment, a senior Koor official said: "Koor Industries denies it is representing South African steel in Europe." The official would not comment any further on the matter.

Koor Industries is owned by the Labour Party dominated Histadrut trade union of Israel, and has already several joint ventures with South Africa. Vast amounts of Iscor steel are imported to Israel and a joint Iscor-Koor steel services centre is due to be opened in Israel this year.

When this deal was announced here in May 1976, it was also reported that South Africa was extremely interested in the completion of the project because of Israel's export potential to the EEC.

The Israeli-South African steel centre will open in Kiryat Gat south of Tel Aviv and imported South African semi-processed steel and iron will be rolled, cut to size, and exported.

The added value would then presumably be sufficient to qualify for the EEC preferential trade tariffs—boosting both Israel's and South Africa's economies.

Iscor steel made up over 40 percent of South Africa's total exports to Israel during fiscal 1975/76.

Current bilateral trade during January-December 1976 topped the R80m mark.

f. South Africa Gains Arms and Trade As Israel Link Hardens*

John F. Burns

JOHANNESBURG, May 20 — Last year two South Africans—an Afrikaner and a Jew—arrived simultaneously at the Yad Vashem memorial in Jerusalem. The Jew watched uneasily as the Afrikaner mounted the steps to pay homage to the six million Jews who died in the Nazi death camps.

"It struck me as most incongruous," said Richard Lampert, a rabbi whose vacation in Israel coincided with Prime Minister John Vorster's controversial visit there last year. "Here was a man who was interned during the war for German sympathies paying tribute to the victims of those same Germans."

Mr. Vorster has insisted that the activities that led to his intern-

*New York Times, Saturday, May 21, 1977

ment in 1942 were anti-British, not pro-German. Nonetheless, the reaction of the rabbi, one of 118,000 South African Jews, reflected the complex political and philosophical issues raised by the close ties between South Africa and Israel.

Most whites here celebrate the growth of the relationship over the last three years. It has given South Africa access to armaments that are increasingly difficult to get elsewhere, as well as opening healthy trade in other items. Moreover, it has offered South Africa diplomatic comfort at a time when its old friends in the West have become increasingly alienated by *apartheid*.

Among Jews the relationship has raised deeper concerns. Some, conservative on racial questions, are enthusiastic about it. Others, weighing their national interest as South Africans against their moral qualms, give it qualified endorsement. A few, mostly rabbis and intellectuals like Mr. Lampert, have spoken openly of their disquiet.

"I'm upset that Israel, founded on the ashes of six million people done to death in the name of racism, should have to find her benefactor in South Africa," said the rabbi, head of one of this city's principal synagogues. "After all, this country is founded on everything Israel must be against."

Mr. Lampert said he agreed that Israel, short of allies, particularly in Africa, has had to be expedient in its diplomacy. "However," he added, leaning forward across his desk, "I just don't believe that it's necessary for the heads of government to sit down to dinner together."

Yitzhak Rabin, then Israeli Prime Minister, played host at a dinner for Prime Minister Vorster during his four-day visit last April. Billed as private, the visit swiftly became semiofficial, with the two leaders conferring at length and agreeing to establish a joint ministerial committee to review the relationship annually.

The visit culminated an extraordinary turnaround in relations after the war in October 1973. Field Marshal Jan Christiaan Smuts, Prime Minister of South Africa in the 1920's and again in the 40's, was an early supporter of Zionism through his contacts in London during World War I with Dr. Chaim Weizmann, later the first President of Israel, and South African Jews played a prominent role in the 1947-48 conflict that followed the establishment of the state. However, relations during its first 25 years were cool and sometimes chilly.

Some awkwardness between Afrikaner nationalists and South African Jews, amounting occasionally to overt anti-Semitism, played its part. More important was Israel's habit of supporting anti-*apartheid* resolutions in the United Nations. In the 1950's Erik Louw, then Foreign Minister, as much as threatened the Jews here with retribution if they failed to persuade the Israelis to change their stand.

In 1971 a $2,000 Israeli contribution to the Organization of African Unity's liberation committee, its principal anti-*apartheid* instrument, brought the issue to a climax. The South Africans briefly halted the flow of Jewish donations to Israel and Jewish businessmen, particularly in rural Afrikaner strongholds, faced a customer boycott.

Elaborate Diplomatic Courtship

The contribution was part of an elaborate diplomatic courtship, promoted with generous aid funds, that had given Israel an extensive network of relationships in black Africa. However, the network collapsed at the outbreak of the 1973 war, with all but three black states—Malawi, Lesotho and Swaziland, all of which have close ties to South Africa—severing relations.

As long as the ties with the black states lasted, they were incompatible with a fuller relationship with South Africa. The war not only removed the impediment; it acted as a catalyst in the thinking of South African officials, who had a growing sense of affinity with Israel as a fellow outcast. The similarities, as the South Africans saw them, were that both countires were bastions of European civilization surrounded by culturally and politically hostile neighbors; that both faced adversaries with overwhelming numerical superiority; that both had become targets of Soviet expansionism; and that both, encountering declining support from their traditional allies, had need of new friends.

Beyond all this, Afrikaners saw an analogy between their historical experience and that of the Jews. As the Jews had their escape from Egypt, so the Afrikaners had their trek from the Cape of Good Hope. In each case there was the promised land, and this each lost, recovering it again only after lengthy travail.

There was, too, the Old Testament bond. The towns that mark the path of the Afrikaners' Great Trek—Bethlehem, Bethal, Benoni—have their counterparts in Israel. Mr. Vorster, like the Israeli Prime Minister, alienates religious leaders at his cost.

Big Expansion of Trade

In 1974 the congruence of interests led the two nations to raise their relations to the ambassadorial level. This was accompanied by a swift expansion of commercial, scientific and military ties. Between 1968 and 1976 trade soared from $9 million to $97 million, excluding the biggest single item in the exchange, weapons.

Each country saw the other as the ideal trading partner. In South Africa Israel found a reliable source of relatively cheap essential materials, especially sugar, coal and steel, that were either unobtainable or too expensive elsewhere. For its part South Africa offered a ready market for Israeli chemicals and textiles, as well as high-technology products, particularly electronic equipment.

An agreement on scientific and technological exchanges, formalized during the Vorster visit, led to an intensification of existing contacts. One rumored program, cooperation on the development of nuclear weapons, has been insistently denied. In any event, Israeli experts are working with South Africans on a wide range of human problems, from bilharzia, a disease common among South African blacks, to soil erosion and water desalinization.

A major benefit for Israel has been the flow of funds out of South Africa. For many years contributions by South African Jews have made them, in per capita terms, the most generous Jewish community. Since the improvement in diplomatic relations South Africa has opened the financial gates wider, permitting its citizens to invest in Israel. The investment opening, unique to Israel, has been tightly controlled. Projects are carefully reviewed, with priority given to those that will employ South African expertise or raw materials. Until the black riots last year only $8 million out of an approved ceiling of $25 million had been taken up; in the months that followed $12 million more was invested.

Eluding Tight Exchange Controls

For the South African Jews it is a valuable concession. Although dividends and profits must be repatriated, it is commonly assumed here that in an extreme crisis for the white community the principal would be recoverable in Israel, providing a means for anxious people to elude tight foreign-exchange controls.

From the South African viewpoint the biggest material dividend of the relationship is almost certainly the access gained to Israeli weapons and military expertise. Details are closely guarded, but one contract, under which South Africa is buying six corvettes equipped with surface-to-surface missiles, totals approximately $500 million. Other contracts provide for the manufacture of Israeli-designed equipment under license.

g. No Curbs Are Seen in Israel's Trade*

JERUSALEM, May 20 — Israel is not curbing its growing commercial and trade links with South Africa, in the view of a number of Israeli officials and members of the foreign diplomatic community based here.

Reports, which have circulated in Johannesburg as well as in

New York Times, May 21, 1977.

Israel, assert that Israel is retrenching in its dealings with South Africa because it wishes to avoid incurring the disfavor of the Carter Administration, which has sharply criticized South Africa's racial policies as part of President Carter's campaign for human rights.

The recent postponement of visits by ranking Israeli officials to South Africa to sign trade and investment pacts are cited as evidence that Israel is backtracking in its dealings with South Africa—dealings the Israelis have fostered in the past couple of years.

The official reason for the postponements was that the officials were needed at home during the election campaign.

Deference to Carter Administration

According to foreign diplomats and Israeli officials, Israel appears to be muting the public aspects of its relations with South Africa in deference to the Carter Administration without, so far, initiating any substantive shift in its dealings with the regime of Prime Minister John Vorster. At the same time, middle-level officials have been going to South Africa on business trips, according to sources here.

Officials here also feel that pressure and arm-twisting from the Americans may well be forthcoming in the near future.

"I do not detect any backtracking—that is not my impression at all," a South African embassy official said. "There has been no cancellation of trade agreements and everything is going ahead as planned."

At a recent luncheon with foreign reporters, the acting Prime Minister, Shimon Peres, was asked about Israel's relations with South Africa.

No Changes Seen by Peres

"I do not see any changes in the present policy," Mr. Peres replied.

Similarly, a ranking Foreign Ministry official said, "There's no new policy—no new decisions—nothing is new."

Israel's growing ties to South Africa have been controversial for some time, and there is by no means unanimity in Israel about the propriety of maintaining links with a country that espouses *apartheid*.

In addition to growing commercial links, there have been reports in the press that Israel also is selling substantial amounts of military equipment to South Africa in exchange for much-needed raw materials.

Government officials here stress that they have long opposed the racial policies of the Vorster Government and continue to do so but that a tenet of Israel's foreign policy sanctions diplomacy with any nation wishing to pursue diplomatic relations with Israel.

4 UNITED NATIONS AND INTERNATIONAL RESPONSE

[1] Situation in South Africa Resulting from the Policies of Apartheid

General Assembly Resolution 3151 (XXVIII)
of 14 December 1973

The General Assembly,
Recalling its resolutions on the policies of *apartheid* of the Government of South Africa and the relevant resolutions of the Security Council, ...

4. *Condemns* the actions of those States and companies which continue to provide to the South African regime military equipment and supplies, and assistance for the local manufacture of such equipment and supplies, or other forms of military co-operation in violation of the resolutions of the General Assembly and the Security Council;

5. *Condemns,* in particular, the unholy alliance between Portuguese colonialism, South African racism, zionism and Israeli imperialism; ...

[2] Situation in South Africa

General Assembly Resolution 3324E (XXIX)
of 16 December 1974

The General Assembly,
Having considered the reports of the Special Committee on *Apartheid,*
Recalling its resolutions on the policies of *apartheid* of the Government of South Africa and its decisions at the current session concerning the representation of South Africa, ...

5. *Condemns* the strengthening of political, economic, military and other relations between Israel and South Africa; ...

[3] Resolution on the Question of Palestine
AHG/OAU Resolution 77 (XII) August 1975

The Assembly of Heads of State and Government of the Organization of African Unity, meeting in its Twelfth Ordinary Session from 28 July to 1 August 1975 at Kampala, Uganda, ...

Considering that the racist regime in occupied Palestine and the racist regimes in Zimbabwe and South Africa have a common imperialist origin, forming a whole and having the same racist structure and being organically linked in their policy aimed at repression of the dignity and integrity of the human being, ...

[4] Elimination of all forms of Racial Discrimination
General Assembly Resolution 3379 (XXX) of 10 November 1975

The General Assembly,

Recalling its resolution 1904 (XVIII) of 20 November 1963, proclaiming the United Nations Declaration on the Elimination of All Forms of Racial Discrimination, and in particular its affirmation that "any doctrine of racial differentiation or superiority is scientifically false, morally condemnable (and) socially unjust and dangerous" and its expression of alarm at "the manifestations of racial discrimination still in evidence in some areas in the world, some of which are imposed by certain Governments by means of legislative, administrative or other measures,"

Recalling also that, in its resolution 3151 G (XXVIII) of 14 December 1973, the General Assembly condemned *inter alia* the unholy alliance between South African racism and zionism,

Taking note of the Declaration of Mexico on the Equality of Women and their Contribution to Development and Peace proclaimed by the World Conference of the International Women's Year, held at Mexico City from 19 June to 2 July 1975, which promulgated the principle that "international co-operation and peace require the achievement of national liberation and independence, the elimination of colonialism and neo-colonialism, foreign occupation, zionism, *apartheid,* and racial discrimination in all its forms as well as the recognition of the dignity of peoples and their right to self-determination,"

Taking note also of resolution 77 (XII) adopted by the Assembly of Heads of State and Government of the Organization of African Unity held in Kampala from 28 July to 1 August 1975 which considered "that the racist regime in occupied Palestine and racist regimes in Zimbabwe and South Africa have a common imperialist origin, forming a whole and having the same racist structure and being organically linked in their policy aimed at repression of the dignity and integrity of the human being,"

Taking note also of the Political Declaration and Strategy to strengthen International Peace and Security and to intensify Solidarity and Mutual Assistance among the Non-Aligned Countries, adopted at the Conference of Ministers for Foreign Affairs of Non-Aligned Countries held in Lima, Peru, from 25 to 30 August 1975, which most severely condemned zionism as a threat to world peace and security and called upon all countries to oppose this racist and imperialist ideology,

1. *Determines* that zionism is a form of racism and racial discrimination.

[5] Situation in South Africa

General Assembly Resolution 3411 (XXX)
of 10 December 1975

The General Assembly,
Having considered the report of the Special Committee against Apartheid...

Reaffirming that the continued collaboration of some States and of economic and other interests with the racist regime of South Africa impedes the efforts for the eradication of apartheid, ...

4. *Again condemns* the strengthening of relations and collaboration between the racist regime of South Africa and Israel in the political, military, economic and other fields; ...

[6] Collaboration Between Israel and South Africa

Statement by H.E. Mme. Jeanne Martin Cisse (Guinea), Chairman of the United Nations Special Committee Against *Apartheid* (October 1975 – April 1976), on April 14, 1976, *International Solidarity with the Struggle for Liberation in South Africa,* April 1976 pp. 20-22.

A few days ago, I was obliged to issue a press statement expressing grave concern over the further strengthening of relations between Israel and South Africa. The General Assembly has repeatedly condemned the increasing collaboration between the Government of Israel and the racist regime of South Africa—most recently in resolution 3411 G (XXX) adopted on 10 December 1975. However, one month after the passage of that resolution, South Africa elevated its Consulate-General in Israel to an embassy. On 26 and 27 March, Mr. C.P. Mulder, the South African Minister for Interior and Information, visited Israel and is reported to have had long meetings with the Prime Minister and Foreign Minister of Israel. He was followed by a visit of the Prime Minister of the racist regime of South Africa, Mr. Balthazar Vorster, who arrived in Israel on 9 April.

Nor can the claim that Mr. Vorster's visit, described by some newspapers as a pilgrimage to holy places, be upheld. Long meetings with the Prime Minister of Israel and visits to military bases are no part of a Christian pilgrimage!

Only a few days ago, the Security Council had to consider successively complaints by the Arab States against Israel and by African States against the South African regime. Why is it that at this time, Israel which continues its occupation of territory in the northeast of Africa and the South African regime which continues its illegal occupation in the southern tip of Africa have found a need to have high-level discussions? I believe that there are two main reasons.

I would recall a report on the Jerusalem radio on 18 January 1976, which said:

> "The (Israeli) Foreign Minister said at today's cabinet meeting that the standoff in which the Organization of African Unity conference over Angola ended was an accomplishment for the moderate camp among the countries of the continent. This is an achievement of American diplomacy, the Foreign Minister said, and a prospect exists that the moderate camp among African countries will also influence relations with Israel."

Is it that the two countries are continuing their vain efforts to divide Africa, with the hope of support from elsewhere?

At the end of March, the South African regime increased its military budget by over 40% from 948 million rand to 1,350 million rand. South Africa's military budget, I may recall, was 44 million rand in 1960, the year of the Sharpeville massacre. It is now thirty times that figure. It is thrice the military budget for 1973-74 and twice the figure for 1974-75. The South African regime has decided on this enormous increase in the military budget, as an immediate reply to the condemnation of its aggression in Angola, in spite of the serious economic crisis in the country. According to authoritative estimates, there will be a lowering of standards of living in South Africa this year, and we have every reason to fear that the Blacks will be the worst sufferers.

The racist regime plans to acquire more military equipment—especially missile boats, corvettes and long-range aircraft. The timing of Mr. Vorster's visit to Israel would seem to indicate that South Africa hopes to use Israel for breaking the arms embargo.

The two governments have found a community of interest. Only a few weeks ago, on 2 February 1976, Major-General Neil Webster of the South African Defence Force delared:

> "South Africans, like the Israelis, must get used to the idea of living with the war-like situation for some years to come."

Mr. Vorster is reported to have told the press on 10 April that relations between South Africa and Israel have never been so good. He also claimed that this would not harm South Africa's relations with its Arab oil suppliers.

[7] Resolution on the Middle East

Fifth Conference of Heads of State or Government of Non-Aligned Countries, Colombo, 1976

The Fifth Conference of Heads of State or Government of the Non-Aligned countries meeting in Colombo, Sri Lanka from 15-19 August 1976, ...

9. *Condemns* the collusion between Israel and South Africa confirmed by the similarity of their policies of aggression and racism as well as their collaboration in all fields with a view to threatening African and Arab security and independence, ...

[8] Ever Closer Collaboration Between Israel and South Africa

UN Special Committee Against Apartheid Unanimously Adopts Report on the Relations Between Israel and South Africa, on August 19, 1976.

REPORT ON THE RELATIONS BETWEEN ISRAEL AND SOUTH AFRICA

I. BACKGROUND

1. In recent years, the General Assembly has expressed increasing concern over the intensification of political, military and other relations between Israel and South Africa.

2. In resolution 3151 G (XXVIII) of 14 December 1973, the General Assembly condemned "the unholy alliance between ... South African racism ... and Israeli imperialism."

3. In resolution 3324 E (XXIX) of 16 December 1974, the General Assembly condemned "the strengthening of political, economic, military and other relations between Israel and South Africa."

4. In resolution 3411 G (XXX) of 10 December 1975, the General Assembly again condemned "the strengthening of relations and collaboration between the racist regime of South Africa and Israel in the political, military, economic and other fields."

5. The Special Committee against *Apartheid* has constantly followed the development of relations between the two regimes with increasing concern and reported to the General Assembly as appropriate.

6. In March 1974, following the decision of the Government of Israel to upgrade its diplomatic mission in South Africa to an embassy, the Special Committee requested its Sub-Committee on the Implementation of United Nations Resolutions and Collaboration with South Africa to prepare a report on recent developments in relations between Israel and South Africa. The report of the Sub-Committee was issued as document A/AC.115/L.383.

7. The Chairman of the Special Committee sent a letter on 2 April 1974 to the Permanent Representative of Israel to the United Nations stating that "the raising of the level of the diplomatic mission in South Africa is a flagrant violation of the resolutions of the General Assembly" and requesting him to convey to his Government the great concern of the Special Committee and its hope that the Government would reconsider its decision and terminate its diplomatic, consular and other official relations with the South African racist regime in accordance with the relevant resolutions of the General Assembly. While the Permanent Representative of Israel acknowledged receipt of the Chairman's letter, no reply was ever received from the Government of Israel.

8. In October 1974, the Special Committee decided to publish a comprehensive study of the development of relations between Israel and South Africa from 1967 to 1974 prepared for the Committee by an expert, Mr. Peter Hellyer. The study was issued as document A/AC.115/L.396.

9. In June 1975, the attention of the Special Committee was drawn to press reports that the South African Minister of Interior and Information had arrived on a "private" visit to Israel on 17 June 1975 and that the South African Consulate-General in Israel would be elevated to an embassy. Disturbed by the evidence of further increase in links between the two countries, the Committee requested its Rapporteur to prepare a report on recent developments concerning military, diplomatic, economic and other collaboration between South Africa and Israel. The report was issued as document A/AC.115/L.411.

10. Following another visit by the South African Minister of Interior and Information, Mr. C. P. Mulder, to Israel in March 1976, and in the light of reports of an impending visit to Israel by the Prime Minister of South Africa, Mr. B. J. Vorster, the Chairman of the Special Committee, Mme. Jeanne Martin Cisse (Guinea), issued a press statement on 7 April 1976. She expressed the hope that all Governments and organizations would condemn the actions of the Government of Israel in developing closer collaboration with the Pretoria regime in defiance of United Nations resolutions, and exercise their influence to persuade the Government of Israel to desist from its present course.

11. At its 321st and 322nd meetings on 14 and 30 April 1976, the Special Committee discussed the growing collaboration between Israel and South Africa, following Prime Minister Vorster's visit to Israel from 9 to 12 April 1976, and the conclusion of a wide-ranging co-operation agreement between the two countries. The Committee requested its Sub-Committee on the Implementation of United Nations Resolutions and Collaboration with South Africa, to prepare, as a matter of priority, a report on the increasing collaboration between Israel and South Africa, with a view to transmitting it to the General Assembly and the Security Council, as well as the Organization of African Unity, the Conference of Non-aligned Countries, and the League of Arab States.

12. On 11 August 1976, the Chairman of the Special Committee, Ambassador Leslie O. Harriman (Nigeria), attending the non-aligned ministers' meeting in Sri Lanka, issued a statement condemning the reported sale of two missile boats by Israel to South Africa. The statement read as follows:

> "Announcement by Israel of proposed sale to South Africa of two corvettes equipped with missiles represents flagrant violation of United Nations resolutions and cynical and hostile act against African people now engaged in heroic struggle for freedom in face of massacres by *apartheid* regime. It also constitutes threat to independent African states and challenge to efforts to establish Indian Ocean zone of peace. I call on all Governments and people to denounce this action and growing Israeli collusion with *apartheid* regime and demand cessation of all collaboration with Pretoria. I feel certain that non-aligned ministers now meeting here in Colombo will give this growing threat to Africa the attention which it deserves."

II. Introduction

13. The purpose of the present report is to give an account of the growth in relations between South Africa and Israel. The report contains information on the historical background of collaboration between South Africa and the Zionist movement prior to the formation of the State of Israel. It reviews developments in all areas of collaboration between the two countries between 1948 and the present.

14. The report shows that relations between South Africa and Israel, which have ideological and historical roots, acquired new dimensions and were greatly intensified after the June 1967 war in the Middle East and even more after the October 1973 war. Differences between the two regimes caused by diverging foreign policy objectives toward the Arab and the African countries were set aside when the African States broke diplomatic relations with Israel. Weakened by the advances of the liberation struggle and forced into increasing isolation by growing Arab-African solidarity and world condemnation of their racist policies, the two regimes have resorted to an ever closer collaboration in all areas. (a) Politically,

this collaboration has aimed at driving a wedge between the African countries and between them and the Arab countries, and at linking southern Africa and the Middle East as common strategic concerns of the Western Powers. South Africa expects substantial political dividends from closer association with Israel, and co-operation in undermining the boycott campaigns; (b) In the military sphere, this growing collaboration has provided each country with an additional source of arms supplies and technological know-how, as well as access to classified information on strategies and tactics; (c) Economically, Israel has benefited from raw materials vital to its economy, while South Africa has derived substantial advantages from its favourable balance of trade with Israel and from the possibility of using that country as a springboard both for evading the international boycott and for circumventing high European Economic Community tariffs. Investment has increasingly taken the form of joint projects by public corporations drawing on the complementarity of the two economies—South Africa's raw materials and Israel's scientific know-how—to promote industrial expansion schemes of benefit to both countries; (d) In the cultural field, exchange programmes and other activities have promoted closer ideological identification between the two countries and have served to further South African propaganda.

III. Development of relations: General

15. The rapidly increasing collaboration between the *apartheid* regime in South Africa and the Government of Israel reached a new stage in April 1976 when Prime Minister B. J. Vorster visited Israel, and concluded agreements on economic, scientific and industrial collaboration between the two countries. Press reports and subsequent developments also showed that the two countries had agreed on intensifying military collaboration.

16. It may be recalled that relations between the minority racist regime in South Africa and Israel have deep historical and ideological roots. General Jan Smuts, Minister of Defence in the Union Government and a member of the Imperial War Council in 1917, was one of the chief architects of the Balfour Declaration on the establishment of a "Jewish homeland" in Palestine.[1]

17. The Nationalist-Labour coalition Government under General J.B. M. Hertzog fully supported the creation of a "Jewish homeland" in Palestine, adopting a resolution to that effect in 1926. It also promised to support the Zionist aims before the League of Nations.[2] In the United Nations, South Africa actively supported the project of the partition of Palestine. One of the first acts of the National Party after coming to power in 1948 was to extend *de jure* recognition to the newly-established State of Israel. Dr. D. F. Malan was the first Prime Minister in the British Com-

monwealth to pay a courtesy visit to the new State. In addition, he permitted South African Jewish reserve officers to serve in Israel, and approved transfer of funds and goods to Israel despite South Africa's financial difficulties at the time.[3]

18. In line with its support for the State of Israel, the National Party reversed its previous policy toward the Jewish minority in South Africa, which had been marked by rabid anti-Semitism. Soon after taking office, Dr. Malan declared that both he and his Government stood for a policy of non-discrimination against any section of the white population and looked forward to the day when there would no longer be any talk of the "Jewish question" in the country.[4] The ban on Jewish membership in the National Party was lifted and prominent Jews were appointed to important governmental positions.[5]

19. The new policy of the National Party was apparently motivated not only by a desire to strengthen white solidarity, but also by a recognition of the important role that the Jewish community had come to play in South Africa's economy. The leaders of the Party feared that any implementation of discrimination against Jews would drain South Africa of Jewish capital. It has also been pointed out that Afrikaner support for zionism had a basis in the common opposition to the British at the time, as well as the common feeling of being "chosen people" with a biblical mission.[6]

20. Through its support for Israel and its official abrogation of anti-semitism internally, the National Party was able to secure acceptance of its *apartheid* policies at all levels of formal Jewish expression. The sizeable Jewish community in South Africa had always been strongly Zionist and had maintained close ties with the thousands of South African Jews who had emigrated to Israel, some of whom had come to occupy prominent positions in the new State. In response to Dr. Malan's new policy, the Jewish associations toned down their previously outspoken criticisms of racial discrimination. While individual Jews maintained their anti-*apartheid* stand and even joined the liberation struggle, the official Jewish organizations followed the South African Jewish Board of Deputies in taking the position that, as non-political bodies, they would "refrain from taking any position on party political issues" and would not "express views on the various race policies being advocated."[7]

21. As Rabbi Dr. M. C. Weiler put it in a speech to the Eighth International Conference of the World Union for Progressive Judaism in London in July 1953:

> "The Jews as a community had decided to take no stand on the native question, because they were involved with the problem of assisting Jewry in other lands. South African Jewry was doing more to help Israel than any other group. The community could not ask for the Government's permission to export funds and goods and at the same time, object to the Government."[8]

22. The South African Jewish press and the Board of Deputies did not

break their silence even on the occasion of the Sharpeville massacre of 1960. In return, the South African Zionist Federation was allowed to continue sending substantial funds to Israel every year—making the South African Jewish community the greatest *per capita* contributor to Israel in the world.[9]

23. The community of interests between the State of Israel and the *apartheid* regime was therefore established from the very beginning, with the South African Jewish community serving as the link between the two countries, in spite of some transitory difficulties. As Peter Hellyer has noted:

> "The differing political objectives of the two States, particularly in sub-Saharan Africa, from 1960 to 1970, have caused problems from time to time, but they have shown themselves to be essentially transitory, and capable of being subordinated to an over-all policy of the continued development of ties."[10]

24. Israel's attempt to establish diplomatic and other links with independent African countries in the 1960s led it to declare opposition to *apartheid* in the United Nations and other forums. In retaliation, in 1962, the South African regime rescinded the special concessions in foreign currency regulations which had allowed the free transfer of funds to Israel.[11] The South African Jewish organizations attempted to influence Israel to abstain "with the other Western nations" in the votes on anti-*apartheid* resolutions in the United Nations.[12] They also turned themselves into instruments of South African propaganda by deciding that "the Jewish community should take steps to explain South Africa's position to Jews overseas and at home."[13]

25. The underlying community of interests between the two Governments despite divergencies over foreign policy, was shown by South African support for Israel during the 1967 war. Special regulations to allow free transfer of funds to Israel were quickly reinstated, and other forms of material aid were made available. The war led to increasing recognition of the basic similarity of the two countries in international politics and the resulting need to co-operate. *Die Burger,* organ of the National Party in Cape Province, decribed the situation as follows:

> "Israel and South Africa have a common lot. Both are engaged in a struggle for existence, and both are in constant clash with the decisive majorities in the United Nations. Both are reliable foci of strength within the region, which would, without them, fall into anti-Western anarchy. It is in South Africa's interest that Israel is successful in containing her enemies, who are among our own most vicious enemies; and Israel would have all the world against it if the navigation route around the Cape of Good Hope should be out of operation because South Africa's control is undermined. The anti-Western powers have driven Israel and South Africa into a community of interests which had better be utilized than denied."[14]

26. The same argument was reiterated by *Jewish Affairs,* the official organ of the South African Jewish Board of Deputies:

> "The argument that Israel and South Africa have a basic community of interest in the Middle East and further south has more than a grain of truth in it. There is nothing secret or sinister about it. The strong ties between the two countries, closer than ever since the 1967 war, are inseparable from their geographical and strategic position, from their anti-communist outlook, and from all the realities of their national existence... In short, the destinies of the two countries, so different in many wars, but so alike in the fundamental conditions of their survival, are interwoven in a much more meaningful sense than any enemy propagandist could conceive, or, for that matter, would be happy to see."[15]

27. Economic, political and military links between the two countries grew rapidly in the subsequent years, despite some new temporary strains occasioned by Israel's overtures toward independent Africa. In 1971, the South African regime again suspended the free transfer of money to Israel in protest against Israel's offer of $5,000 to the OAU Assistance Fund for the liberation movements. Israel was then obliged to withdraw the offer.

28. The October 1973 war was a major milestone in the process of growing identification between the two countries. Most African States broke relations with Israel during or after the war, thus putting an end to Israel's need to maintain a facade of opposition to *apartheid.* This was immediately evident in Israel's voting on anti-*apartheid* resolutions in the United Nations: since 1973, Israel has either been absent, has abstained or has voted against these resolutions.[16] South Africa openly expressed its support for Israel during the war: Mr. P. W. Botha, South African Minister of Defence, declared that "within our means, and without declaring war", his Government would provide assistance to Israel. Prime Minister Vorster stated that if Israel lost the war, its defeat would have important consequences for South Africa.[17] Accordingly, South Africa immediately lifted exchange controls to allow free transfer of funds to Israel and provided various forms of material assistance, including military assistance. After the war, South Africa became, in the words of an observer, "Israel's sole substantive supporter on the African continent and one of the few Governments anywhere not calling for its withdrawal from occupied Arab territory."[18]

29. In the years since the 1973 war, the two countries have rapidly moved towards the establishment of an ever closer alliance in defence of common interests, and the formalization of their links. They upgraded the level of their diplomatic relations from the legal of legations to that of embassies. Several joint investment projects were undertaken by para-statal corporations in both countries, and commercial and scientific ties were strengthened with the creation of appropriate organs and the exchange of high-level visits. Political contacts were greatly intensified. Among the

high-ranking Israeli officials who have visited South Africa since 1974 are Gen. Moshe Dayan, former Minister of Defence, Gen. Meir Amit, former head of Israel's intelligence services and present Chairman of Koor Industries; and Gen. Chaim Herzog, then military commentator on the Israeli radio and now Permanent Representative of Israel to the United Nations. While such Israeli visitors had in the past usually been admitted to South Africa in connexion with functions involving the local Jewish community, this limitation was reportedly dropped in 1974.[19]

30. Dr. C. P. Mulder, South Africa's Minister of Interior and Information, visited Israel twice, in June 1975 and in March 1976, and met with the Prime Minister and the Foreign Minister of Israel.[20] His visits apparently paved the way for a formal invitation by Prime Minister Yitzhak Rabin to Prime Minister J. B. Vorster, who visited Israel for four days in April 1976. Mr. Vorster, who was accompanied by Foreign Minister Mr. Hilgard Muller, Secretary for Foreign Affairs, Mr. Brand Fourie and others, held talks with the President of Israel, with the Prime Minister, the Foreign Minister, the Defence Minister and other high officials in the Israeli Government. He toured strategic areas in the southern Sinai (reportedly the first foreign Prime Minister to do so), and visited a military aircraft factory.[21]

31. During Mr. Vorster's visit, a wide-ranging agreement on economic, scientific and industrial collaboration was concluded between South Africa and Israel. Announcing the agreement at a press conference held on 12 April in Jerusalem, Mr. Vorster stated that the two Governments had decided to establish a Ministerial Joint Committee comprising Ministers of South Africa and Israel, which would meet at least once a year to review the situation of economic relations between the two countries and to discuss ways and means to expand economic co-operation between the two countries, in particular the encouragement of investments, development of trade, scientific and industrial co-operation and joint utilization of South African raw materials and Israeli manpower in joint projects. A steering group would be established in order to regulate the exchange of information and ideas, and committees would be established in both countries.[22] It was expected that, from the South African side, the committee would include the Ministers of Defence, Finance, and Economic Affairs.[23] Press reports indicated that the pact might also involve "a major expansion of the arms supply relationship," although both Governments denied that this was discussed. The subsequent announcement that Israel was building two missile boats for the *apartheid* regime made it clear that military co-operation is being rapidly strengthened following Mr. Vorster's visit.[24]

32. While the agreement aroused world-wide condemnation, it was welcomed jubilantly by most sectors of the South African white community, in particular the Jewish organizations, which hailed Vorster as "an outstanding statesman" and called the pact "a most imaginative act of

statesmanship on the part of both countries."[25] The Johannesburg *Star* commented:

> "Clearly the pact goes well beyond the usual trade and co-operation agreements which normally round off a state visit between friendly countries ... at the root of the pact is a mutual exchange of materials with military know-how which both countries desperately need. For both, it is virtually a question of survival. Very likely that is the stongest imperative of all."[26]

An editorial in the *Rand Daily Mail* stated:

> "There is no gainsaying the signal nature of Mr. Vorster's triumph this week. By achieving a publicly announced economic, scientific and industrial pact with Israel he has done far more than merely formalize bonds that have, in any case, been growing stronger. He has, in fact, acquired for South Africa a public friend, an avowed ally, at a time when this country confronts an increasingly hostile world and an increasingly aggressive Black Africa."[27]

33. Closer association with Israel has also important political advantages for South Africa. In an interview with a group of Jewish newspaper editors from the United States of America, published in *Jewish Press* of 18 June 1976, the Israeli Ambassador to South Africa, Mr. Yitzhak Unna, made it clear that he expected the agreement to influence the attitudes of the international Jewish community towards South Africa favourably.

IV. Diplomatic and consular relations

34. Israel has maintained a Legation in Pretoria and a Consulate-General in Johannesburg since 1949. Being a member of the Commonwealth at the time, South Africa chose initially to be represented through the United Kingdom in order to promote links with the Arab countries. In 1961, following the severance of diplomatic ties by the United Arab Republic and the break with the Commonwealth, South Africa sought a closer association with Israel. Israel, however, had adopted a policy of wooing the newly independent African States: consequently, it recalled its Minister in Pretoria, and left the mission under a Charge d'affaires. The over-all strengthening of relations between the two countries subsequent to the June 1967 war led to the general upgrading of Israel's level of representation: in 1969, Israel appointed a Charge d'affaires with the personal rank of ambassador. In April 1973, it expanded its Consulate-General. Following the October 1973 war, Israel decided to elevate its diplomatic mission to a full-scale embassy, and appointed Mr. Yitzhak Unna, a former Consul-General, as its first ambassador.[28]

35. South Africa reciprocated by establishing a Consulate-General in Tel Aviv in 1971, headed by a Consul-General with the personal rank of ambassador. In 1975, South Africa established an embassy in Tel Aviv,

and its first Ambassador to Israel presented his credentials in January 1976.[29]

V. Military collaboration

36. Military collaboration between South Africa and Israel dates back to the very beginning of the State of Israel. Several hundred South African volunteers fought with the Zionists after November 1947, and South Africa sent food, medical and other supplies to the Zionists during the 1948 war. The first pilot to fall in battle in the Israeli Air Force was a South African volunteer. Other South African pilots have reportedly died fighting for Israel.[30]

37. Military contacts between the two countries were intensified during and after the 1967 war, leading to the establishment of ever closer relations in the military sphere. While professing neutrality, South Africa provided material support for the Israeli war effort in 1967, most importantly by relaxing controls on the transfer of funds. The sum involved, though never officially disclosed, is estimated to have been over R 21 million.[31] In addition, the official South African blood transfusion service loaned blood to the Israeli medical services.[32] Spokesmen from all white political parties expressed sympathy for Israel and participated in various support activities.[33]

38. Jewish volunteers from South Africa served in Israel during the 1967 war, officially in non-military posts, replacing Israelis who had been called up for combat duty. The South African Zionist Federation launched a special fund for Israel. In addition, many other sectors of the white South African community became involved in support for Israel.[34]

39. South Africa's support for Israel during the October 1973 war was even more extensive, marking a new stage in the development of relations. The South African Government relaxed all exchange control regulations to allow immediate cash transfer to Israel of all money raised. Although the total amount was not disclosed, press reports have indicated that it may have been as high as $30 million. As during the 1967 war, collection of funds and support activities were carried out by all sections of the white community, not just Jewish groups.[35]

40. A considerable number of South African volunteers went to Israel during and after the war to take part in combat and other duties. Press reports have indicated that hundreds of South Africans, both Jewish and non-Jewish, volunteered to fight in Israel in October 1973. At least one report put the number of men with South African connexions in the Israeli armed forces during the war at 1,500.[36] Following the war, hundreds of volunteers from South Africa went to Israel to replace kibbutz workers who were still in the armed forces.[37]

41. There were indications that South Africa may have played an even more direct role in the October 1973 war. The Egyptian Government announced that a Mirage jetfighter of South African origin had been shot down on the Suez front during the war. A subsequent report in the London *Daily Telegraph* suggested that South Africa had sent several Mirage jets via the Azores to aid Israel. These reports were subsequently denied by both Israel and South Africa.[38]

42. In addition to providing assistance during the wars, South Africa was reported to have supplied military equipment to Israel, but these reports were denied by Israel. In January 1970, for instance, the Jewish Telegraphic Agency reported that the South African Government was exporting giant 65-ton tanks, designed after the British "Chieftain" Tank, to Israel. The Israeli Foreign Ministry refused to comment on the report, which was denied by the Israeli representative to the United Nations.[39]

43. There has been increasing evidence of Israel's military co-operation with the *apartheid* regime, in the form of supplies of military equipment and of assistance in counter-insurgency training and in the use of sophisticated weaponry.

44. In the early 1960s, South Africa obtained from a Belgian company a licence to manufacture the *Uzi* submachine gun, of Israeli design.[40] This is now standard equipment in the South African Army.

45. South Africa has long been interested in obtaining military aircraft from Israel. The first contacts between the Israeli Aircraft Industries and South Africa's Atlas Aircraft Corporation were reported to have taken place in 1967, concerning the possibility of export to South Africa of the new Israeli plane, the "Arava", specially suited for counter-insurgency operations. The "Arava" was taken to South Africa for test trials, and there have been unconfirmed reports that South Africa may have bought the plane.[41]

46. Another indication that Israel may have supplied military aircraft to South Africa came in May 1971, when Israel was reported to have offered to replace three airplanes of the South African Air Force which had crashed into Table Mountain.[42]

47. There have also been reports that Israel might supply the "Gabriel" sea-borne missile, manufactured in Israel, to South Africa. These reports were also denied by a spokesman for the Israeli Aircraft Industries in September 1974. Shortly thereafter, however, the London *Daily Telegraph* indicated that six missile boats then being built in South Africa would probably be equipped with the "Gabriel".[43]

48. An important element of Israel's military collaboration with South Africa has been the sharing of expertise in counter-insurgency techniques and sophisticated modern weaponry. A South African mission was reported to have flown to Israel in June 1967 to study the use of weapons and the tactics of lightning strikes during the six-day war.[44] After the war, the Chief of Staff of the Israeli Air Force visited South Africa to explain in

detail the lessons of the war to the South African staff college.[45]

49. Gen. Meir Amit, former head of Israel's intelligence services and present chairman of Koor Industries, disclosed during a visit to South Africa in July 1975 that senior Israeli military officers visit South Africa regularly to lecture South African officers on modern warfare and counter-insurgency techniques. Although declining to give details, Gen. Amit stated that the South African Defence Force was benefiting from Israel's experience and know-how in the field of military electronics manufacture.[46]

50. On 3 April 1976, the Johannesburg correspondent of the *Daily Telegraph* reported that Israeli officers had been closely involved with South African Army planning in the Angolan campaign. According to the report, Gen. R. H. D. Rogers of the South African Air Force had stated that one reason why South African casualties in the campaign had been so light was because Israeli techniques for evacuation and treatment of front-line casualties had been closely followed.

51. Marcia Freedman, Opposition member in the Israeli Parliament, asserted in June 1976 that hundreds of Israeli soldiers were attached to South African Army units as instructors and participated in training manoeuvres. The report was denied by the Israeli Defence Minister.[47]

52. Desire to share in Israel's expertise in military technology and modern warfare was reportedly an important element in Mr. Vorster's visit to Israel in April 1976.[48] Press reports indicated that South Africa was prepared to finance an expansion of Israel's arms-producing capacity, and even to supply Israel with uranium, in return for the Israeli *Kfir* jetfighter and other arms. Mr. Vorster denied these reports, but toured the *Kfir* factory. A representative of the Israeli Aircraft Industries was known to have visited South Africa in January 1976. According to the *Times* of London, "informed sources" indicated that arms from Israel were already on their way to South Africa even before Mr. Vorster's trip.[49]

53. In August 1976, the Israeli radio announced that Israel was building two long-range gunboats armed with sea-to-sea missiles for the South African Navy. Unofficial sources were quoted as having said that 50 African naval officers and their families had arrived in Israel and would take delivery of the boats in January. Press reports have indicated that Israel is building "several" missile boats for the *apartheid* regime, and in return will receive steel and coal.[50]

VI. Trade

54. Trade between Israel and South Africa has increased rapidly in recent years, especially since the June 1967 war in the Middle East, and has almost doubled in the aftermath of the October 1973 war. The following table shows the growth in trade between the two countries over the ten-

year period ending in 1974, the last complete year for which statistics are available:

	Israel's exports to South Africa	Israel's imports from South Africa
	(in million US dollars)	
1965	2.7	4.3
1966	2.3	4.5
1967	4.0	3.4
1968	5.7	5.2
1969	8.2	5.8
1970	10.7	10.2
1971	9.4	8.1
1972	8.8	11.6
1973	12.0	34.3
1974	28.7	43.1

56. In 1974, the main South African imports from Israel were chemicals, textiles, rubber goods, pharmaceuticals, electronic equipment and machinery. South Africa's main exports consisted of steel, cement, timber and sugar. Coal and other raw materials are expected to be added to the list in the near future.[51]

57. Israel's largest import from South Africa is raw diamonds, which are not included in statistics for trade between the two countries since sales are carried out through the London-based Central Selling Organization (CSO), an arm of De Beers. Israel, which is one of the world's leading diamond processors, reportedly buys almost half of its raw diamonds from the CSO for an amount exceeding $100 million a year.[52]

58. Although trade links between the two countries were established immediately after the creation of the State of Israel, trade remained minimal until the opening of the Straits of Tiran as a result of the 1956 tripartite aggression against Egypt.[53] It was only after the 1967 war in the Middle East that concerted efforts were made to formalize and strengthen commercial relations between the two countries. A delegate from the Israeli Ministry for Commerce and Industry was sent to South Africa for a four-month period at the end of 1967. Representatives of Israeli business and shipping interests also visited South Africa with a view to promoting trade.[54]

59. Several associations aimed at promoting trade between the two countries were set up in the aftermath of the war. The Israel-South Africa Friendship League was established in Israel in January 1968, with a membership which included several politicians, local councillors and businessmen. The organization pledged to work to increase trade and to improve relations between the two countries.[55] The South Africa Foundation, an

organization of prominent South African and international businessmen devoted to promoting South Africa's interests abroad, established an Israeli-South African "Man-to-Man Committee" whose membership included high-ranking former Israeli politicians and military men. The Committee was instrumental in promoting exchanges or visitors at the highest levels and in furthering economic links between the two countries.[56] An Israel-South Africa Trade Association (ISATA) was also established in 1968, and was reported to have been a key factor in the subsequent rapid increase in trade between the two countries.[57]

60. In June 1968, Israel appointed a trade commissioner to South Africa. [58]

61. An Israel Fashion Week was held in Johannesburg and Cape Town in August 1968. This was the first major fashion promotion of its kind by Israel in South Africa, organized by the Israeli Export Institute. More Israel Weeks were held in South Africa in the following years.[59]

62. In July 1970, the South African State-owned Industrial Development Corporation (IDC) signed an agreement with the Foreign Trade Bank of Israel extending a guaranteed line of credit for R 10.7 million to promote South African capital exports to Israel. The first South African trade mission to Israel was organized shortly thereafter by ISATA, with the participation of the Federated Chamber of Industries, the IDC, and some of South Africa's largest companies and banks. The mission's goal was to ensure that the line of credit would be fully taken up, and to strengthen economic links between the two countries.[60]

63. A new line of credit for $14.9 million was made available to Israel by the IDC at the beginning of June 1971. The agreement was followed by another South African trade mission to Israel in early 1972, with the purpose of further boosting South African exports.[61]

64. The October 1973 war in the Middle East marked another major turning point in commercial relations between South Africa and Israel. In January 1974, the Israel-South Africa Chamber of Commerce was formed in Tel Aviv. At the inauguration ceremony, the South African Consul-General predicted that trade between the two countries would increase considerably during the year (as in fact it did). The Chamber was joined by nearly 100 Israeli firms. Its immediate success led to the formation of a South Africa-Israel Chamber of Commerce in Johannesburg shortly thereafter.[62]

65. In 1974, Israel and South Africa undertook a joint campaign to promote Jaffa and Outspan oranges and orange juice in the United Kingdom.[63]

66. Israel had a pavilion at the Easter Rand Show—South Africa's largest industrial fair—in the spring of 1974, for the first time in 10 years. In 1976, Israel was reportedly one of the major overseas exhibitors at the Show, with electronic and control equipment.[64]

67. In April 1975, South Africa was designated a "preferred export

target" by the Israeli Ministry of Trade and Industry, and Israeli exporters were granted special financial concessions. [65] A high-level trade promotion mission from the Johannesburg Chamber of Commerce visited Israel in June 1975.[66]

68. Trade between South Africa and Israel was given another major boost by the co-operation agreement signed by Prime Minister Vorster during his visit to Israel in April 1976. The agreement was expected to lead to an expansion of two-way trade, the exchange of trade missions, and an increase in South Africa's exports of raw materials to Israel, in particular coal from the new Richards Bay harbour. The development of Richards Bay was expected to be accelerated as a result. There was speculation in the South African press that closer ties with Israel would result in a two-way shipping traffic in which vessels would carry coal from South Africa to Israel and return with oil for South Africa.[67]

VII. Investment

69. South African investment in Israel has grown rapidly since the early 1970s, and in particular after the October 1973 war. This growth was stimulated by a decision of the South African Government, in May 1971, to relax controls on direct investment by South African companies in Israel, raising the ceiling to R 10 million. The ceiling was raised again to R 20 million in May 1974, and it is expected to increase to R 32 million in 1977.[68]

70. Israeli interests are also increasingly channelling capital to South Africa, both as direct investment and in the form of loans. Japhet Bank and Bank Leumi established offices in South Africa in 1971 and 1973, respectively.[69] The United States subsidiary of Bank Leumi was involved in a secret loan to the South African Finance Ministry in 1972, with a share of $2 million.[70] Bank Leumi recently sent one of its top executives to South Africa to explore further investment possibilities.[71]

71. Direct investment by either country in the other has taken place primarily through joint undertakings by public and private corporations. Both South African and Israeli leaders have often pointed out that the economics of the two countries are complementary and that their potential can best be realized through partnership arrangements. As the former Israeli Consul-General to South Africa put it: "With South Africa's abundance of raw materials, and Israel's know-how, we can really go places if we join forces."[72] The Israeli Trade Consul in South Africa pointed out recently that South Africa was rich in cheap labour, which Israel lacked.[73]

72. A major advantage for South Africa of partnership arrangements with Israeli companies has been that Israel is thereby used as a manufacturing base from which to evade the boycott against the *apartheid* regime. For example, South Africa manufactures textiles, chemicals and fertilizers

in Israel for export to Africa and other countries.[74] In addition, South Africa is using Israel as a springboard for circumventing high European Economic Community and United States tariffs on its products. South African semi-finished goods can be exported to Israel and finished there to qualify for an Israeli certificate of origin, thus taking advantage of Israel's free-trade agreements with the Community and the United States.[75]

73. The co-operation agreement between Israel and South Africa concluded on the occasion of Prime Minister Vorster's visit to Israel in April 1976, is expected to lead to a significant increase in these joint investment projects. The South Africa-Israel Chamber of Commerce is reportedly considering sending a high-level mission to Israel to study the most effective ways to implement the agreement. Mr. E. Hausmann, President of the Transvaal Chamber of Industries, said that the Chamber had been approached by a number of industrialists eager to explore investment opportunities in Israel, and was considering sending an industrial mission there. Several major companies already involved in joint undertakings have announced expansion schemes. The pact is also expected to lead to an agreement to avoid double taxation in the near future.[76]

74. While the actual extent of investment by either country in the other is not known precisely, a list of the known projects is given here:

(a) South African investments in Israel

75. Steel Pipe Industry (Pty.), a subsidiary of African Gate Holdings, entered into a partnership with Middle East Tube Co. of Haifa to build a R 250,000 spiral steel pipe mill.[77]

76. Africa-Israel Investments, a major Israeli firm in which South African interests have a 25 per cent stake, participated in a project in Venezuela with financing by the South African Industrial Development Corporation.[78]

77. The Desiree Clothing group of Cape Town established a textile venture in Israel called Cecil Knits.[79]

78. Undisclosed South African interests have invested 400,000 pounds sterling in an Israeli factory to make cotton prints for the black South African and independent African market. This was reportedly only one of six or seven such projects in the pipeline.[80]

79. The South African Iron and Steel Corporation (Iscor), a State-owned company, entered into a partnership with Koor Industries, a major industrial investment company owned by a syndicate of Israeli trade unions. The new company, Iskoor, with a share capital of R 1 million (owned 51 per cent by Koor and 49 per cent by Iscor), distributes steel in Israel. The company's success was such that a steel-processing plant is now being built at Kirjat near Ghaza. The company has lately made a substantial investment in a ware-house and a steel servicing centre.[81]

80. Dorbyl, one of South Africa's largest heavy engineering companies, has established a subsidiary in partnership with the Israeli company Koor to tender on engineering construction projects. The first contract obtained by the new company was a R 9.2 million project for the construction of steel tank farms in Israel.[82]

81. The South African Railways and companies Dorman Long and Union Carriage are building a railway line to the Red Sea port of Eilat.[83]

82. Other South African projects undertaken in Israel include the following: "South Africa House," a 26-story office and shops complex in Tel Aviv; a petro-chemicals complex in Haifa; a factory complex at Holon, near Tel Aviv, for rental to light industry; the manufacture of agricultural machinery in Eilat; a plant to make welded mesh fencing in Ashdod; a rice-milling plant in Haifa; a non-ferrous metal works; and participation in the redevelopment of the port at Eilat and of other Israeli ports.[84]

(b) Israeli investments in South Africa

83. Israeli investments in South Africa have remained modest until recently, when Koor Industries set up an agency in Johannesburg—Afrita—with the specific purpose of promoting economic relations between the two countries, and in particular joint investment projects.[85] The expansion of ties, however, has led to the establishment of several major joint ventures in South Africa.

84. In June 1974, Koor Industries made its first investment in South Africa by joining in a partnership with the South African Adcock-Ingram group for the construction of a R 2.5 million agricultural chemicals plant at the Berlin "border area", near the Transkei. A new company, Agbro (Pty), was formed to establish and run the factory, which would be the first of its kind in South Africa. Koor was to hold 25 per cent of the equity, with the South African group holding the difference. The factory was expected to have sufficient capacity to supply the needs for herbicides of South Africa and neighbouring territories, as well as "countries further afield." [86]

85. Assia Chemical Laboratories, another Israeli chemicals company, has established a subsidiary in South Africa, called Denkavit, for the manufacture of balanced feeds. Assia holds a 25 per cent share in the venture, with the option to purchase the remaining 75 per cent.[87]

86. Israeli interests are building a seawater desalination plant in South Africa.[88]

87. Tadiran, Israel's leading manufacturer of advanced electronic equipment, is to establish a R 1.7 million plant at Rosslyn, in a "border area." The plant, which will produce nickel cadmium products and batteries, will reportedly be fitted with the latest equipment from Israel. Tadiran is also to assemble emergency lighting equipment in partnership

with Conlite South Africa at a plant in Johannesburg.[89]

88. Earlier, and smaller, Israeli ventures in South Africa include: Electra, a manufacturer of air-conditioners; Car Part Industries, in partnership with a South African company; and a joint venture between Shabal Engineering Works and the South African Power Tool and Equipment Co. for the manufature of tools under licence.[90]

89. Israel has recently shown interest in investing in the "bantustans." *Ha'aretz,* an influential Israeli newspaper, has suggested that Israel could help "develop" the African reserves through its know-how in modern agricultural techniques and in combating soil erosion.[91] In April 1976, a delegation from Israel attended a three-day symposium organized in Umtata, Transkei, by the South African Foreign Affairs Association.[92]

VIII. Collaboration in science and technology

90. In the past few years, South Africa and Israel have established increasingly closer ties of scientific and technological collaboration. According to Dr. van der Merwe Brink, president of the South African Council for Scientific and Industrial Research (CSIR), a para-statal agency, this co-operation extends to such areas as water resources management, agriculture, building and construction, oceanography, the manufacturing industry including chemicals, fertilizers, electronics, aeronautical engineering and others.[93]

91. The first steps towards such collaboration were taken in 1972, with the exchanges of missions by scientists and technicians to study various areas of interest. In June 1972, the South African Minister for Water Affairs and Forestry visited Israel to study Israeli methods of water conservation and held talks with his Israeli counterpart, with a view to establishing collaboration with Israel in this field.[94]

92. A year later, a 15-man mission from South Africa visited Israel for two weeks to study methods of establishing new towns, urban renewal schemes, emergency building schemes, and industrialized buildings. The mission was headed by Dr. T. L. Webb, director of the National Building Research Unit of the CSIR.[95]

93. In July 1974, Dr. E. J. Kruger, senior professional officer at the Lowveld Fisheries Research Station of the Transvaal Nature Conservancy Division, visited Israel to attend a fisheries seminar.[96]

94. In 1975, steps were taken to put these initial contacts on a more formal basis. A South African Committee of the Weizmann Institute was formed under the chairmanship of Prof. S. S. Israelstam, chemistry professor at Witwatersrand University. One of the first tasks of the Committee was the organization, in co-operation with the CSIR, of the Weizmann Centenary Science Conference, held in Johannesburg in April 1976 with the participation of leading scientists from South Africa and

from the Weizmann Institute of Science in Israel.[97] The establishment of the Committee was followed by a visit to Israel of Dr. C. van der Merwe Brink, president of CSIR, and Dr. W. A. Verbeek, South African Secretary for Agriculture, to promote scientific co-operation. Early in 1976, the visit was returned by Dr. E. Tal, director of the Israeli National Council for Research and Development, Mr. Y. Saphir, director of international affairs of the Council, and Prof. S. Lavee, chief director of the Department of Horticulture, who travelled to South Africa as guests of the CSIR.[98]

95. The strengthening of scientific and technological co-operation was one of the aims of the agreement with Israel signed by Prime Minister Vorster on the occasion of his visit to Israel in April 1976. In June, it was announced that a research exchange agreement had been reached between the SCIR and the Israeli scientists and for a symposium of interest to both countries to be held annually. The first symposium was already held in Israel in November 1975 on the recycling of waste water. The next symposium would reportedly be held in South Africa in 1977, again on a topic of equal importance and common to the national interest of both countries. A similar agreement was also reached between the Israeli Agricultural Research Organization and the South African Department of Agricultural Technical Services. According to Dr. Meiring Naude, scientific advisor to Prime Minister Vorster, South Africa expects to gain tremendous scientific advantages from closer co-operation with Israeli scientists and technologists.[99]

96. A further area in which South Africa is apparently interested in tapping Israeli know-how is that of scientific management. It was reported in April 1976 that Mr. Israel Meidan, head of the Israeli Productivity Institute and reportedly one of the world's top productivity experts (the Institute itself is said to be the largest of its kind in the world) had been invited to speak at a country-wide series of seminars in South Africa at the end of 1976. Mr. Meidan would seek to apply Israel's experience in raising productivity to the South African situation. While in South Africa, he would be the joint guest of the National Productivity Institute in Pretoria and the National Development and Management Foundation.[100]

IX. Airline and shipping connexions

97. Regular airline connexions between Israel and South Africa are provided by El Al, the Israeli airline. Following the increase in relations between the two countries after each major war in the Middle East, El Al stepped up its flights from Tel Aviv to Johannesburg to twice weekly in 1968, and thrice weekly in November 1973. The shorter route made possible by the Israeli occupation of the Sinai peninsula has reportedly led to a rapid increase in the volume of traffic carried by the airline.[101]

98. Shipping connections are provided by Zim, the Israeli shipping line. The line plies regularly between Israel and South Africa.[102]

X. Cultural relations

99. Social and cultural relations have been intensified with the strengthening of political, economic and military ties between South Africa and Israel. For instance, tourism increased rapidly after the 1967 war, with the number of South African visitors to Israel rising by 35 per cent in one year, and continuing to increase steadily thereafter. This rapid growth resulted in the establishment of an Israeli Government tourist office in South Africa in 1968.[103] In 1972, South African tourists to Israel numbered 15,319.[104] In the same year, 2,601 Israelis visited South Africa.[105]

100. Visits by Israeli artists to South Africa have become increasingly common since 1968. In that year, the Karmon Israeli Singers and Dancers and the comedian Shimon Dzigan toured South Africa.[106]

101. Two leading musicians from the Israeli Philharmonic Orchestra played in Johannesburg in August 1970.[107]

102. In 1974, the Israeli Philharmonic Orchestra toured South Africa for two weeks. It was a major cultural event for South Africa, which reportedly had not entertained a visiting orchestra of comparable size and stature for 18 years.[108]

103. In 1976, the Bat Dor Dance Company of Israel toured Johannesburg, Cape Town and Bloemfontein.[109] An exhibition of paintings of some of Israel's most prominent artists was held in Johannesburg in March 1976.[110]

104. Another instance of increasing cultural relations was a twin-city agreement between Cape Town and Haifa signed in February 1975. The mayor of Cape Town visited Haifa on the occasion and stated that the agreement had the consent of the Government of Israel and the South African Department of Foreign Affairs. The agreement was expected to lead to intensified exchanges between the two cities. One result of the agreement was the establishment of a cultural exchange society at the University of Haifa aiming to promote closer ties with South Africa. The director of foreign affairs at the University of Haifa toured South Africa for three weeks in June 1976 to promote the aims of the Society, in particular by starting an exchange programme between South African professors and students and the University of Haifa, and by setting up a correspondence course in Jewish affairs in South Africa.[111]

105. Among other instances of cultural collaboration are reported to be the following:

> "In Israel there are countless foundations established by South Africans: the parasitology laboratory of Hebrew University is entirely financed by a South African foundation; the Bialik chair of Hebrew; the Ruth Ochberg chair of agriculture; the Cootcher Museum; an entire wing of the national library; the Silas S. Perry foundation for biblical research..." [112]

106. In addition, it was disclosed in 1975 that a wealthy Israeli arts dealer, after a trip to South Africa, had offered a $2.3 million book collection to the Hebrew University to establish a department devoted to the promotion of closer ties between Israelis and Afrikaners.[113]

107. Cultural relations between the two countries have at times concerned Namibia. In 1971, a study group from Tel Aviv University visited Namibia as guests of the Windhoek Rotary Club to study the socio-economic and political structure of the country.[114]

XI. Collaboration in sports

108. Sports ties between the two countries, which had been dormant since the mid-1950s, were intensified since 1970. In March of that year, the Israeli Lawn Tennis Association declined to use its proxy vote at the Davis Cup meeting in London which was to decide on participation by Rhodesia and South Africa.[115]

109. In 1971, the official Israeli judo team visited South Africa, the first international judo team to do so.[116] The Israeli basketball team Maccabi Tel Aviv played matches against all-white teams in South Africa in July-August 1971.[117] In November, two Israeli athletes participated in multiracial athletic meetings in Cape Town.[118]

110. An official Israeli women's tennis team went to South Africa in March 1972 to participate in the Federation Tennis Cup.[119]

111. In July 1973, a team of 120 athletes from South Africa competed in the Maccabiah Games in Israel commemorating the 25th anniversary of the establishment of Israel.[120] In December of the same year, the Israeli Sports Federation sent a team to compete in the international gymnastics competition in Johannesburg.[121]

112. The Northern Transvaal rugby team toured Israel in January 1976.[122]

---

[1] Richard P. Stevens, *Weizmann and Smuts: A study in Zionist-South African co-operation* (Beirut, Institute for Palestine Studies, 1975); Gustav Saron and Louis Hotz, *The Jews in South Africa* (Cape Town, London, New York, Oxford University Press, 1955) pp. 281 ff. General Smuts, a close personal friend of Chaim Weizmann, the Zionist leader, was to remain one of the strongest supporters of the Zionist cause until his death.
[2] Antoine J. Bullier, "Les relations entre l'Afrique du Sud et Israel," *Revue francaise d'etudes politiques africaines*, No. 119, November 1975.
[3] Richard P. Stevens, "Zionism, South Africa and apartheid—the paradoxical triangle," *The Arab World*, vol. XVI, No. 2, February 1970.
[4] Henry Katzew, "Jews in the land of *Apartheid*," *Midstream*, vol. 8, December 1962.
[5] Stevens, *op. cit.*
[6] Ibid.; Leslie Rubin, "Afrikaner nationalism and the Jews," *Africa South*, vol. 1, No. 3, April-June 1957; Interview with Mr. Yitzhak Unna, Israel's Ambassador to South Africa, in *Jewish Press*, 18 June 1976.
[7] Katzew, *op. cit.*
[8] Quoted in Stevens, *op. cit.*
[9] Stevens, *op. cit.*; Saron and Hotz, *op. cit.*

United Nations and International Response 223

[10] Peter Hellyer, "Israel and South Africa—Development of relations 1967-1974," paper prepared for the Special Committee against *Apartheid,* A/AC.115/L.396, p. 2.
[11] Stevens, *op. cit.*
[12] Henry Katzew, "South Africa: a country without friends," *Midstream,* Spring 1962.
[13] *Jewish Chronicle,* London, December 1962.
[14] *Die Burger,* Cape Town, 29 May 1968.
[15] *Jewish Affairs,* November 1970.
[16] Israel's voting record on anti-*apartheid* resolutions in the United Nations General Assembly since 1973 has been as follows:
28th session—Resolution 3055, absent; resolution 3151A, absent; resolution 3151B, absent; resolution 3151C, absent; resolution 3151D, abstaining; resolution 3151E, abstaining; resolution 3151F, absent.
29th session—Resolution 3324A, no vote taken; resolution 3324B, absent; resolution 3324C, absent; resolution 3324D, abstaining; resolution 3324E, against.
30th session—Resolution 3411A, no vote taken; resolution 3411B, no vote taken; resolution 3411C, absent; resolution 3411D, absent; resolution 3411E, no vote taken; resolution 3411F, abstaining; resolution 3411G, against.
[17] *Rand Daily Mail,* Johannesburg, 15 October 1973; *South African Digest,* Pretoria, 19 October 1973; *Die Transvaler,* Johannesburg, 9, 13 and 15 October 1973.
[18] *New York Times,* 18 April 1976.
[19] *Jewish Chronicle,* London, 2 August 1974.
[20] Jerusalem Radio, 17 and 19 June 1975; *The Star,* Johannesburg, weekly airmail edition, 27 March 1976.
[21] *Herald Tribune,* Paris, 10 April 1976; *New York Times,* 18 April 1976; *Times,* London, 9 April 1976; *The Star,* Johannesburg, weekly airmail edition, 17 April 1976; *Comment and Opinion,* Pretoria, 16 April 1976.
[22] *House of Assembly Debates (Hansard),* 22 April 1976, Speech by the Prime Minister, Col. 5200.
[23] *The Star,* Johannesburg, weekly airmail edition, 24 April 1976; *Rand Daily Mail,* Johannesburg, 14 April 1976.
[24] *New York Times,* 18 April 1976, 9 August 1976; *Christian Science Monitor,* 12 August 1976.
[25] *The Star,* Johannesburg, weekly airmail edition, 17 April 1976.
[26] *The Star,* Johannesburg, weekly airmail edition, 17 April 1976.
[27] *Rand Daily Mail,* Johannesburg, 14 April 1976.
[28] *The Star,* Johannesburg, weekly airmail edition, 3 January 1969, 16 March 1974, 10 April 1976; Republic of South Africa, Pretoria, *Government Gazette,* 27 April 1973, 9 August 1974.
[29] *House of Assembly Debates (Hansard),* Questions and answers, 13 May 1975, cols. 151-2; Jerusalem radio, 12 January 1976.
[30] Antoine J. Bullier, "Les relations entre l'Afrique du Sud et Israel," *Revue francaise d'etudes politiques africaines,* No. 119, November 1975.
[31] *South African Digest,* Pretoria, 25 October 1970.
[32] *Rand Daily Mail,* Johannesburg, 19 June and 6 August 1967.
[33] *Ibid.,* 6 June 1967.
[34] *Ibid,* 31 May, 3, 6-9 June 1967; *The Star,* Johannesburg, weekly airmail edition, 10 June 1967.
[35] *Cape Times,* 16 October 1973; *The Star,* Johannesburg, 2 October, 7, 9 November 1973; *Rand Daily Mail,* Johannesburg, 9 October 1973.
[36] *The Star,* Johannesburg, weekly airmail edition, 13 October 1973; *Rand Daily Mail,* Johannesburg, 9 October 1973.
[37] *The Star,* Johannesburg, weekly airmail edition, 1 December 1973.
[38] *Daily Telegraph,* London, 31 October 1973; *The Star,* Johannesburg, 3 November 1973.
[39] *Jewish Telegraphic Agency,* 20 and 21 January 1970.
[40] *New York Times,* 30 April 1971; *Rand Daily Mail,* Johannesburg, 11 September 1971.
[41] *Sunday Times,* Johannesburg, 10 October 1967; *The Star,* Johannesburg, 25 May 1973; Peter Hellyer, "Israel and South Africa—development of relations, 1967-1974,"(A/AC.115/L.396), p. 25.
[42] *Rand Daily Mail,* Johannesburg, 11 September 1971; Hellyer, *op. cit.,* p. 18.
[43] *The Star,* Johannesburg, 9 September 1974; *Daily Telegraph,* London, 3 March 1975.
[44] *New York Times,* 30 April 1971.
[45] *Rand Daily Mail,* Johannesburg, 10 October 1967.
[46] *Rand Daily Mail,* Johannesburg, 7 July 1975; *Washington Post,* 8 July 1975; *New York Post,* 14 July 1975.

[47] *New York Times*, 1 June 1976; *Jerusalem Post*, 29 June 1976.
[48] *Times*, London, 3 April 1976.
[49] *New York Times*, 10 and 18 April 1976; Jerusalem Domestic Service, 12 April 1976; *Times*, London, 3 April 1976; *Daily Telegraph*, London, 3 April 1976.
[50] *Christian Science Monitor*, 12 August 1976.
[51] *The Star*, Johannesburg, weekly airmail edition, 24 April 1976; *Rand Daily Mail*, Johannesburg, 14 April 1976.
[52] *Rand Daily Mail*, Johannesburg, 3 February 1972; *To the Point International*, 22 February 1974.
[53] Hellyer, *op. cit.*
[54] *Rand Daily Mail*, Johannesburg, 25 October 1967; *Sunday Times*, Johannesburg, 10 December 1967.
[55] *Rand Daily Mail*, Johannesburg, 14 March 1968 and 26 January 1969.
[56] *Sechaba* (publication of the African National Congress of South Africa), April 1970; *Rand Daily Mail*, Johannesburg, 4 and 27 April 1968.
[57] *American-Jewish Yearbook*, 1969, p. 454.
[58] *Today's News*, published by the South African Embassy, London, 3 July 1968.
[59] *Rand Daily Mail*, Johannesburg, 16 July and 13 August 1968; *American-Jewish Yearbook*, 1970, p. 535.
[60] *Rand Daily Mail*, Johannesburg, 15 July 1970; *South African Financial Gazette*, 17 July 1970, 22 January and 28 May 1971.
[61] *Christian Science Monitor*, Boston, 5 June 1971; Johannesburg Radio, 19 April 1972.
[62] *South African Digest*, Pretoria, 22 February 1974; *Financial Mail*, Johannesburg, 17 March 1974; *Sunday Times*, Johannesburg, 17 March 1974; *Rand Daily Mail*, Johannesburg, 19 June 1974.
[63] Anti-*Apartheid* Movement, Communication to the Special Committee against *Apartheid*, 9 September 1974 (A/AC.115/L. 389).
[64] *Jewish Chronicle*, London, 5 April 1974; *Financial Mail*, Johannesburg, 15 April 1976.
[65] *South African Digest*, Pretoria, 25 April 1975.
[66] *Financial Mail*, Johannesburg, 13 June 1975.
[67] *The Star*, Johannesburg, weekly airmail edition, 17 April 1976.
[68] *South African Financial Gazette*, Johannesburg, 28 May 1971; *Financial Mail*, Johannesburg, 7 June 1974; *The Star*, Johannesbrug, weekly airmail edition, 24 April 1976.
[69] *South Africa Digest*, Pretoria, 7 May 1971; *South African Financial Gazette*, Johannesburg, 5 January 1973.
[70] Frankfurt Documents, published by the Corporate Information Centre of the National Council of Churches, New York, *CIC Brief*, July 1973.
[71] *South Africa Foundation News*, Johannesburg, January 1976.
[72] *Financial Mail*, Johannesburg, 7 June 1976.
[73] *The Star*, Johannesburg, weekly airmail edition, 17 April 1976.
[74] *Ibid.*, 9 June 1973, 15 and 16 October 1974.
[75] *Rand Daily Mail*, Johannesburg, 14 April 1976.
[76] *The Star*, Johannesburg, weekly airmail edition, 17 and 24 April 1976; *Rand Daily Mail*, Johannesburg, 14 April 1976; *South African Digest*, Pretoria, 30 April 1976.
[77] *The Star*, Johannesburg, weekly airmail edition, 3 October 1970.
[78] *Rand Daily Mail*, 25 February 1971.
[79] *South African Financial Gazette*, Johannesburg, 28 May 1971.
[80] *The Guardian*, London, 2 June 1973.
[81] *Sunday Times*, Johannesburg, 16 September 1973 and 24 March 1974; *The Star*, Johannesburg, weekly airmail edition, 24 April 1976; *South African Digest*, Pretoria, 11 June 1976.
[82] *The Star*, Johannesburg, weekly airmail edition, 24 April 1976.
[83] *Financial Mail*, Johannesburg, 15 April 1976; *South African Financial Gazette*, Johannesburg, 9 April 1976.
[84] *Sunday Times*, Johannesburg, 24 March 1974; *Financial Mail*, Johannesburg, 15 April 1976.
[85] *The Star*, Johannesburg, weekly airmail edition, 24 April 1976.
[86] *Sunday Times*, Johannesburg, 16 June 1974. Recent reports indicate a similar project in Berlin by the Israeli company Machteshim and the South African company Sentrachem. It is not clear whether these companies have joined the earlier undertaking, or whether this is a different project. (See *The Star*, Johannesburg, weekly airmail edition, 24 April 1976; *Financial Mail*, Johannesburg, 15 April 1976.)
[87] *The Star*, Johannesburg, weekly airmail edition, 24 April 1976.

United Nations and International Response   225

[88] *Rand Daily Mail*, Johannesburg, 7 July 1975; *South African Digest*, Pretoria, 23 April 1976.
[89] *South African Digest*, Pretoria, 14 May 1976.
[90] *Rand Daily Mail*, Johannesburg, 16 October 1973; *Sunday Times*, Johannesburg, 17 and 24 March 1974.
[91] Quoted in *South African Digest*, Pretoria, 30 April 1976.
[92] *The Star*, Johannesburg, weekly airmail edition, 24 April 1976.
[93] *The Star*, Johannesburg, weekly airmail edition, 8 May 1976.
[94] *Kuwait Times*, 13 June 1972.
[95] *Rand Daily Mail*, Johannesburg, 12 May 1973.
[96] *The Star*, Johannesburg, weekly airmail edition, 20 July 1974.
[97] *Rand Daily Mail*, Johannesburg, 14 April 1976.
[98] *The Star*, Johannesburg, weekly airmail edition, 24 April 1976.
[99] *Rand Daily Mail*, Johannesburg, 14 April and 1 June 1976; *The Star*, Johannesburg, weekly airmail edition, 5 June 1976; *New York Times*, 1 June 1976.
[100] *The Star*, Johannesburg, weekly airmail edition, 17 April 1976.
[101] *Rand Daily Mail*, Johannesburg, 25 October 1968; *The Star*, Johannesburg, 27 September 1973; Bank of Israel, Jerusalem, *Annual Report*, 1968.
[102] *South African Financial Gazette*, Johannesburg, 9 April 1976.
[103] *Rand Daily Mail*, Johannesburg, 28 October 1969; Bank of Israel, *Annual Report*, 1968.
[104] Central Bureau of Statistics, *Statistical Abstract of Israel*, 1973.
[105] Department of Statistics, Pretoria, *Bulletin of Statistics*, quarter ended September 1973.
[106] *Rand Daily Mail*, Johannesburg, 16 April and 19 July 1968.
[107] *Ibid.*, 11 August 1970.
[108] *Jerusalem Post*, 13 August 1974.
[109] *South African Digest*, Pretoria, 13 February 1976.
[110] *Ibid.*, 5 March 1976.
[111] *South African Digest*, Pretoria, 28 Feburary 1975 and 18 June 1976; Jerusalem radio, 17 and 19 June 1975.
[112] Bullier, *op. cit.*
[113] *Rand Daily Mail*, Johannesburg, 8 July 1975.
[114] *Windhoek Advertiser*, 11 March 1971.
[115] *Rand Daily Mail*, Johannesburg, 17 March 1970.
[116] *Ibid.*, 1 September 1971.
[117] *Today's News*, 3 August 1971.
[118] *Report from South Africa*, South African Embassy, London, February 1972.
[119] *Jewish Chronicle*, London, 24 March 1972.
[120] A/9022, para. 120-1
[121] *Jewish Chronicle*, London, 7 December 1973.
[122] *South African Digest*, Pretoria, 30 January 1976.

[9] Afro-Arab Condemnation of Apartheid in South Africa and Zionism in Palestine

The Declaration of Sharjah, Issued by the Afro-Arab Symposium, Held in Sharjah, United Arab Emirates, December 14-19, 1976.

Principles:

1. The Symposium affirms that the African and Arab peoples have had profound historical and cultural links in the past, experienced similar fates and struggles, and now share similar problems and aspirations. Therefore, the Symposium endorses the principle that the future of Africa and of the Arab World of Africans and Arabs throughout the world is organically linked; and neither can nor should seek a separate destiny.

2. The Symposium fully endorses and supports the African and Arab commitment to promote social, political, economic and cultural liberation and full independence in Africa and the Arab World. In particular, the Symposium supports the African Liberation movements and the Palestine Liberation Movement in their militant efforts to dismantle the colonial settler regimes of Israel and that of the Republic of South Africa and its control of Namibia, Rhodesia. The Symposium calls upon all African and Arab States to support by all means these national liberation movements and appeals to all anti-colonial states and peoples to endorse the principles of the African and Arab National Liberation Movements and to render them full support. . . .

5. The Symposium categorically condemns all forms of racism and racial discrimination throughout the world, including *apartheid* in South Africa and Zionism in Palestine. The Symposium supports and urges support for all international, regional, and national efforts to combat these doctrines and the states upholding them, by all means including sanctions boycotts and embargoes. . . .

[10] For a Closer Cooperation Between the African and Arab Peoples

Political Declaration of the First Afro-Arab Summit Conference Meeting Held in Cairo From 7 to 9 March 1977.

5. The African and Arab Heads of State and Government reaffirm the need to strengthen their peoples' united front in their struggle for national liberation and condemn imperialism, colonialism, neocolonialism, zionism, *apartheid* and all other forms of discrimination and racial and religious segregation, especially under the forms in which they appear in Southern Africa, Palestine and the other occupied Arab and African Territories. In this connection they express their full support for the struggle of the peoples of Palestine, Zimbabwe, Namibia, South Africa and the so-called French Somaliland (Djibouti) for the recovery of their legitimate national rights and the exercise of their right to self-determination and affirm their support for the political unity and territorial integrity of the Comoros . . . .

10. The Afro-Arab Summit Conference, after a thorough examination of the situation, expressed great concern about the problems of Palestine, the Middle East, Zimbabwe, Namibia and South Africa. Fully convinced that these causes are Afro-Arab causes, the Summit decides to extend its total support to the peoples struggling against the racist and zionist regimes and to the Frontline States bordering confrontation zones for their assistance to the National Liberation Struggle . . . .

INDEX

Absentee Property Law (1950) 28, 29
African National Congress 31, 62, 172, 174-176
Afrikaners 27, 30, 51, 59-60, 63, 67, 70, 74-75, 113, 143, 154, 193, 206
Afro-Arab Summit Conference (1977) 15, 191, 226
Alexander, Bernard 47-48, 115
Aliens Act (1936) 57
Allon, Yigal 160, 178, 188
American Jewish Congress 11, 69, 181, 187
Amit, Meir 80, 152-153, 154, 209, 213
Anglo-American Inquiry Committee 44
Angola 11, 80, 146, 157, 168, 170, 176, 179, 180, 201
Apartheid 7, 9, 11, 12, 13, 23, 24, 26, 31, 62, 63, 64, 65, 66, 68, 69, 70, 72, 75, 76, 77, 109, 110, 119, 123, 125, 142, 143, 148, 149, 150, 153, 157, 164, 165, 167, 169, 170, 171, 172, 173, 174, 176, 181, 182, 186, 187, 189, 194, 195, 197, 202, 204, 206, 208
Arab States, League of 163, 204
Arafat, Yasser 158
Ashkenazim 19-20, 22-23, 29, 153
Balfour Declaration 9, 22, 27, 38-39, 42, 45, 50, 52, 53, 74, 99-103, 113, 114, 205
Bandung Conference 74
Bantu Investment Corporation 190
Bantu Law Amendment Act (1964) 31
Bantu Urban Areas Consolidated Act (1964) 31
Bantustans 29, 31, 70, 148-150, 151, 156, 175, 176, 190, 219
Bar Lev, Haim 193
Ben Gurion, David 21, 22, 29, 74, 103, 106-107, 123, 153
Black Africa
  relationship with Israel 8, 9, 11, 65, 76, 121, 129, 136-138, 145, 152, 157, 164, 168, 169, 174, 186, 187, 196, 201, 204, 207, 208, 210
  relationship with South Africa 11, 71, 75, 136-139, 145, 168, 174, 178, 187, 210
  support of Nasser 70, 121, 122, 130
Black South Africans
  demonstrations against apartheid 186
  education 33, 168, 170
  effect of increased military expenditures 201
  governmental control of political activity and freedom of movement 31-32
  Natives Land Act (1913) 27
  segregation 28-29, 30, 31
  struggle against white racist regimes 175
  see also African National Congress; Apartheid
Botha, Louis 36, 37, 75, 113
Botha, P.W. 208
Botha, Stephanus 179
Botswana 11, 71, 149
British Mandate 27, 32, 45, 53
Cairo Summit Conference (1977): see Afro-Arab Summit Conference
Carter, Jimmy 197
Chamberlain, Joseph 20, 102
Colonialism
  Africa 7, 9, 18-24, 27, 30-33, 36, 74-75, 81, 136, 225
  Israel 7, 9, 18-28, 30-33, 70, 74-76, 81, 170, 225
  see also Zionism
Comay, Michael 51, 107
Commerce: see Economic relationship between Israel and South Africa; Economy, South African
Common Market, European 117-118, 172, 192, 210
Crossman, Richard 40
Dayan, Moshe 22, 127, 150-151, 152-153, 209
DeBeers Group 141-142, 214
De Passe family 85, 96, 98
Declaration of Sharjah (1976) 225
Diplomatic relationship between Israel and South Africa 50-51, 65-66, 76, 120-121, 134-136, 143, 160-174, •177-178, 184
Eban, Abba 20, 22-23, 51
Economic relationship between Israel and South Africa
  condemned by UN 200,202
  diamond industry 139-142, 143, 168, 191
  discussed by UN Special Committee against Apartheid 203, 205, 208, 213-219
  Economic-Cooperation Pact 76, 161-163, 167, 171, 172, 182, 185, 209, 216, 220
  Israeli investments in South Africa 216, 218-219

Israeli re-export of South African products 78, 164, 171, 172, 191, 192, 216-217
Israeli-South African Trade Association 77
South African investments in Israel 216-218
steel industry 152, 162, 177, 183
trade, balance 70, 135-136, 154, 168-169, 171, 172, 177-178, 183, 191, 195, 196, 214
Weizmann's plan for development 106
Economy, South African
  agriculture 98-99, 151
  Bantustans 149-150
  Black African trade 187
  commerce 84-86, 93, 95
  controlled by whites 175
  diamond industry 8, 90, 139-142, 191
  European trade 173
  gold mining 8, 86, 89-92
  Jewish contribution 84-89
  post World War II status 103-106
  retail and wholesale trade 94-95
  see also Economic relationship between Israel and South Africa
Egypt 65, 70, 127, 130, 139, 144
European Common Market: see Common Market, European
Flesch, Fritz 68, 109-112
Freedman, Marcia 80, 172, 213
George, Lloyd 38, 39, 102
Givat Educational Foundation 173
Goldreich, Samuel 101, 102-103, 114
Greenberg, L. 53-54, 115
Group Areas Act 31
"Herrenvolk" democracy 26, 30, 33
Hertzberg, Arthur 187
Hertzog, J.B.M. 57, 75, 113, 205
Herzl, Theodor 9, 10, 20-21, 52, 100-101, 102, 114
Herzog, Chaim 209
Histadrut 32, 153, 193
Hod, Mordechai 78
Hotz, Louis 63, 69, 134, 136, 146
ISCOR: see Iron and Steel Corporation
Imperialism: see Colonialism
Industrial Conciliation Act (1956) 32
International Women's Year, World Conference of 199
Iron and Steel Corporation (ISCOR) 153, 173, 192, 193, 217
Israel-South Africa Friendship League 214
Israel-South Africa Trade Association 215
Israeli economy: see Economic relationship between Israel and South Africa
Israeli-South African Committee 70
Jabotinsky, Vladimir 21
Javits, Jacob K. 109, 110
Jewish Board of Deputies, South African 23, 51, 59, 61, 62-63, 65-66, 67, 68, 110, 121, 123, 132, 182, 206, 208
Katzew, Henry 62-63, 67
Katzir, Ephraim 160, 165
Kaunda, K. 174
Kirschner, N. 75, 112
Kollek, Teddy 160, 165
Koor Industries 80, 153, 154, 192, 209, 213, 217, 218
Lampert, Richard 193, 194
Law and Order Maintenance Act 31
Law of Return 30
League of Nations 12, 103
Lesotho 11, 71, 149, 164
Louw, Eric 65, 66, 119, 120, 122, 194
Malan, Daniel F. 51, 57, 60, 61, 63, 69, 76, 110, 113, 143, 154, 161, 205-206
Malawi 71, 164
Meir, Golda 29, 184
Military relationship between Israel and South Africa
  Amit's comments 154
  condemned by 1976 Conference 202
  condemned by UN 198, 200, 202
  development 75, 78-80, 81, 103, 107-109
  importance 135, 136-137, 154
  Israeli sale of military equipment to South Africa 163, 177, 178, 179, 191, 193, 209, 211, 213
  Israeli training of South African military 153, 172, 173, 177, 178, 179, 211, 212, 213
  purported by South-West Africa People's Organization 180
  South African support of Israel in 1967 War 128, 129, 133, 211

227

South African jet downed over Egypt (1973) 145, 152, 212
UN Special Committee against Apartheid 203, 204, 205, 208, 211-213
Vorster's visit to Israeli naval base 162, 165, 171, 178, 185, 192, 209
Mozambique 11, 174, 187
Mulder, C.P. 203, 209
Muller, Hilgard 152, 160, 165, 209
Namibia 80, 179, 180
Nasser, Gamal 65, 70, 121, 122, 126, 127, 130
National Party (South African) 51, 57, 59-63, 65, 70, 76, 125, 134, 143, 205, 206
Natives Land Act (1913) 27
Nordau, Max 18
Oppenheimer, Ernest 92, 141
Organization of African Unity 139, 148, 150, 163, 176, 195, 201, 204, 208
Palestine 7, 10, 20, 22, 24, 27, 28, 29, 30, 34, 35, 41, 42, 43, 45, 46, 47, 48, 49, 50, 51, 52, 70, 74, 100, 103, 104, 143, 173, 205, 226
Palestine Liberation Organization (PLO) 157-159, 174, 176
Pan-African Congress 31
Passfield White Paper (1930) 38, 39
Peled, Mattityahu 75, 171
Peres, Shimon 78, 197
Prohibition of Improper Interference Bill (1966) 31
Publications and Entertainment Act (1950) 31
Quota Act (1930) 57
Rabin, Yitzhak 159, 160, 161, 164, 171, 172, 173, 178, 182, 194, 209
Rabinowitz, L.I. 63, 109
Racism: see Apartheid; Colonialism
Rhodes, Cecil John 81
Rhodesia: see Zimbabwe
Royal Commission Report (1937) 38, 41
Rustin, Bayard 12, 187
Sadat, M. Anwar 145
Schweizer, A. 152
Sephardim 19-20, 22-23, 153
Sharett, Moshe 69, 76
Sharpeville Massacre (1960) 63, 201, 207
Shertok, Moshe 51
Smuts, Jan Christian 10, 23, 34, 54, 60, 62, 64, 65, 75, 113, 114, 115, 138, 155, 161, 194, 205
South Africa Foundation 70, 153, 214-215
South African economy: see Economic relationship between Israel and South Africa; Economy, South African
South African Palestine Enterprise (Binyan) Corporation 47, 77
South-West Africa People's Organization 160, 179-180, 192
Stone, Phineas 186-187
Suppression of Communism Act (1950) 31
Suzman, Arthur 66
Swaziland 11, 71, 149, 164
Tanzania 73, 180
Trade: see Economic relationship between Israel and South Africa; Economy, South African
Truman, Harry 22
Ungar, Andre 37, 58, 68
United Nations Educational, Scientific and Cultural Organization (UNESCO) 158, 159
United Nations General Assembly 12, 13, 46, 48, 74, 119, 126, 155, 156, 157, 158, 169
see also United Nations Resolutions
United Nations Reports
Report on the Relations between Israel and South Africa 11, 202
United Nations Resolutions
1947: partitioning Palestine 28, 48, 143
1961: deprecating South Africa's policy of apartheid 65, 119, 129
1963: Elimination of All Forms of Racial Discrimination 199
1964: condemning apartheid 12
1973: condemning the alliance between South African racism and Zionism 198, 202
1974: condemning relationship between Israel and South Africa 198, 202
1975: Question of Palestine 199
1975: equating Zionism with racism 13, 154, 157, 158, 169, 171, 172, 173, 182, 199

1975: condemning relationship between Israel and South Africa 200, 202
United Nations Security Council 50, 130, 131, 158-159
United Nations Special Committee against Apartheid 11, 200, 202
United Nations Special Committee on Palestine 45-46, 48
Unlawful Organization Act (1960) 31
Unna, Yitzhak 74, 164, 181, 182, 183-186, 210
Verwoerd, Hendrik F. 57, 61-62, 66-67, 70, 117, 120, 123-125
Vorster, Balthazar John 13, 75, 78, 79, 80, 81, 124, 125, 136, 143, 144-146, 148, 150, 151, 160-168, 170-174, 176, 177-180, 182, 184, 185, 187, 192, 193, 194, 196, 200, 201, 203, 204, 205, 209, 210, 211, 216, 220
Wars
 1948 Palestine War 28, 107, 116, 131, 211
 1967 Six-Day War 8, 28, 32, 70, 126-132, 136, 204, 207, 208, 210, 211, 212, 213, 214, 221
 1973 October (Yom Kippur) War 77, 144-148, 152, 165, 194, 204, 208, 210, 211, 212, 213, 215, 216
 Anglo-Boer War 36, 101, 112-113, 128
 Kaffir Wars 27
Weizmann, Chaim 9, 10, 21-23, 34-54, 60, 76, 102, 103, 114, 116, 194
Weizmann, Vera 39-40
White Paper (1922) 38
White Paper (1939) 39, 42, 45, 46
Wiener, Ludwig 85, 95
Woodhead Report 41
World Jewish Congress 68, 111
Zambia 11, 75, 152, 174, 176, 179, 180
Zangwill, Israel 29, 35
Zimbabwe (Rhodesia) 12, 26, 27, 28, 30, 31, 114, 144, 148, 160, 226
Zionism
 condemned by 1975 Declaration of Mexico on the Equality of Women 199
 condemned by 1975 Political Declaration by Conference of Ministers of Foreign Affairs of Non-Aligned Countries 199, 204
 condemned by Political Declaration of Cairo Summit Conference (1977) 226
 condemned in Declaration of Sharjah 225
 effect of 1967 Six-Day War 8
 equated with racism in UN 9, 13, 154, 158, 159, 169, 171, 172, 173, 182
 founded by Herzl 9
 response to apartheid 12
 roots in 19th century imperialism 13, 18-24, 35-36
 settler land acquisition in Palestine 27, 28, 30, 43-44
 statement by African National Congress of South Africa 174-176
 UN resolution condemning alliance between South African racism and Zionism 198, 199
 see also Herzl, Theodor; Weizmann, Chaim; Zionism in South Africa
Zionism in South Africa
 Afrikaans press support 51
 Afrikaner support 74
 development 112-117
 effect of Israeli vote on 1961 UN resolution against apartheid 122
 financial support of Israel 12, 169, 178, 183, 184, 207
 politics 8
 praised by Yitzhak Rabin 161
 resolution of South African Cabinet in support 103
 Smuts' support 9, 10, 36-38, 46, 47, 50, 51, 62, 63, 64, 65, 194, 205
 South African Jewish support 58-59, 61, 62, 64, 68, 70, 76, 77, 78, 101, 102, 103, 107, 110, 154
 South African Palestine Enterprise (Binyan) Corporation 47, 77
 support of formation of Israel 48, 52, 78, 101, 102, 107, 206, 211
 support of Israel in 1967 War 127-132, 133
 support of Jewish settlement of Uganda 10
Zionist Federation, English 35
Zionist Federation, South African 22, 23, 51, 52, 59, 61, 65, 66, 67, 101, 103, 112, 115, 120, 153, 169, 207, 211
Zones of Security Regulations (1949) 32